THE PSYCHOLOGY OF EMBARRASSMENT

THE PSYCHOLOGY OF EMBARRASSMENT

Robert J. Edelmann
University of Surrey, UK

JOHN WILEY & SONS
Chichester · New York · Brisbane · Toronto · Singapore

Library of Congress Cataloging-in-Publication Data:

Edelmann, Robert J.
   The psychology of embarrassment.

   Bibliography: p.
   Includes index.
   1. Embarrassment.   I. Title.—[DNLM: 1. Anxiety—
physiology.   2. Emotions.   BF   575.E53 E21p]
BF 575.E53E33   1987   152.4   86–28208

ISBN 0 471 91429 0

British Library Cataloguing in Publication Data:

Edelmann, Robert J.
   The psychology of embarrassment.
   1. Embarrassment
   I. Title
   152.4   BF575.E53

ISBN 0 471 91429 0

Printed and bound in Great Britain

Contents

Acknowledgements viii

CHAPTER 1: Introduction 1
A. The concept of embarrassment............................. 1
    1. Shyness and audience anxiety 3
    2. Embarrassment and shame 4
B. Theoretical perspectives 7
    1. Psychoanalytic theories 7
    2. Existential approaches 10
    3. Behavioural approaches 11
    4. Interpersonal approaches............................. 13
C. Plan of the book... 16

CHAPTER 2: Self-Presentation and Embarrassment 19
A. Identity and the phenomenal self......................... 20
B. Self-presentation.. 22
    1. Self-presentation strategies.......................... 23
    2. Protective self-presentation 25
    3. Self-handicapping..................................... 26
C. Self-awareness and self-presentation 28
D. Factors influencing the adoption of a protective self-presentation
    style.. 30
    1. Characteristics of the target audience 30
    2. The interaction context............................... 33
    3. Individual differences 35
        (a) Need for social approval 35
        (b) Fear of negative evaluation 36
        (c) Self-consciousness 36
        (d) Self-monitoring 38
E. Summary.. 39

CHAPTER 3: Social Predicaments and Embarrassment 41
A. The rules of conduct 41
    1. Knowledge of social rules............................ 41
    2. Degree of intent...................................... 44
B. Categories of predicament 47
C. Explanations for conduct.................................. 54
    1. Varieties of remedial tactics......................... 55
        (a) Apologies 55

(b) Accounts 57
   (i) Excuses 57
   (ii) Justifications 60
2. Selecting explanations 64
D.   Summary 66

CHAPTER 4: Physiological and Behavioural Concomitants of
             Embarrassment 68
A.   Physiological reactions 68
1. Blushing 68
2. Skin conductance and heart rate 71
B.   Nonverbal reactions 73
1. Eye contact, body motion and speech disturbances 73
2. The recognition of embarrassment 79
3. Smiling and laughter 80
4. Laughter as a coping response 84
C.   Summary 87

CHAPTER 5: Embarrassment: Private Feeling or Social Act? 88
A.   Embarrassment as an emotion 89
B.   Emotion as a process 91
1. The role of nonverbal behaviour 93
2. Cognitions and embarrassment 98
3. Self-focus and the perception of bodily states 101
C.   Towards a model of embarrassment 103

CHAPTER 6: Developmental and Individual Differences 108
A.   Age and embarrassment 108
1. Age and self-presentation 111
2. Role-taking and self-consciousness 113
3. Knowledge of social rules 116
4. Summary and conclusions 118
B.   Individual differences in embarrassment 119
1. Embarrassibility scale 120
2. Self-monitoring 124
3. Self-consciousness 125
4. Social anxiety 126
5. Extraversion 127
6. Neuroticism 128
7. Empathy 128
8. Other personality factors 130
C.   Summary 131

CHAPTER 7: Social Implications of Embarrassment 132
A.   Embarrassment and helping 133

B. Help-giving 134
    1. Situational and audience factors 134
        (a) Audience effects 135
        (b) Ambiguity of the situation 136
        (c) Embarrassing situations 137
    2. Characteristics of the target 139
    3. Characteristics of the help-giver 141
C. Help-seeking 142
    1. Audience effects 144
    2. Characteristics of the helper 146
    3. Characteristics of the help-seeker 149
D. Summary 151

CHAPTER 8: Clinical Issues 153
A. Embarrassment as a clinical phenomenon 153
B. Theoretical explanations of social anxiety 156
    1. Classical conditioning 156
    2. Skills deficit model 157
    3. Cognitive factors 160
        (a) Negative self-evaluations 161
        (b) Negative self-statements 162
        (c) Irrational beliefs 163
        (d) Selective memory 164
C. Dealing with embarrassing events: cognitive or behavioural
    difficulties 166
D. Blushing and physiological aspects 170
E. Intervention issues 171

CHAPTER 9: Therapeutic Intervention 174
A. Treatment of social anxiety 174
    1. Behavioural approaches 176
        (a) Exposure-based methods 176
        (b) Social skills training 178
    2. Treatment of chronic blushing 181
    3. Cognitive approaches 184
B. Reducing self-attention 189
C. Embarrassment as an aversive stimulus 192
D. Summary 194

CHAPTER 10: Concluding Comments 196

References 199

Index 216

Acknowledgements

I would like to thank a number of friends and colleagues who have provided suggestions and criticisms both on my research reported in the book and on the book itself. Sarah Hampson played an important role in the early stages of my research and has continued to provide insightful comments and encouragement. I am also grateful to Padmal de Silva who provided comments on some of my research reported in this book, and Kevin Connolly whose interest in my work was largely responsible for seeing this project reach fruition. The interest and comments by many friends on my research has also provided constant stimulation. In addition I am especially grateful to Chris Spencer who read the entire manuscript, and Peter K. Smith who read the developmental section, both of whom made excellent criticisms which led to significant improvements. However, in the final analysis I must take responsibility for the views expressed, together with any errors or omissions contained in this work. I also owe much to Gay Rich for patiently typing the final version from my barely legible first draft. Last, but by no means least, I would like to thank Susan E. Vivian for keeping my feet firmly placed on the ground.

Preface

The main purpose of this book is to integrate a diverse body of research investigating the phenomenon of embarrassment. The systematic study of embarrassment, as with related areas such as shyness and social anxiety, has made rapid advances in recent years. While review monographs covering the latter areas have been produced, an integrative overview of embarrassment has been lacking. This book aims to fill that gap.

Many lines of research provide an understanding to key components of embarrassment. Self-presentational concerns, the organization and structure of rule-governed behaviour, and physiological and behavioural responses associated with embarrassment all provide clues to an understanding of what embarrassment is, when it will occur and how it is experienced. The very experience of embarrassment can also have a very dramatic effect on our day-to-day lives. It is systematically built into our social system, controlling and occasionally inhibiting our everyday behaviour and in particular our social behaviour. Fear of behaving in a way which will be embarrassing forms a central component of social anxiety. The study of the phenomenon of embarrassment is thus of considerable theoretical and practical importance. Not only does it highlight some of the important preconditions for normal social interaction it also suggests methods of coping with or resolving embarrassment. This book is about all these aspects of embarrassment fused together to give a theoretical and empirical overview.

My own research interest in embarrassment spans a period of eight years during which time I have tested a number of hypotheses on undergraduates, the general public and clinical populations. The initial investigations were concerned with an everyday phenomenon: embarrassment resulting from a *faux pas*, social predicament or social rule transgression. It almost goes without saying that each one of us can be placed in a situation or can perform an act defined by either ourselves or others present as embarrassing. It also seems that embarrassment is associated with a definable non-verbal display: reduced eye contact; increased body motion and speech disturbance. In addition, blushing has been referred to as the hallmark of embarrassment. Yet there are wide individual variations in the extent to which embarrassment is experienced and the associated behaviours displayed. Some people claim that they are never embarrassed while others suffer personal agony over the slightest social predicament.

During the conducting and publishing of my research I have received many letters from chronic sufferers and during the past two years have seen a number of such people in my clinical work. A remark made by all these sufferers is that they feel unable to tell even their closest friends or family about their problem. After all, everyone is faced by an embarrassing incident at some time in their lives, so sufferers feel that others will not take them seriously. Chronic blushing and fear of embarrassment can present genuine difficulties for such people. It is particularly towards this issue that my most recent research has been directed. This book is thus about both an everyday phenomenon and, in its chronic form, a disabling condition each of which require an explanatory framework.

Of course there are still gaps in our understanding of embarrassment and many avenues of research remain to be pursued. There is little work on the changing experience of embarrassment in childhood and adolescence, little by way of a systematic appraisal of the part played by blushing in the experience of embarrassment, and only three single case reports detailing therapeutic intervention with chronic blushers. As well as integrating a diverse body of knowledge and presenting a theoretical framework for this research, perhaps this book will also act as a stimulus to other researchers to fill in some of the remaining gaps.

Robert J. Edelmann
Department of Psychology
University of Surrey
November 1986

CHAPTER 1

Introduction

Consider each of the following situations: you fall over in a public place, spilling your shopping everywhere; you are about to introduce a speaker to a large audience when you realize you have forgotten his/her name; you are being particularly rude about a colleague behind his/her back, when you discover he/she has overheard you.

All these situations have one common feature—they are all potentially embarrassing. Each represents a situation which is likely to engender a feeling in the central character that he/she has behaved in a way which is discreditable in the eyes of an observer. They also represent situations with which everyone is familiar—embarrassment is a common and often dramatic experience. It can induce a highly uncomfortable psychological state which can have a severely disruptive effect upon social interaction. Not only can certain situations disrupt our behaviour, inducing a state of embarrassment, some people have a chronic fear of embarrassment; a fear which can lead to anxiety about, or avoidance of, social encounters and social situations.

The study of the phenomenon of embarrassment is thus of considerable theoretical and practical importance. It could not only highlight some of the important preconditions for normal social interaction, but also suggest ways of coping with or resolving embarrassment for those who are particularly fearful or anxious about social encounters.

This book is about all aspects of embarrassment: it will examine the complex interaction of events and experiences which give rise to the process of embarrassment; the existence of developmental and personality differences in the likelihood that we will experience embarrassment; the behavioural and social implications of embarrassment; and ways of intervening with those who fear embarrassment in social encounters.

It is important to begin, however, by placing embarrassment in its psychological context. Is it possible to distinguish between embarrassment and related psychological constructs?

A. THE CONCEPT OF EMBARRASSMENT

Within the recent psychological literature embarrassment is generally regarded as a form of social anxiety closely related to shyness, audience anxiety and shame (Buss, 1980; Schlenker and Leary, 1982). Social anxiety has been variously defined as:

1

> Anxiety resulting from the prospect or presence of personal evaluation in real or imagined social situations. (Schlenker and Leary, 1982, p. 642).

> The tendency to be made anxious by social situations. (Argyle, 1981, p. 167).

> Being upset or disturbed by others' scrutiny or remarks, or merely because others are present. (Buss, 1980, p. 204).

European researchers have long recognized the fact that for some people social encounters may be stressful and anxiety-provoking. Marks (1970) refers to 8 per cent of his clients treated at a general psychiatric hospital as socially phobic; defined as clients with excessive anxiety and a tendency to avoid certain inter-personal situations. Similar prevalence rates for social anxiety have been found in the USA. Curran *et al.* (1980a) estimated that 7 per cent of a psychiatric population struggled with such difficulties. It is only in the past few years, however, that social phobia has been included as a new diagnostic category within DSM-111. Here social phobia is defined as:

> A persistent, irrational fear of, and compelling desire to avoid, situations in which the individual may be exposed to the scrutiny of others. There is also fear that the individual will behave in a manner that will be *humiliating or embarrassing*. (DSM-111, 1980, p. 227—present author's italics).

The fact that fear of embarrassment seems to play a central role in the experience of social anxiety is a theme returned to later in the book, particularly in relation to clinical intervention with clients who most fear embarrassment in social encounters (i.e. those who are likely to be referred to as socially anxious or socially phobic).

Interestingly, while social phobia is one of the newest additions to the DSM-III it does have a preliminary data base to suggest that it is a clearly differentiable category of anxiety reaction. Marks (1970) suggests that, on the basis of behavioural reactions, social phobics can be readily distinguished from simple phobics and agoraphobics; more recently Amies, Gelder, and Shaw: (1983) also found that social phobics and agoraphobics could be reliably discriminated, with the former being more likely to experience flushing and muscle twitching. The specific stimulus situation of exposure to interpersonal evaluation also sets social anxiety apart from other fear-inducing situations.

The attempts to separate social anxiety into different classes have also tended to emphasize the type of situation in which the anxiety occurs. Bryant and Trower (1974) found two major clusters of situation in their analysis of data obtained from a student sample. Each subject was asked to rate 30 situations according to the extent that:

> The situation makes you feel anxious or uncomfortable, either because you don't know what to do, or because you feel frightened, embarrassed or self-conscious. (Bryant and Trower, 1974, p. 15).

The first cluster of situations consisted of those involving initial contact with strangers, particularly of the opposite sex, while the second consisted of situations involving intimate social contact. In a further study, Richardson and Tasto (1976) developed a social anxiety inventory of 166 items from which they found seven clear dimensions.

1. Fear of disapproval or criticism by others.
2. Fear of social assertiveness and visibility.
3. Fear of confrontation and anger expression.
4. Fear of heterosexual contact.
5. Fear of intimacy and interpersonal warmth.
6. Fear of conflict and/or rejection by parents.
7. Fear of interpersonal loss.

There are a number of other studies which suggest the existence of similar dimensions (Stratton and Moore, 1977; Hodges and Felling, 1970; Magnusson and Ekehammar, 1975). These dimensions match, to a certain extent, the many labels used in the clinical and social psychological literature to refer to different categories encompassed by the umbrella term, social anxiety. These include: stage fright, audience anxiety, embarrassment, shame, shyness, dating anxiety, hetero-sexual social anxiety, communication apprehension and reticence. Many of these terms clearly overlap and can usefully be encompassed by the four terms referred to previously: shyness, audience anxiety, embarrassment and shame. Although these four types of social anxiety have many overlapping features, there have been attempts in the literature to highlight crucial differences.

1. Shyness and audience anxiety

The clear linking of shyness and audience anxiety, on the one hand, and embarrassment and shame, on the other, has been noted by a number of authors (Buss, 1980; Schlenker and Leary, 1982).

Buss (1980) regards both audience anxiety and shyness as traits which appear to possess consistency over time and across situations, a consistency which, he suggests, neither embarrassment nor shame possess. As we shall see in Chapter 6, however, an individual's susceptibility to embarrassment (i.e. embarrassibility) may also be a measurable and consistent trait.

A more useful working distinction takes as its starting point the fact that all social difficulties are related to self-presentational problems (Leary and Schlenker, 1981; Schlenker and Leary, 1982). In social situations we attempt to control images of self, or identity-relevant information, before real or imagined audiences (Schlenker, 1980, 1982). Social anxiety occurs either because we doubt that we will be able to convey the image we would wish, or because an event occurs which prevents us from so doing.

It has been argued that those who *anticipate* a discrepancy between their perceived self-presentation and their desired self-presentation are likely to

4

experience shyness or audience anxiety (Schlenker and Leary, 1982; Asendorpf, 1984) depending upon the nature of the encounter.

In our interactions with others we must be continually responsive to their actions and reactions. Our behaviours are *contingent* upon the responses of others. Actors who do not possess, or believe that they do not possess, the necessary repertoire of behaviours to participate effectively in social encounters anticipate a discrepancy between the way they expect to present themselves and the way they would wish to present themselves. The label 'shy' is often applied to such people.

Encounters which are guided primarily by internal plans, such as those involving the delivery of a prepared speech or a performance in a play, are likely to be only minimally responsive to the reaction of the audience. Those who do not possess, or believe that they do not possess, the necessary repertoire of behaviours for performing in such *non-contingent* encounters are likely to experience audience anxiety. Shyness and audience anxiety can thus be said to arise when a discrepancy between one's standard for self-presentation and one's actual self-presentation is *anticipated* in *contingent* or *non-contingent* encounters.

The extent to which we are likely to experience either shyness or audience anxiety is likely to vary considerably from individual to individual. Zimbardo (1977), for example, suggests that shyness spans a wide psychological continuum, varying from occasional feelings of awkwardness in the presence of others all the way to traumatic episodes of anxiety which totally disrupt a person's life. At the one end we have shy people who enjoy their solitude, feeling more comfortable with books, ideas and objects than with other people. At the other end are those who will do anything to escape from or avoid social contact, simply because it is terrifying to be with people, although they would dearly love to be.

Of the various terms used to describe aspects of social anxiety, it is likely that speech anxiety and reticence correspond very closely to shyness. Questions about shyness are usually contained in speech anxiety questionnaires (McCroskey, 1977) and a trait called reticence, which appears to be very similar to shyness, has been described by Phillips and Metzger (1973).

2. Embarrassment and shame

Cutting across the shyness, audience anxiety dimensions are social emotions which result from unintentional and undesired predicaments or transgressions (Semin and Manstead, 1981, 1982; Schlenker and Leary, 1982). Social anxiety which results from such predicaments has been termed 'embarrassment' or 'shame', depending upon the nature of the event. Thus, when an undesirable event, such as a *faux pas*, impropriety, accident or transgression occurs it is likely to cause a *perceived* discrepancy between one's current unintended self-presentation and one's desired self-presentation (Asendorpf, 1984).

The literature distinguishing shame from embarrassment is rather more confusing than that distinguishing shyness from audience anxiety. In fact the terms embarrassment and shame are often used interchangeably. English (1975) states that 'embarrassment is a euphemism for shame' (p. 25) while Baldwin and Levin's (1958) definition of shame could equally apply to embarrassment:

> Shame is an emotional state which occurs when one's defects, poor abilities or bad intentions are made public. (p. 363).

Lynd (1958), on the other hand, suggests that:

> Embarrassment is often an initial feeling of shame before shame is covered up or explored as a means of further understanding oneself and of the situation that gives rise to it. (p. 38).

A similar suggestion is made by Modigliani (1966), who makes the point that:

> In common usage one is primarily ashamed of *oneself*, while one is primarily embarrassed about one's *presented* self. This may mean that shame is the more personal extension of embarrassment, or it may mean that it is a quite distinct psychological state. (p. 10).

This suggestion of overlapping but differing concepts is also raised by Vallelonga (1976), who collected 40 written descriptions each of being ashamed and being embarrassed. He thus defines shame as:

> to perceive suddenly, in and through one's behaviour, an extremely unpleasant discrepancy between who one is and who, according to one's lived self-projects, one 'must' be. (p. 57).

He suggests that embarrassment, on the other hand, always entails at least three constituents:

> (1) interpersonal exposure—with the presence of a *thematic other*, whether that presence be 'actual, presumed or fantasised' . . . (2) either a concern for one's face . . . or the experience of 'losing face' (diminishing in the other's esteem or regard); and (3) a desire to escape, hide or 'disappear'. (p. 57).

Embarrassment in this sense, while involving the discrepant self-image present in shame, involves in addition the exposure of this discrepancy to the scrutiny of others. This difference is highlighted by Goffman (1956), who suggests that the term 'shame' should be restricted to those instances which refer to personal feelings, with the resultant public presentation of this state giving rise to embarrassment, discomfiture and uneasiness:

> Embarrassment has to do with the figure the individual cuts before others felt to be there at the time. (p. 98).

In a more detailed comparison of shame and embarrassment, Buss (1980) points to a number of similarities between the two affects:

> Common to both is gaze aversion, covering of the eyes or face and parasympathetic reactivity. Both affects may be caused by a person's own acts or by the scrutiny of others. Both may result from disclosure of socially unacceptable behaviour or from ridicule from others. And both may cause a drop in self-esteem. (p. 161).

(It should be noted that research does not support the notion that embarrassment results in a loss of self-esteem (Modigliani, 1966, 1968).)

In spite of these similarities, however, Buss regards shame and embarrassment as different in a number of respects: thus embarrassment sometimes involves blushing and smiling or laughing, whilst shame does not; embarrassment usually involves a feeling of foolishness, whilst shame involves regret; a *faux pas* or social accident is likely to result in embarrassment, letting the group down or being caught in a cowardly or immoral act is likely to give rise to shame.

It is interesting to note that while Buss recognizes a number of distinguishing features, he does not concur with the difference between shame and embarrassment noted by Goffman (1956), Modigliani (1966), and Vallelonga (1976), i.e. that shame is a private feeling, while embarrassment involves interpersonal exposure. This is somewhat surprising as embarrassment is most likely to occur in some form of real or imagined social interaction, while one can feel ashamed of oneself for a private act.

Embarrassment in these terms thus results when a perceived discrepancy occurs between one's current self-presentation and one's standard for self-presentation, as a result of an undesired and unintentional social accident or predicament. While the anticipated–perceived and contingent–noncontingent dimensions offer a useful conceptual distinction there is little by way of empirical work examining the differences and similarities between forms of social anxiety. Thus, while embarrassment certainly can result from a perceived discrepancy between one's current unintended self-presentation and one's desired self-presentation there are also likely to be cases when the anticipation of embarrassment can occur. As mentioned, the DSM-111 definition of social phobia states:

> There is also fear that the individual will behave in a manner that will be humiliating or embarrassing.

It seems useful to make a distinction between (a) being in a situation where one's behaviour *is likely to be judged* or evaluated by others, in which case one might fear the negative, possibly embarrassing consequences of failure; and (b) being in a situation where one's behaviour *has already been judged* as inadequate by others; such an event being labelled 'embarrassing' by the actor and/or the observers to the event. Embarrassment then can be both a fear occasioned by the anticipated occurrence of a social transgression, *faux pas* or accident, or an emotional state occasioned by a social transgression, *faux pas* or accident which *has* occurred. It may be that those referred to as shy or anxious in front of audiences or with members of the opposite sex fear the negative and embarrassing consequences of failure. In the same way that agoraphobia may involve 'fear of fear' or fear of one's own physiological reaction involved in a panic attack, (e.g. Goldstein and Chambless, 1978; Mavissakalian, 1983), social anxiety may involve a fear of the anticipated embarrassing consequences of failure.

It seems then that embarrassment is likely to be a complex phenomenon, the key components of which need to be carefully unpacked before a clear understanding can be achieved. Careful attention needs to be paid to (1) the interaction between the eliciting circumstances and the characteristics of the individual concerned; (2) the core reaction and the possibility that the reaction itself generates further discomfort; and (3) the social implications of the reaction of embarrassment. A number of theorists have in fact offered explanations for the occurrence of embarrassment. These will be overviewed briefly before leading to an outline of the overall plan which will be adopted in this book.

B. THEORETICAL PERSPECTIVES

1. Psychoanalytic theories

Psychoanalytic approaches to embarrassment are usually concerned with the neurotic or exaggerated form of blushing referred to as erythrophobia—a neurotic state in which social anxiety predomintes (Sattler, 1966). Embarrassment is also referred to in the psychoanalytic literature, generally in relation to dreams. Freud (1900) first mentions embarrassment in a section of *The Interpretation of Dreams* devoted to typical dreams of nakedness or of being inappropriately clothed (pp. 242–8). He noted that the dreamer's embarrassment usually occurs in the presence of strangers who take little or no notice of his/her state of bodily exposure. The dreamer generally feels too inhibited to cover or correct his/her state of undress. The suggestion was that behind these dreams is a wish to exhibit oneself to a parental figure. It should be noted that generally Freud did not differentiate between embarrassment and shame, and that apart from the pages referred to above:

> Freud writes only of shame and does not employ another word that might be translated as embarrassment. (Dann, 1977, p. 454)

Following Freud, several psychoanalytic authors comment on embarrassment in dreams (e.g. Altman, 1969; Gutheil, 1939; Lowy, 1942) especially in relation to dreams involving nakedness. The main focus of this approach is that the need to satisfy socially unacceptable sexual impulses or exhibitionistic tendencies is met by covert processes such as dreams—the content of which the client finds embarrassing and distressing.

Gutheil (1939), for example, suggests that embarrassment in dreams may not only reveal conflict over exhibitionistic tendencies, but also reveal feelings of guilt and inferiority. Saul (1966), in an article on embarrassing dreams of nakedness, classifies these dreams into defences against derivatives of infantile exhibitionism, and other ego meanings. In dreams under the second category, the exhibitionism itself or the embarrassment can be defensive against current reality concerns, against various oedipal and pre-oedipal conflicts, and especially against transference wishes and fears. Saul gives as an example the case of a woman who was so distressed by her sexual daydreams that she was in a continual state of embarrassment.

Dreams of nakedness and an inability to clothe oneself in the presence of strangers are in fact fairly common. In one report this type of dream was recorded as being present in the dreams of 20 per cent of hospitalized psychiatric patients (Ward, Beck and Roscoe, 1961). Dann (1977) describes a case of a woman in her thirties who requested help for sexual difficulties and for mild depressive episodes alleviated by approval from others. He describes her as having:

> a rather normal sex life, but intermittently she was distressed by sexual daydreams . . . she imagined being observed masturbating, belly dancing and stripping, and had urges to observe men and couples undressing and involved in sexual activities. (p. 457).

He discusses the patient's problem as embarrassment resulting from fantasies that were linked to exhibitionistic and scopophilic (sexual-aggressive) conflicts.

References to erythrophobia are also generally linked with the need to satisfy socially unacceptable sexual impulses and exhibitionistic tendencies. Feldman (1941) suggests that there are three important factors which play a part in blushing:

> (i) a predisposing libidinous situation, (ii) local sexual and social traumata of the face, and (iii) general social traumata with confusion in building up the superego. (p. 254).

In this sense the facial display represents repressed libidinal excitement, i.e. blushing is a sign of repressed libidinal excitement displaced upwards due to fear of castration. Benedek (1925) also took this view, and describes the case of a 26-year-old woman with a fear of blushing which she suggests was due to apprehension concerning preadolescent masturbation, a castration complex, a strong sense of guilt and scopophilia.

Hitschmann (1943) also stressed the significance of exhibitionism and scopophilia, which he suggests develops from maternal condemnation for genital exhibitionism. Blushing then represents the displacement upwards of the repressed wish to exhibit the genitals.

A slightly different view was adopted by Bergler (1944), who suggests that the primary defect in blushing is an excessively strong voyeur component.

Thus, the repression of phallicized exhibitionism and aggression is replaced by the symptoms of erythrophobia (i.e. blushing as exhibitionism):

> A displacement from below upward phallicizes the face, whereby unconscious exhibitionistic and punishment wishes are satisfied (p. 43).

> By blushing the erythrophobe makes himself really conspicuous, i.e. exhibits himself. (p. 45).

Many of the concepts used by these earlier authors were incorporated into the writings of Fenichel (1945), who suggests that for erythrophobics the idea of being judged by others supplants the idea of sexual contact with others. Thus in severe cases of fear of blushing an individual:

> may be inhibited to such an extent that they withdraw from social contact; they anticipate possible criticisms to a degree that makes them hardly distinguishable from persons with paranoid trends. Less severe cases are unconsciously governed by the fear that (and the desire that) their masturbation may be found out by sexual (scopophilic) aggressive strivings. (p. 180).

For Fenichel, as with the previous analytic authors referred to, the major components of erythrophobia revolve around unconscious strivings against erotic temptations, fear of castration and suppression of exhibitionistic needs.

This brief summary of a psychoanalytic perspective on embarrassment and blushing suggests that this school of thought had many adherents in the 1930s and 1940s with decreasing numbers in recent years. The idea that embarrassment and blushing are always linked with exhibitionistic or sexual tendencies is of course fanciful, to say the least. Karch (1971) himself writing in a psychoanalytic journal, points out:

> Most theories which have been proposed are based on the study of individuals who have sought psychiatric help. . . . Almost one hundred years ago Darwin established the fact that virtually everyone blushes, and it is difficult to accept the concept that everyone suffers from superego immaturity or scopophilia. (p. 46).

There is indeed no empirical evidence to support the claims of the psychoanalytic writers made on the basis of a few subjective single case reports. The outcome of psychoanalytic interventions for chronic blushers or those who fear embarrassment is also difficult to evaluate; most again are based upon individual therapists' comments. Further, many of the explanations offered would be wholly unacceptable to a large number of clients.

Even if one were to accept certain aspects of this position it is difficult to see how it could account for some of the fundamental aspects of embarrassment and blushing: (1) almost everyone is embarrassed at some stage in their lives and everyone is capable of blushing (2) embarrassment occurs in a fairly well-defined range of situations—only a few of these are associated with sexuality or sexual connotations and could have little to do with exhibitionistic or scopophilic tendencies except in one's wildest imaginings. It is fair to say that the psychoanalytic approach to embarrassment has not been a fruitful one. There has been general confusion between the terms 'shame' and 'embarrassment', a tendency to de-emphasize the important situational determinants of embarrassment; and with the emphasis on a subjective description of specific cases no real attempt to offer a generalizable explanation of a widely experienced phenomenon.

2. Existential approaches

In contrast to the psychoanalytically oriented theorists, existential theorists tend to emphasize the importance of the environment in which blushing or embarrassment occurs, and how this relates to the nature of man/woman.

Sartre (1956), for example, discusses blushing as a state which occurs when the individual becomes aware of the alienation of his body. That is, when the person becomes aware of his or her body as it appears to an observer rather than the way it appears to the actor himself or herself. Describing the wish to disappear from sight following embarrassment, Sartre writes:

> When he longs 'not to have a body anymore', to be 'invisible', it is not his body-for-himself which he wants to annihilate, but his inapprehensible dimension of the body-alienated. (p. 353).

Thus the actor wishes to hide his/her embarrassed self from the eyes of the observer.

Buytendijk's (1950) view closely parallels that of Sartre, although he tends to place rather more emphasis upon the situational component. He thus describes situations in which the actor might find himself-herself being unmasked or exposed as unworthy. These situations might include breaking the rules of convention, being excessively praised or wrongly accused. It is in these situations that blushing represents a sign of one's feeling of existential unworthiness. As will be seen in Chapter 3, the situations referred to above are indeed those which in empirical studies tend to be associated with embarrassment.

De Beauvoir (1957) has extended the existential viewpoint to examine the occurrence of increased social distress and blushing during adolescence. She describes the adolescent girl's body as

> getting away from her, it is no longer the straightforward expression of her individuality; it becomes foreign to her; and at the same time she becomes for others a thing; on the street men follow her with their eyes and comment on her anatomy. She would like to become invisible; it frightens her to become flesh and to show her flesh. (p. 308).

Again this description highlights a number of points made later in this book. Adolescence is widely regarded as a peak period for embarrassment; embarrassment does seem to be associated with the tendency to be made the centre of attention and does seem to be associated with a discrepancy between one's desired role or presentation and one's actual role or presentation.

The issue of blushing in adolescent girls is also taken up by Van den Berg (1955), who refers to an adolescent girl's blush as resulting from an estrangement from her body and a new intimacy with her body. No longer being a child and not yet an adult the adolescent has yet to develop a familiar repertoire of behaviours.

The general theme of existential writers thus concerns feelings of discovery, unmasking, unworthiness and exposure which create the state of embarrassment. Blushing signifies an awareness of the alienation of one's body, as the actor becomes aware of how he/she is viewed by an observer and communicates to the observer that he/she has been affected by the situation.

This descriptive approach gives us a useful account of the experience of embarrassment. Certainly embarrassment has to do with 'unmasking'—with an observation that we have not acted or behaved in the way we would have wished. Certainly blushing is a visible sign of this state and almost certainly embarrassment is more prevalent during adolescence. The description does, however, leave a number of gaps in our knowledge of the experience of embarrassment. Why, for example, does the experience occur? Why should the observation that we have not acted or behaved in the way that we would have wished give rise to a state which is labelled 'embarrassment'? Is blushing always associated with embarrassment? If so, is it just a sign of embarrassment or does it serve some further communicative or alternative function? How and why does embarrassment first develop? Is it an innate state or is it a learnt emotion? What is the precise social function of the state labelled 'embarrassment'? Any comprehensive model of embarrassment must be able to answer all these questions.

3. Behavioural approaches

Skinner (1953) and Gordon (1963) are representative of the behavioural orientation to embarrassment, both focusing on the importance of punishment. Thus Skinner states: 'Behaviour that has been frequently punished may be emitted in a form called "timid", or "embarrassed" ' (p. 169). Further, shame which is seen as closely related to embarrassment represents 'the conditioned aversive stimulation generated by bad behaviour as a result of punishment'.

Thus learning involved in the experience of embarrassment takes place via a series of steps:

1. We undergo a series of negative consequences for behaving wrongly (either by direct punishment or as a result of watching others punished).
2. Timidity, embarrassment, or shame becomes the conditioned aversive consequence gradually replacing direct punishment.

12

3. Situations which might provoke timidity, embarrassment, or shame are avoided.

It is in fact possible to short-cut stage 1 and use ridicule, laughter or embarrassment as the initial punishment. A clear illustration of how this can work in society is provided by the Eskimo culture (English, 1975). If a young child should venture onto thin ice with the result that he/she falls through, the rest of the village will gather round laughing, ridiculing, in short embarrassing the child for his/her behaviour. As a result the child is likely to avoid thin ice in future and hence avoid the trauma caused by embarrassment. This explanation has a lot in common with Mowrer's (1950) two-stage theory of fear acquisition. In Mowrer's view, classically conditioned fear motivates avoidance behaviour which leads to a reduction of fear and a strengthening of the avoidance behaviour. According to this theory, anxiety and avoidance are causally linked, and avoidance should be reduced as soon as anxiety is eliminated. In terms of embarrassment and social anxiety one could postulate a critical link between the two constructs. Through ridicule, rejection or failure in social situations we learn to experience embarrassment—we thus avoid social situations to avoid the embarrassing consequences of failure. Reducing fear of embarrassment should result in reduced avoidance of social situations.

This two-stage theory of learning has, however, been disputed by several lines of evidence (e.g. Eysenck, 1976). First, a traumatic experience relating to the genesis of fears and phobias often cannot be found; second, apart from the famous 'Little Albert' experiment of Watson and Raynor (1920), who conditioned a phobia in a 1-year-old child, there have been repeated failures to condition phobias under laboratory conditions. While it is easy to see how negative, embarrassing experiences in social situations may condition a person to fear embarrassment in similar future situations, a crucial issue remains unanswered: why should embarrassment occur in the first place?

Two alternative behavioural–cognitive models, the skills deficit model and the cognitive model, suggest explanations. The former model presupposes that individuals may not possess the necessary behavioural repertoire to meet the demands of the situation. Thus an unskilled actor may receive negative reactions from others—in the conditioning sense the actor may learn to fear embarrassment in social situations simply because he/she behaves in a way which is unsuitable or unacceptable, both to the actor and the observer. The cognitive model on the other hand suggests that faulty patterns of self-perception or faulty cognitions play a central part. Thus, an actor who possesses the necessary repertoire of behaviours, may nevertheless regard his/her performance as inadequate and embarrassing. Thus, social anxiety may result from a fear of embarrassment generated as a direct result of negative expectations about one's own performance.

This issue is obviously a complex and critical one in our understanding of embarrassment and social anxiety which has only been hinted at in this section. The question of behavioural explanations for social anxiety, which are closely linked with possible explanations for the genesis of embarrassment, form a central clinical issue dealt with in detail in Chapter 8.

While it is clear that embarrassment might be learnt in one or more of the ways suggested above, it is still important to unravel the nature of the experience itself. In this sense, embarrassment is unlikely to be a discrete entity, but a reaction which changes and develops over time. The importance of the individual's own perception of the circumstances in which the event occurs, as well as his/her perception of his/her reaction to the event and the reaction of the observers present, should thus form a central component of any theoretical explanation for the experience of embarrassment. While the existential approach offers a useful descriptive account of the experience of embarrassment, and the behavioural approach offers a useful analysis for the possible generation of embarrassment and related trepidation in social situations, a clearer understanding of the nature of embarrassment as a changing and developing experience is required. The final theoretical perspective, the interpersonal approach, goes some way towards providing this understanding.

4. Interpersonal approaches

The nature of embarrassment has been most often and most clearly defined in the context of interpersonal processes. Many of the theorists subsumed under this rubric agree that a necessary condition for embarrassment to occur is the presence of one or more other persons. Thus Heider (1958) describes an important precondition for the experience of embarrassment as:

> The disintegrating effect of self-consciousness produced by the seeming exposure of oneself to the perception of another (p. 17).

He also cites Hellpach (1913), who states that embarrassment implies: (a) the presence of another person; (b) an awareness that the attention of other people is directed toward the subject, and (c) empathy, if present, furthering the embarrassment.

Baldwin (1955), writing about shyness, embarrassment and shame in children, also makes a number of important points concerning the link between an evaluative audience and the experience of embarrassment. He thus suggests that for a child to be embarrassed he/she must be aware of his/her conspicuousness or visibility, with a number of facets of the audience influencing the degree of embarrassment experienced. Thus, embarrassment is likely to decrease as the size and/or status of the audience decreases. The issue of the nature of the target audience and its effect upon the embarrassment potential of the situation is discussed in Chapter 2.

Ausubel (1955) has also emphasized the role of an audience's presence in the generation of embarrassment (which he refers to as 'nonmoral shame').

He suggests that embarrassment results from an impropriety or bodily exposure which the actor feels will be labelled by an observer as a display of incompetence or ignorance. Many of the behaviours of the embarrassed person then constitute attempts to avoid this observation and evaluation (i.e. looking away, covering the face, turning away, etc.).

Goffman (1955, 1956) has also suggested that embarrassment only occurs when an individual is felt to have projected an incompatible image of himself/herself before those present. Thus, embarrassment is caused by our projected image (i.e. the image of ourself available to others) being discrepant from our own standard for self-presentation. Sattler (1966), overviewing interpersonal approaches to embarrassment, suggests three key factors which are necessary for embarrassment to occur: (1) the presence of another person, or at least the thought of another person; (2) the person becoming aware that he/she is the centre of attention; and (3) the person feeling that he/she is being judged. Embarrassment then reflects a failure to present oneself in the way one would have wished. As such it is likely to be built up of several components rather than reflecting a clearly definable and discrete state. Thus an act must occur which is defined as being potentially embarrassing by the actor; he/she must be aware of, and recognize the importance of, an evaluative audience—the actor must appraise and react to the audience's reaction; the actor is likely to react behaviourally and physiologically, and must also appraise and if necessary change and/or acknowledge his/her own reaction. Embarrassment is thus likely to involve a complex process or interlinking package of events, each component of which any adequate model must take into account.

There have, in fact, been a number of attempts to conceptualize the process underlying embarrassment, most of which encapsulate elements of the interpersonal approach. Modigliani (1968, 1971) has suggested a three-part model of embarrassment, as an extension of Goffman's (1955, 1956) suggestion that embarrassment involves our projected image being discredited. The basic features of this model are:

1. An assumption that the incident which is the immediate cause of embarrassment involves a failure on the part of the individual concerned to fulfil certain social expectations.
2. The fact that this failure leads to a diminution in the individual's perceived public esteem.
3. The fact that this diminution in turn leads to a diminution in the individual's esteem.

In an investigation of this proposition, Modigliani (1966) studied the relationship between embarrassibility (i.e. a measure of a person's general susceptibility to embarrassment—the embarrassibility scale is discussed in detail in Chapter 6 where it is presented in full), general self-esteem (i.e. how one rates oneself in relation to others), and instability of general self-esteem (i.e.

a feeling of inadequacy about one's general adequacy). The results showed that self-esteem was only moderately correlated and instability of self-esteem uncorrelated to embarrassibility. (This study will be examined in more detail in Chapter 6.)

An experimental study also only yielded partial support for Modigliani's theory (Modigliani, 1971). In neither of the above two studies was embarrassment found to be accompanied by the loss of self-esteem.

More recently, Semin and Manstead (1981, 1982) have proposed that states such as embarrassment, which are experienced after an unintentional violation of social norms, arise as a consequence of a discrepancy between the negative public image the actor assumes that he/she has projected and the actor's self-image which, it is argued, is unaffected by the incident. This proposition has found support in both a correlational study (Manstead and Semin, 1981) and an experimental study (Semin and Manstead, 1981).

Within this model there are four main conditions which are held necessary for social transgressions to result in embarrassment:

1. The occurrence of public violation of a taken-for-granted social rule which is part of the actor's repertoire.
2. The rule in question must have been violated unintentionally.
3. The actor must be aware that a violation has occurred.
4. The violation must be witnessed by others.

This model has a number of features in common with the self-presentational model of social anxiety suggested by Schlenker and Leary (1982), Leary and Schlenker (1981), and Leary (1982). According to their model, the different forms of social anxiety result from the joint effects of two sets of factors. Thus it is suggested that people become socially anxious when they are firstly motivated to make particular impressions on others, but secondly doubt that they will be able to do so, with the result that they will obtain less than satisfactory reactions from others. Should a social accident or predicament occur, this will contradict the actor's desired identity (i.e. there will be a discrepancy between his or her own standards and his or her social performance). Since the personal consequences of failing to project desired self-presentations are often negative, people who are motivated to make particular impressions become apprehensive and socially anxious, at the prospect of failing to do so. The actual perception that a projected self-presentation is negative is likely to give rise to self-attention and embarrassment. The precise nature of self-presentational concerns involved in the experience of embarrassment are examined in detail in the following chapter.

While the interpersonal approaches do then attempt to specify the antecedents of embarrassment, it is questionable whether the causes of embarrassment or factors which maintain fear of embarrassment in social encounters are clearly specified. A behavioural explanation is required at some point to specify these factors and to generate programmes for intervention. In view of the emphasis upon the need for the actor to evaluate and appraise his reaction and that of others, a cognitive–behavioural explanation is likely to prove most fruitful. The interpersonal approaches also expand upon the descriptions offered by the existential theorists (i.e. alienation of the body) but de-emphasize the existence of a definable state. Instead, embarrassment is clearly recognized as a process or sequence of cognitive experiences which any adequate model will need to take into account.

At least three of the theoretical explanations offered for the experience of embarrassment thus go some way toward giving an explanation for the phenomenon. It may well be the case that one type of theory on its own cannot explain all facets of embarrassment. A multifaceted approach combining a behavioural and interpersonal perspective could offer the most fruitful conceptualization by recognizing the importance of both learning and experience. As mentioned, careful attention needs to be paid to (1) the eliciting circumstances; (2) the core reaction and the possibility that the reaction itself generates further discomfort; and (3) the social implications of embarrassment.

C. PLAN OF THE BOOK

The overall aim of this book is to present a comprehensive and coherent account of all aspects of embarrassment. In order to do this the book is structured into two halves, with Chapter 5 acting as a pivotal chapter. The aim of the pivot chapter is to provide an analysis of embarrassment as a process or chain of events, some aspects of which may be more salient to some individuals than to others. One side of the pivot (Chapters 2, 3 and 4) outlines critical features of the components giving rise to the experience of embarrassment: self-presentational concerns and their relationship with the experience of embarrassment; the nature of rule-governed behaviour and predicaments giving rise to embarrassment; the physiological and behavioural reaction associated with embarrassment and explanations for this reaction. The other side of the pivot (Chapters 6 to 9) examines ways in which embarrassment affects our everyday lives: the way in which we differ with regard to age and personality in our susceptibility to the experience of embarrassment; the way in which this experience can control our behaviour in certain settings; the way in which fear of embarrassment can inhibit our social behaviour, and ways of rectifying these inhibited thoughts and behaviours. Further details of each chapter are as follows.

Chapter 2 examines the implications of self-presentational styles for the experience of embarrassment. Self-presentation refers to the attempts we make to control the self-relevant images that we project to others. A number of authors have recognized the existence of self-presentational styles, classifiable according to the attribution sought by the presenter. One style may be more appropriate on one occasion than another, or may be more appropriate for one person than another. Should a particular self-presentation be inappropriate or otherwise fail, then embarrassment is a possible consequence.

Situations in which an inappropriate self-presentation is more likely to be selected involve those without clearly prescribed goals and rules. Any ambiguous or novel situation will thus present the greatest risk of self-presentational difficulties and potential embarrassment. These instances are likely to further our self-presentational concerns, particularly concerns about how others are perceiving and evaluating us. This concern with the public aspect of our identity or public self-attention seems to play a central role in the generation of embarrassment.

Interrelated with self-presentation concerns is our desire to behave in a way which is generally consistent with social rules. The structure of rule-governed behaviour is so closely linked with embarrassment that classifications of embarrassing events are often based upon the types of rule violations which give rise to identity-threatening predicaments. In order to examine the type of rule-breaking which gives rise to embarrassment, Chapter 3 examines in some detail the various classes of embarrassing incident. Once an embarrassing event has occurred we are likely to make attempts to remedy the situation and re-establish for ourselves a more acceptable image. The second half of Chapter 3 examines the various attempts to classify verbal accounting strategies which might be used by the actor to mitigate the negative circumstances associated with the embarrassing event. As well as having a number of social causes, embarrassment also has a number of physical symptoms and behavioural signs. Blushing, gaze aversion, gesturing, speech disturbances and smiling or laughter have all been suggested as composing a typical embarrassment display. As well as describing studies designed to investigate the precise nature of the physiological and behavioural display of embarrassment, Chapter 4 examines the possible functions of these behaviours: as cues for the recognition of embarrassment, nervous responses or face-saving strategies.

In spite of the usefulness of the various self-presentational approaches to the study of embarrassment, there are still a number of gaps in our knowledge of the process involved. In an attempt to draw together research outlined in the first three chapters, Chapter 5 examines embarrassment as an emotion involving a chain of events. The nature of this process is examined in relation to a recently proposed model of embarrassment (Edelmann, 1984, 1985a). This model is an attempt to present a comprehensive account of the experience of embarrassment. The role of non-verbal behaviours, cognitions and self-focus in the generation and labelling of the subjective state of embarrassment is examined.

In Chapter 6 various aspects of the development of embarrassment are outlined in relation to specific components of the model. Whether embarrassment first appears during the learning of social rules or whether it is related to awareness of oneself as a social object is examined. Recent research examining the emergence and development of embarrassment, factors underlying its development, and how and when impression management strategies are learnt is discussed. Chapter 6 also outlines personality differences in susceptibility to embarrassment, discussing recent research findings and examining the embarrassibility scale used to assess these differences.

A central component of the model of embarrassment proposed in Chapter 5 is the relationship between embarrassment and social rule transgression. An implicit assumption is that fear of embarrassment can be viewed as a way of constraining our behaviour. Research suggests that we do, in fact, tend to avoid social situations which might engender embarrassment. Chapter 7 examines how fear of potential embarrassment can influence the amount of help we give to others and cause apparently negative responses to the physically disabled or those with a physical stigma.

The final two chapters of the book introduce a number of clinical issues. It has long been recognized that, because the behavioural signs of embarrassment are difficult to conceal, the actor will make a number of efforts to restore his/her public image, in order to remedy the situation and recreate a more favourable presentation of self. Whether individuals differ in their ability and/or confidence in their ability to deal with embarrassing events forms the central theme of Chapter 8. The skills deficit or cognitive models of social anxiety are of particular relevance to embarrassment as a clinical phenomenon. A related issue concerns clients who are chronic blushers and the problem of dealing with 'subjective' as opposed to situationally induced embarrassment.

The final chapter addresses the issue of clinical intervention and embarrassment. The question of social skills training versus cognitive control/self-attention reduction draws on issues raised in the preceding chapter. As well as the question of alleviating embarrassment, the very experience of embarrassment can itself be used as an aversive experience. The way in which fear of embarrassment constrains our behaviour will be discussed in Chapter 7—this same fear of embarrassment can be used to constrain clinically undesirable behaviour. Studies emphasizing teaching clients to experience embarrassment in order to eliminate exhibitionism are described in Chapter 9.

This book presents a range of ideas that firstly serve to organize and integrate various concepts and components of a complex cognitive process. Some of these ideas are speculative; all of them lead to directly testable hypotheses. Secondly, developing from the model presented are various further ideas and studies that aim to expand and clarify central issues involved in the process of embarrassment. Finally, having examined the psychology of embarrassment, further predictions can be made and implications for clinical intervention, social and personality processes evaluated. Chapter 2 then outlines the central aspects of our everyday self-presentation that lead to risks of embarrassment.

CHAPTER 2

Self-Presentation and Embarrassment

> Whatever else, embarrassment has to do with the figure the individual cuts before others felt to be there at the time. The crucial concern is the impression one makes on others in the present—whatever the long range or unconscious basis of this concern may be. (Goffman, 1956, p. ff 265)

No-one would seriously question the fact that we make inferences about what someone is like on the basis of their behaviours and actions, or that we feel it to be important that we attempt to control, in some way, the inferences that others make about us as a result of our own actions. Goffman crystallized one viewpoint on this need to manage the way in which we present ourselves in his dramaturgical account of embarrassment in 1956, as well as in his later writing (1959). In effect, his writings gave us the label 'self-presentation'.

The possibility that all the different forms of social anxiety may be related to self-presentational problems has been raised by Schlenker and Leary (1982). Certainly the notion of self-presentation, and the many facets that this involves, is likely to play a central part in the experience of embarrassment. How do we view ourselves? What view of ourselves do we wish to make available to others? What happens if we are unsure which image it is appropriate to present? What happens when we are made aware of how others regard us? Each of these questions holds part of the key to a clearer understanding of why we become embarrassed.

The first question—'How do we view ourselves?'—has to do with our awareness of the image we have of ourselves. Our own view of our identity; our awareness of our own beliefs, values and attitudes. Whenever we are in the presence of others, it is usually in our best interests to convey particular aspects of our identity or to portray ourselves in a particular way. Thus, the second question, 'What view of ourselves do we wish to make available to others?'; some projected images will be appropriate to the situation, creating the desired impression, with the result that we will gain the approval or at least not disapproval of others. If, on the other hand, the projected image is inappropriate, we are likely to create an undesired impression and may well generate undesired reactions. This may well be an important precursor of embarrassment.

The problem of conveying the appropriate image is of particular relevance in situations which create uncertainty—perhaps in situations we have not encountered before or with people with whom we are not familiar. It is in these situations that the risk of behaving inappropriately is at its most extreme. We have fewer clues about how we should respond, and hence there is an increased risk of 'doing the wrong thing' leading to disapproval from others, and hence the possibility of embarrassment.

The final question—'What happens when we are made aware of how others regard us?'—raises a further central issue. While we are concerned with our own image for ourselves, we are also concerned with which image, or which aspect of ourselves, to convey to others. The very presence of others can make us more concerned with presenting an image which is consistent with their expectations. The nature of the audience in terms of its status or numbers present can increase this desire to 'perform' adequately. Some people are also more likely to focus on the image they convey to others regardless of the type or size of audience. Again, the extent to which we are made aware of our actions, particularly if we are unsure which actions are appropriate, increases our concern with our behaviour and its appropriateness, and hence increases the risk of being embarrassed.

The four central features introduced in this chapter refer to the concepts of identity (Schlenker, 1980, 1982, 1983) or the phenomenal self (Jones and Gerard, 1967); self-presentation or impression management (Goffman, 1959; Schlenker, 1980; Jones and Pittman, 1982), uncertainty and ambiguity (Buss, 1980; Zimbardo, 1977) and self-attention (Buss, 1980; Carver, 1979; Duval and Wicklund, 1972; Fenigstein, 1979; Fenigstein, Scheier, and Buss, 1975; Carver and Scheier, 1981).

Each of these concepts and their relationship to embarrassment will be discussed in turn. Several of the key issues raised in this chapter will also recur at later points in the book—for example, the issue of self-attention as a pre-disposition will be discussed in Chapter 6; the role of ambiguity or uncertainty and resultant embarrassment as an inhibitor of help-seeking or help-giving will be discussed in Chapter 7. The present chapter thus raises many of the fundamental issues about embarrassment.

A. IDENTITY AND THE PHENOMENAL SELF

Identity is a theory (or schema) that is constructed about how one is and should be perceived, regarded, and treated in social life.' (Schlenker, 1980, 1982)

One's identity then is a composite of all aspects of an individual which go towards creating our own view of ourselves as well as how we are viewed by an audience. Schlenker (1980) suggests that all aspects of our appearance (e.g. type of dress, bodily size and shape, hair colour); background (e.g. home environment); apparent personal characteristics (e.g. intelligence); and behaviour in general (degree of anxiety), serve to build up this image or identity.

Within this general identity, Schlenker (1980, 1982) suggests that we have numerous, less inclusive identity images, each of which might be germane to a particular situation, audience, and behaviour.

Thus, we might be quite sure of ourselves with people we know well, but reserved with strangers; we might be talkative with one or two others, but quiet in the presence of larger groups; we might be assertive with equal or lower-status colleagues, but not with those of higher status. Schlenker further suggests that

> One's perceived identity is thus a theory about oneself embedded within the larger theory called self-concept. (1982, p. 195).

While it might seem that the view of a self-concept is broader than that of identity, the notion of one's *phenomenal self* has a great deal in common with Schlenker's theory. The phenomenal self was defined by Jones and Gerard (1967) as

> each person's awareness of his own beliefs, values, attitudes, the links between them, and their implications for his own behaviour. (p. 182).

In this sense then, each of us has a potentially available over-arching cognition of his or her interrelated dispositions or identities. Tedeschi and Riess (1981a) comment that:

> Controlling the identities perceived by others has the effect of defining the situation and thereby establishes the norms and behaviors that are appropriate for the interacting persons. (p. 15).

Identities can then act as a guide or script by which we can direct our behaviour. This allows us to form some sort of *standard* by which we are able to evaluate our current behaviour. It is as if we have a notion of what we are like, an image that we wish to project and expose to the evaluation of others. It is perhaps not difficult to see how this notion is related to the experience of embarrassment. Take as an example people who view themselves as being humorous—they have established a standard image for themselves, an image that they wish to present to others. Imagine that their behaviour leads to a failure to meet this standard—perhaps they forget the punchline of a joke or tell a joke which is wholly inappropriate to the situation. Whatever the failure, they perceive that others view them as far from humorous. They are in fact likely to be evaluated negatively—an evaluation which may generate anxiety, feelings of incompetence, unworthiness (Carver, 1979; Schlenker and Leary, 1982) and perhaps embarrassment. The converse obviously applies in that meeting or living up to a standard is likely to generate a positive affect.

The starting point for our exploration of an understanding of the experience of embarrassment then lies in the existence of a self- and identity-linked standard which we carry round with us. In order to avoid embarrassment we need to behave in a way which is consistent with this standard: in other words we try to manage the impressions of ourselves that we convey to others; we try to control the image of ourselves that we make available for other's scrutiny.

B. SELF-PRESENTATION

Self-presentation is the attempt to control identity-relevant information before real or imagined audiences. (Schlenker, 1982, p. 197).

Impression management consists of any behavior by a person that has the purpose of controlling or manipulating the attributions and impressions formed of that person by others. (Tedeschi and Riess, 1981a, p. 3).

Tedeschi and Riess (1981a) suggest six underlying reasons why people engage in self-presentation and impression management. (1) To create definitions of the situation and social identities for the actor, thus influencing which interactions are appropriate and which inappropriate; (2) to avoid blame and social disapproval by disassociating themselves from negative actions and conversely to gain social approval by associating themselves with positive ones; (3) to maintain self-esteem; (4) to influence the interaction; (5) to establish power and influence over the target person; or (6) to create connotative impressions of being good–bad or strong–weak.

A number of these research areas have clear implications for the experience of embarrassment. For example, if doubt is cast on the image the person is trying to present he/she may well experience negative, perhaps embarrassing, consequences. Attempts may then be made by the actor to remedy the situation, perhaps to avoid blame for the negative event or to gain approval for his/her remedial actions. The use of remedial tactics for overcoming embarrassment is discussed in the following chapter. First, however, we need to address ourselves to the precise link between self-presentational concerns and embarrassment.

It has widely been assumed that people will use self-presentational strategies both to avoid blame and social disapproval by dissociating themselves from negative actions and outcomes, and also to actually gain credit and social approval by associating themselves with positive ones (Jones and Pittman, 1982; Tedeschi, 1981; Schlenker, 1982). Most research on self-presentation does seem to emphasize the fact that individuals appear to strive to convey the most positive presentation of self, the presentation of self that would result in the most social approval. It is generally recognized, however, that there are a number of self-presentations which are likely to vary as a result of the situation. There are occasions when assertiveness or hostility may be appropriate, and other occasions when creating an impression of weakness and dependency may be the most desirable presentation to adopt.

1. Self-presentational strategies

Jones and Pittman (1982) in fact suggest five different self-presentational strategies which an actor may use according to the type of image he/she wishes to project (that is the attributions that the actor wants the observer to make about him/her).

The first strategy, *ingratiation*, involves attempts by the author to influence the observers liking for him/her (i.e. influencing attributions of likeability). These attempts may take the form of favours, paying attention to or flattering others, or conforming to expectations. Obviously, should these behaviours be excessive or show signs of ulterior motives they may well generate a negative response. Factors which might influence the selection of strategies of ingratiation, as well as the way in which they are evaluated by the observer, include the extent to which the actor wishes to be liked, the likelihood that the strategy will be executed effectively and whether it will be perceived as being genuine.

The second strategy is *intimidation*, which refers to attempts by the actor to convince the observer that he/she is dangerous. Unlike the ingratiator, who wants to be liked, the intimidator wants to be feared and believed. It would commonly be the person of higher power or status who would be likely to adopt such a strategy, appearing to be gruff, impatient and severe.

The third strategy, *self-promotion*, refers to attempts by the actor to be perceived as effective, whether with reference to general ability level (intelligence, knowledge or athletic prowess) or to a specific skill (piano-playing ability, typing excellence). It is also possible for self-promotion to have certain features of both ingratiation and intimidation. Thus, an actor making claims to intelligence may wish to be liked because he/she perceives intelligence as an attractive personal quality and also to be respected because intelligence is a particular talent.

There are also many contexts in which we might be eager to impress others with our competence: students confronting lecturers, applicants before an interview panel, making our first date with the opposite sex. In all cases the self-promoter must cope with the problem that many areas of competence can either be objectively diagnosed or the validity of claims made can be tested against future performance. Thus, the interviewee who claims competence in an area has to later live up to these claims in his work; the student claiming to be knowledgeable can be assessed by objective examinations, whilst the person making claims to a potential partner will have his/her claims tested by the course of time.

One further problem can be referred to as the self-promoters' paradox—the fact that claims of competence are more likely to be made when competence is in fact shaky rather than when it is secure. The most effective way of carrying out self-promotion is by rather more subtle, indirect means—the persons wanting a job in a particular area may fill in spare time with voluntary work or seek election to various committees of relevance, etc.

The fourth strategy, *exemplification*, refers to attempts by the actor to be admired and respected for his/her integrity and moral rectitude. 'The saint who walks among us, the martyr who sacrifices for the cause' (Jones and Pittman, 1982, p. 245). The effective exemplifier is someone who is, or at least appears to be, the standard bearer of morality—'Look what I have given up, look what I have donated, look what long hours I work', etc. As well as wanting others to think of him/her as competent (self-promotion) and likeable (ingratiation) the exemplifier wants to be thought of as honest, generous and self-sacrificing.

The final strategy mentioned by Jones and Pittman, *supplication*, is most often used as a last resort by weak and dependent people. Supplication involves making one's dependence clear in order to elicit help from others. While there may be heavy costs in advertising one's helplessness or incompetence, there may be times when emphasizing stereotypical weaknesses (the woman who cannot repair her car, the man who cannot mend his clothes) can quite easily ensure that someone else will perform chores which we do not wish to perform ourselves. Nevertheless, dependence is a risky strategy which can severely damage one's view of oneself if the image of dependence is mismanaged.

Several factors of importance emerge from this analysis of self-presentational strategies, both in general terms and of direct relevance to the experience of embarrassment.

First, it should be noted that self-presentation involves neither manipulation nor deceit. As mentioned previously, certain images of oneself and hence certain styles of self-presentation are appropriate at different times. Intimidation may be appropriate for the boss at work, but not when he/she arrives home to his/her family in the evening. Further, certain styles may become ineffective if used continuously—it is acceptable for either partner to use supplicatory behaviour at times during their relationship, but should one partner adopt this strategy continuously, overdependence may result.

Second, it is important to note that one style is not necessarily used at the exclusion of others. Thus it is possible for any one individual to be seen as competent (self-promoter), likeable (ingratiator) and morally worthy (exemplifier). Some combinations are obviously more plausible than others—a likeable (ingratiator), fear-inducing person (intimidator) though a possibility is less likely than a competent, likeable person.

What then of self-presentation and embarrassment? Goffman (1956) lends a key to the link:

> During interactions the individual is expected to possess certain attributes, capacities, and information which, taken togeter, fit together into a self that is at once coherently unified and appropriate for the occasion. (p. 270).

> When an event throws doubt upon or discredits these claims, then the encounter

finds itself lodged in assumptions which no longer hold. . . . At such times the individual whose self has been threatened (the individual for whom embarrassment is felt) and the individual who threatened him may both feel ashamed of what together they have brought about. (p. 172).

In Goffman's terms it is the very discrediting of our intended self-presentation which leads to embarrassment. Thus for the ingratiator, whose attempts to be likeable are found to be false; the supplicator, whose attempts to look dependent are seen as attempts to scrounge help; or the exemplifier, who is found to be unworthy and dishonest, the risk of experiencing embarrassment is increased.

That there is more to the story will become evident through the course of this book. Discrediting one's intended self-presentation does, however, present a clear starting point. We thus have an image or view of ourselves, the presentation of which we use to define both ourselves and the situation. If this definition is shown, during the course of the interaction, to be false we are left with a negative, undesired image. This involves the basic assumption, however, that the desire for social approval underlies the individual's behaviour, i.e. attempts are made to convey the most positive presentation of self—the presentation of self that would result in the most social approval. In order to adequately explain the experience of embarrassment two further aspects or styles of self-presentation require explication: protective self-presentation and self-handicapping strategies.

2. Protective self-presentation

The existence of a protective self-presentation style has been suggested by Arkin (1981). The motive underlying protective self-presentation can be characterized as a desire to avoid significant losses in social approval in contrast with the previous self-presentation strategies referred to which emphasize gaining social approval. As mentioned, self-presentations that fail (i.e. are undermined by various facts that fail to support the individual's claim to an identity) are likely to give rise to embarrassment. The potential for disapproval by relevant others is always present but in certain circumstances can be particularly costly in terms of outcome. Thus, with certain target audiences it is difficulty to ascertain which impressions are likely to be judged positively or negatively. In certain interaction contexts, i.e. when faced with an unfamiliar audience or when a particular presentation has to be sustained for long periods of time, there may be particular difficulties in terms of how to present oneself in order to gain approval. Further, the presenter him/herself may not feel able to identify which presentation is likely to be evaluated positively or negatively by the audience, or may feel unable to execute the necessary presentation successfully. In each of these cases, there is an increased likelihood that the individual will fail in his/her self-presentation as well as in the likelihood that embarrassment may be the result.

Arkin (1981) argues that it is under just these circumstances that the actor is likely to adopt a protective self-presentation style. When it is risky to adopt an acquisitive style (i.e. one seeking social approval) then the individual will adopt a protective self-presentational style in order to avoid disapproval, i.e. there is a tendency to take a conservative orientation just to be on the safe side.

This protective, conservative orientation can be portrayed in a number of ways. First, there is the assumption that by remaining relatively quiet one can remain relatively safe. This has been referred to as the 'reticence syndrome' (Phillips and Metzger, 1973) in which individuals sometimes appear reluctant to interact with others. In its extreme form such an orientation can result in complete social avoidance and withdrawal (Watson and Friend, 1969).

Rather than withdraw, we may actively use behaviours that prevent others from challenging us or that create an impression which cannot be questioned. Highly modest portrayals of one's personal characteristics, behaviour and accomplishments may prevent challenge from others. Neutral, uncertain, or qualified expressions of views or opinions render them difficult to question. Conformity and compliance are particularly safe and are unlikely to require much by way of explanation, or justification.

It has been argued (Edelmann, 1985a) that, under those conditions which are likely to give rise to embarrassment, the individual is much more likely to adopt a protective self-presentation style. This suggests that for those most prone to embarrassment (the socially anxious, self-conscious, etc.—see Chapter 6) and in situations in which a risk of embarrassment is increased (the size, status, knowledge, competitiveness of the target audience), a self-protective style of self-presentation is the most likely option. By appearing to be modest, or compliant, or by remaining quiet, a standard is created which is not difficult to meet. Further failure to meet this standard would only result in a minor loss of identity.

3. Self-handicapping

Further important protective self-presentation strategies with relevance to embarrassment are those which serve to disarm information suggesting one's incompetence. Through self-handicapping strategies individuals excuse their inadequate behaviours and therefore attempt to defer others from viewing them as inadequate. As first described and demonstrated by Jones and Berglas (Jones and Berglas, 1978; Berglas and Jones, 1978) a self-handicapping strategy is a self-invoked impediment to performance in evaluative settings. Such an impediment provides the individual with a ready-made excuse for possible failure. Thus, individuals faced with an evaluative situation frequently attempt to structure the situation so as to 'protect their conceptions of themselves as competent, intelligent persons' (Jones and Berglas, 1978, p. 200).

If failure then occurs, it is relatively easy for the individual to attribute this failure to the impediment rather than to the individual's lack of ability. Thus, a guest who is unsure how to behave at a dinner party might comment on the fact that he/she always does something embarrassing in such situations. If the person then does something which is potentially embarrassing he has already generated reasons (e.g. his behavioural tendencies) for his embarrassing behaviour and simultaneously multiplied the positive implications of success at not behaving embarrassingly, i.e. achieved in spite of his behavioural tendencies.

Self-handicapping has been demonstrated in drug choices, alcohol use and, of particular relevance to the present argument, to shyness (Snyder et al., 1986; Snyder and Smith, 1982, 1983).

Performance-related anxieties (e.g. speech anxiety, test anxiety, social anxiety) can serve effectively as alternative explanations because of their acknowledged debilitating effect upon task performance. In more extreme situations these anxiety patterns can serve as reasons for avoiding the situations entirely—social anxiety, perhaps shyness or embarrassment, can thus be viewed as potentially understandable reasons for avoiding difficult social situations: 'I don't go to parties because I find having to talk to people I don't know rather embarrassing.'

In an experimental test of this hypothesis, Snyder *et al.* (1985) found that male subjects who scored highly on measures of social anxiety or shyness would report more symptoms of social anxiety in evaluative settings in which anxiety or shyness could serve as an excuse for poor performance than would individuals in either an evaluative setting in which shyness could not adequately be used as an excuse or in nonevaluative settings. Also, males (but not females) who were not socially anxious did not use shyness as an excuse for their actions. It may be that men have to think of an active excuse for their actions while females can respond with passive accommodation— although other studies have found that women too use self-handicapping strategies (Smith, Snyder and Perkins, 1983). What does seem to be clear is that in situations which are likely to be potentially embarrassing, or in the case of individuals who are characterized by a predisposition to embarrassment, a protective self-presentation style including the possibility of a self-handicapping strategy may be used rather than an acquisitive, self-presentational strategy. Factors which are likely to influence the adopting of a protective rather than an acquisitive style may reside with the target audience (size, status, knowledge, competitiveness), the interaction context (novel or ambiguous situations), or the actor's characteristics (self-consciousness, social anxiety), those context factors or individual characteristics which increase the actor's desire to avoid objective signs of failure. Such signs would be likely to elicit negative self-referent cognitions and arouse affective signs and behavioural consequences of embarrassment. It seems that these factors also serve to increase our concern with the way others perceive us; they make us more self-attentive.

C. SELF-AWARENESS AND SELF-PRESENTATION

A crucial role in activating concern about one's identity appears to be played by self-attention. The starting point for this concept was self-awareness theory (Duval and Wicklund, 1972; Wicklund, 1975), proposing that attention is primarily focused either outward toward the environment or inward toward the self. According to their theory the focusing of attention leads to a comparison between one's present behaviour or state and relevant standards of comparison. The standards which are adhered to will partly be dependent upon the context in which the behaviour occurs. In most interaction contexts the standard would be the image of oneself or one's identity that one wishes to project to others. If a discrepancy is perceived between ongoing behaviour and a standard, negative affect is assumed to be generated, one potential result of which is a tendency to alter the behaviour so that it conforms more closely to the standard regulating it.

The comparisons between present state and standard thus have important self-regulatory consequences. In Duval and Wicklund's view, a negative discrepancy between the two values creates a negative drive state, which can be reduced by altering the behaviour to more closely approximate the standard. Thus awareness of the self leads the person to attempt to conform behaviourally to salient standards. A recent alternative analysis of this self-regulatory process is derived from an examination of control theory or cybernetics. Reduction of discrepancies between sensed states and reference values are explained in terms of a feedback mechanism (Carver, 1979; Carver and Scheier, 1981; Scheier and Carver, 1982). The behavioural consequences of the two models are fundamentally the same. Self-attention appears to prompt people to attend to information from the perspective of its relevance to the self or identity; it increases the importance of one's attempts to adhere to personal or public standards for conduct; it intensifies the process of self-assessment and self-evaluation; and it enhances self-reinforcement when standards are met and negative affect when standards are not met (Schlenker, 1982). The notion of increased attention for information of relevance to one's identity is of central importance to the experience of embarrassment and the likelihood of selecting protective styles of self-presentation. Before discussing this issue, however, a number of important distinctions need to be made about our tendency to seek out information. First, it should be noted that the disposition to be self-attentive has been labelled 'self-consciousness'; the manipulated state (i.e. introduced by outside factors) has been labelled 'self-awareness'.

Further, it has been argued that, when people direct their attention toward themselves, they may be either privately or publicly self-aware. Private self-awareness occurs when people attend to aspects of themselves that can be observed only by the experiencing person (Buss, 1980), e.g. a feeling of resentment or fear, an idea about an item of news, etc. That is, all those which are personal to the individual concerned unless he/she wishes to make them known to us as observers. This can be contrasted with public self-awareness which refers to observable aspects of the actor's actions and behaviours. Thus our facial expressions, gestures, properties of our voice and so on, are available to the observer for interpretation.

In the case of embarrassment it has been argued that the public aspect of the self is of central importance (Edelmann, 1985a). When we are publicly self-aware, attending to the observable aspects of ourselves, we are concerned about the observer's interpretation of this information. The perceptions and evaluations of others thus assume a particular importance (Buss, 1980; Fenigstein, 1979). The individual who is publicly self-focused, simply because he/she is specifically focusing on the way in which he/she is being perceived and evaluated by others, is much more likely to make attemps to control and monitor the identity images he/she is conveying. Thus the mere presence of others who are attending to our physical appearance or the way in which we are conveying ourselves can lead to a state of self-attention. In experimental studies, the presence of observers has in fact been used as a means by which self-awareness can be induced. The crucial point about the situation is that the persons being observed are made to feel that they are indeed being evaluated, i.e. that they are the very centre of attention. In this context, Zimbardo (1977) reports that the single most likely situation making people feel shy is being the centre of attention of a large group. In such a situation our behaviour is being watched, we are usually eager to be seen in the best light (i.e. we wish our behaviour to meet the standards we set for ourselves) and fear that we may not do so. As Schlenker comments:

> Public self-attention focuses people on how their conduct will look to immediate audiences, evoking concerns with maintaining a desirable identity before those others (1982, p. 220).

It is not difficult to speculate from this that we feel more exposed to evaluative observations when confronted by larger audiences, or by high-status, knowledgeable audiences, i.e. the situations where our performance is likely to be under close scrutiny. We may also feel that in novel or ambiguous situations our behaviour is under particular scrutiny, although our own negative thoughts about our performance may influence the outcome of our reactions rather than our behaviour *per se*. Further, as mentioned, the actor's characteristics may predispose him/her to be more or less self-attentive and concerned about his/her presented behaviour (i.e. self-conscious). The set of circumstances outlined above are also the ones proposed as being more likely to evoke a protective rather than an acquisitive self-presentational style. They are the situations where the negative consequences of failure and possibility of embarrassment are likely to be greatest.

It seems then that situations which are more likely to increase our public self-awareness are the ones we find most threatening to the identity image that we with to present. They are the situations and characteristics which induce uncertainty about the way we should be presenting ourselves towards others present. Self-attention (as self-consciousness) can thus be a cause of our feelings of insecurity or a consequence of our feelings of insecurity in front of certain audiences or in certain situations. Given this insecurity it is more likely that we will resort to the conservative, protective styles of self-presenation to see us through. Let us examine these situations and characteristics in more detail.

D. FACTORS INFLUENCING THE ADOPTION OF A PROTECTIVE SELF-PRESENTATION STYLE

1. Characteristics of the target audience

There are a number of aspects of the target audience which are likely to influence the adopting of a protective rather than an acquisitive style—the audience's size, status, whether it is an authoritative, expert audience or an audience of the opposite sex. Two points are of importance here: first, we must actually want to impress the audience with which we are confronted, whilst, secondly, doubting that we will be able to do so. It is under these circumstances that a protective self-presentational style, whilst not being inevitable, is the more likely outcome. These are situations which pose an increased threat to our identity, hence it is better to be safe than sorry. Certainly in case of social anxiety (Zimbardo, 1977) it has been reported that people feel more anxious in front of the type of audiences detailed above—perhaps because the threat of the negative, embarrassing consequences of failure is that much greater. The social implications of this fear of negative evaluation in front of certain types of audiences are discussed in Chapter 7. It seems that fear of embarrassment in such encounters may inhibit the extent to which we offer our assistance to others as well as the extent to which we are prepared to seek help. It may also be the case that fear of embarrassment in such situations is actually a cause of anxious preoccupation about social encounters (i.e. social anxiety).

Before discussing the limited research on the effect of audience characteristics on self-presentational style and embarrassment, we need to ask why the characteristics of others are such an important element in determining how we present ourselves. At the heart of the matter lies the fact that we value the views, impressions, opinions and reactions of others to our behaviour/performance. Should we consider someone to be worth impressing then the salience of these views, reactions, etc., becomes much more important. Should we feel that we have a modicum of talent in conducting a particular skill then the criticism of someone whose opinion we value will be particularly damaging. This includes not only possible rebuffs from a member of the opposite sex whom we find attractive, but criticism from superiors at work, or an observation of our perhaps limited musical or artistic skills, etc, by someone whom we consider to be rather more expert than ourselves. It is more rewarding to be evaluated highly by someone whose opinion we would value, but at the same time the negative and possibly embarrassing consequences are that much greater should we fail. Hence, the likely adoption of a protective self-presentation style under such circumstances. This is particularly relevant with reference to self-handicapping strategies whereby we can explain our failings before they happen (or at least before they might happen). We might comment on how embarrassing it is to display our mediocre drawing or playing skills, etc, in front of such a talented audience, or we might comment to a superior 'Look, I know this is not particularly good but I would value your opinion'. That high-status, expert others, whose opinions, etc., we value pose a greater threat than low-status, inexpert others with the negative consequences of failure and embarrassment in front of the former type of audience being more severe, has been demonstrated experimentally (Brown, 1970; Brown and Garland, 1971; Garland and Brown, 1972).

In the first of these studies (Brown, 1970) subjects performed either an embarrassing task (sucking a pacifier in order to form a detailed impression of it) or a non-embarrassing task (feeling a rubber soldier). They then had the choice of either receiving maximum monetary payoff by describing their reactions publicly or accepting smaller payoffs to avoid public exposure. Half the subjects believed their potential payoffs were announced to an audience, half believed they would remain unannounced. It was found that sacrifice was pronounced when subjects performed the embarrassing task and believed the audience was ignorant of their costs.

In the second part of this study half the subjects were led to believe that the audience had an evaluative role, half to believe that the audience had a non-evaluative role when they described their reactions to the embarrassing task. Sacrificing the tangible rewards referred to above was greater in the evaluative condition, i.e. following an embarrassing event, subjects would rather avoid being evaluated by others.

In the second and third studies (Brown and Garland, 1971; Garland and Brown, 1972), the effect of the audience acquaintance, sex and expertise upon sacrificing tangible rewards to avoid looking foolish was evaluated. Subjects were asked to sing 'Love is a Many Splendored Thing' with longer public singing increasing monetary reward. If the audience was perceived as being competent, and if there was a likelihood that the subject would have to meet them afterwards, then the subject was much more likely to sacrifice the rewards.

This seems to support the notion that evaluation from certain types of audience is perceived as being more threatening and would be avoided if possible. Often it is not possible to avoid such encounters, but by adopting a rather more conservative, protective orientation we can partially guard against the negative and potentially embarrassing consequences of failure in front of such an audience.

The question remains, though, of audience size. Is a larger group of low-status others more threatening than perhaps one other low-status individual? Certainly this is the case with a large group of high-status compared with a smaller group of high-status others. Is it important to avoid looking foolish in front of a larger group of others whose opinion we do not value than a similar but smaller group? In a study evaluating this proposition, Jackson and Latané (1981) studied the effects of audience size and status upon anticipated tension and nervousness. Subjects were told they would have to imagine themselves singing 'The Star Spangled Banner' in front of a variety of different audiences—audiences which consisted of coloured photographic slides of one, three or nine persons standing in a group facing the camera. In the low-status conditions these persons were undergraduates described as 'college students who have been tested and found to be partially tone deaf'. In the high-status conditions, the pictures were of older graduate students, professors and secretaries who were described as professors and graduate students from the Music Department.

As predicted, subjects perceived high-status audiences as eliciting more nervousness and tension than low-status groups. This is consistent with the findings of Brown and his colleagues referred to previously, and does tend to support the view that high-status audiences are perceived as being more threatening. This may increase the possibility of a negative outcome and hence embarrassment, with the likelihood of adopting a protective self-presentational style to guard against such failure.

Audience size was seen to be threatening, however, independently of the status of the group concerned. Respondents perceived larger groups as arousing more nervousness and tension than small groups. It is of interest to note that other research suggests that continued increase in the numbers of others present tends to have an ever-decreasing proportionate increase in anxiety generated. Thus we are unlikely to feel 10 times as nervous at a party with 100 people than we would at a party of 10 people; we are unlikely to feel 8 times more nervous when speaking before 800 than before 100. In a study by Latané and Harkins (1976) college students were asked to imagine that they were reciting a memorized poem in front of an audience of 1, 2, 4, 8 or 16 people. They were to adjust the brightness of a light or the loudness of a tone to indicate nervousness, tension and anxiety. Results showed that estimated nervousness, tension and anxiety was greater before imagined larger audiences, but that although they would feel about twice as nervous in front of 4 than 2 people, they were only about 3 times as tense in front of 8 than 2, and only about 4 times as tense in front of 16 than 2. Nervousness appeared to increase in proportion to the square root of the number of people in the audience.

It seems then that amount of anxiety and nervousness does increase as a function of audience size and status. Although it is also likely that the embarrassment potential of the situation increases in a similar fashion, the results of the studies cited must be treated with some caution. The studies by Brown and Garland, and Hawkins and Latané, used artificial situations.

Neither involved actual sequences of social interaction, and the latter study involved a purely hypothetical self-report of an imagined situation. Neverthe-less, the fact that audeinces make us nervous seems to apply to social anxiety in general. Zimbardo (1977) reports that shy people are more anxious at large parties than small parties. No doubt it is also far more embarrassing to fail in front of a large audience than a small audience even if they are of equal or lower status, although this proposition has not been tested. Why, however, might this be the case? Why should many low-status others be threatening when a single low-status other is not? The threat in this case may well be the threat of losing an expected reward rather than the threat of losing praise. When we value the audience's opinion but expect it to be poor (as with high-status or expert others), then we will try to protect ourselves against failure and possible embarrassment by adopting a conserva-tive, protective, perhaps self-handicapping self-presentation style. If then we are evaluated favourably, we have won through, even though we have already decreased the likelihood of negative evaluation. In front of low-status others, however, we may well expect our own performance to be relatively competent and may not take the precaution of protecting our image. To fail under these circumstances would then be seen as not presenting ourselves in a way which is consistent with our own expectations. That is, we have fallen below our desired standard and hence expect negative evaluation and the consequent embarrassment which accompanies this.

On the one hand then we can adopt the conservative line and present ourselves in a way which decreases the risks—our present image has been excused and is therefore not discrepant from our expectations; on the other hand we can attempt to be acquisitive in our self-presentation style with the accompanying risks of failure.

2. The interaction context

While we may adopt different self-presentation styles depending upon the characteristics of the audience before whom we are performing, there are also occasions when we may not be sure which style to adopt. That is, in situations which are novel or ambiguous—situations where, because we are unsure, we run the risk of presenting ourselves in a way which is inconsistent with the way in which we would wish to appear and hence run the risk of negative and embarrassing consequences of failure. These again then are situations where it is better to be safe than sorry and to adopt a protective self-presentation style.

> Uncertainty should be generated in novel, unusual, unstructured situations, and when people interact with others about whom they know relatively little. When situations are novel or unusual, people cannot rely on previous experience as a guide. (Leary and Schlenker, 1981, p. 348).

In such situations it is fear of presenting oneself inappropriately, and the negative and embarrassing consequences which can result, which often inhibit our interactions with others. The social implications of this are discussed in Chapter 7. There have been many studies and suggestions linking this supposition with anxiety, shyness, reticence, public speaking anxieties and social anxiety in general, but little empirical validation of this supposition in relation to embarrassment. It is nevertheless illuminating to look at the research on the influence of novel and ambiguous situations on other facets of social anxiety and to compare this with the limited work on embarrassment. There are really two issues involved here—firstly the question of 'Who am I?' in relation to the image the actors may feel they want to present; and second, 'What is this situation all about?' in relation to an interaction context which we have not experienced before. Obviously, the two closely overlap.

The question of 'Who am I?' can perhaps arise when we take on a new job or other new role, when we have yet to establish the appropriate way in which we wish to be seen in this role. This may be one reason why embarrassment is so devastating during adolescence. As Buss (1980) points out:

> adolescents, confronted with changes as basic as body image, are driven to wonder about their identity: Who am I; What am I becoming? (p. 244).

The issue of developmental changes in relation to embarrassment will be discussed in full in Chapter 6. Adolescence in particular is a time when novelty, in terms of role and status, can cause problems for adequate self-presentation—not knowing which image to present and how to guard against possible failure.

In the same way that role novelty can present self-presentation difficulties so can ambiguous and unstructured social settings. Self-reports of social anxiety, and in particular shyness, have been found to increase in novel and unstructured situations, and in encounters with relative strangers (Pilkonis, 1977; Zimbardo, 1977). These are situations for which it is difficult to plan one's behaviour or to guess how others present might react or behave. By not knowing how to present oneself it is easy to adopt the wrong approach—being too ingratiating, too intimidating, too self-promoting and so on. No doubt we can all recall times when we have overdone it—perhaps been a bit too pushy or worthy, going beyond the expectations of those present. It is at these times that we may well decide to take the conservative, protective line in an attempt to avoid the possible negative and embarrassing consequences of social failure.

It is of interest to note in this context, that the very experience of embarrassment can give rise to uncertainty. The display of embarrassment is a particular self-presentation in its own right—one which can occasion its own problems for the other interactants present. Should they comment on the reaction? Should they carry on as if nothing has happened? Should they help the actor out of the predicament? The ways in which both the actor and the observer can manage such situations are dealt with in the following chapter.

In the light of the present discussion though it is easy to see how things can quickly get out of hand. Initially the actor may not be quite sure how to deal with a novel situation, and behaves in a way which is out of step with the rules and conventions of the situation—this results in a predicament for the observer—'What should he/she do?'. Observers run the risk of themselves responding inappropriately and only serving to increase the actor's embarrassment and perhaps cause themselves embarrassment. The situation can easily escalate out of control; embarrassment can then grow, engulfing all those who are present in the situation.

Uncertainty of the rules and roles of social encounters is thus one of the prime sources of difficulty in knowing how to present oneself appropriately. This uncertainty has two possible consequences: first, an increased likelihood that one will adopt a protective style of self-presentation, and second, the increased likelihood that we will fail to present ourselves as we would wish, resulting in an increased likelihood of negative consequences and embarrassment.

3. Individual differences

Having examined the interaction context and the target audience as influences upon the selection of a protective self-presentation style, it is important to note that some people, more or less chronically, adopt a protective self-presentation style independently of both context and audience.

Any personality variables which relate to self-doubt, or lack of confidence in one's ability to present oneself adequately, are likely to increase one's concern with disapproval and increase concern about one's identity. These dispositions are likely to have two sets of consequences: first, the individual concerned with the views of others is more likely to guard against failure by adopting a protective self-presentation style; second, should a failure occur (even of a fairly minor variety), over-concern with social approval and with one's identity is likely to give rise to over-concern with the views, reactions and evaluations of others. Over-concern with the negative aspects of these evaluations is likely to enhance the individuals' potential for embarrassment.

Various aspects of personality are likely to be implicated, which will be discussed in some detail in Chapter 6. A summary of the salient features will be presented here.

(a) Need for social approval

It perhaps goes without saying that those who score highly on measures of a need for social approval will be more likely to adopt a protective self-presentation style and be more distressed by the negative consequences of failure. One scale which has been used to measure need for approval is the Social Desirability Scale (Crown and Marlowe, 1964). One problem, however, with people who need approval may be to misrepresent themselves on scales which would show them in a negative light. They may thus respond negatively to questionnaire items such as 'Do you get easily embarrassed?' or positively to 'No matter who I am listening to, I'm always a good listener', and so on, creating a possibly false impression of themselves in order to be seen in a good light. Questionnaire evaluations of the relationship between need for approval and the impact of embarrassing incidents may thus not be particularly fruitful. Consistent with this possibility is the finding that the related construct of shyness is negatively related with need for approval. As Marlowe and Crowne originally proposed that high social desirability scores were evidence of a need for approval, we perhaps need some other indirect means of assessing the relationship between this factor and embarrassibility.

(b) Fear of negative evaluation

Closely related to a need for approval is fear of negative evaluation—in the same way that some individuals may be particularly concerned with engendering others' approval, the converse situation may apply in that individuals may be concerned with avoiding the negative reactions of others. A widely used scale for assessing this tendency is the 'Fear of Negative Evaluation Scale' (Watson and Friend, 1969). Several studies suggest a relationship between this construct and dimensions of importance to the present argument and social anxiety in general.

In a study of highly socially anxious individuals, Nichols (1974) noted that the most common characteristic of these subjects was a sensitivity to, and fear of, receiving disapproval and criticism of others. Scores on the Fear of Negative Evaluation Scale also correlate moderately to highly with several measures of social anxiety, including the Social Avoidance and Distress Scale (Watson and Friend, 1969); the Interaction Anxiousness Scale (Leary, 1983b) and measures of audience anxiety (Leary, 1983b). Fear of Negative Evaluation is clearly implicated as a factor in social anxiety, and is clearly important as a motivator in avoiding disapproval from others. It would seem that this factor is also important as a predisposing characteristic identifying those most prone to the experience of embarrassment. The reasoning behind this is that these individuals are most likely to play safe in terms of the self-presentation adopted when faced with uncertainty, or an audience which presents a threat to one's identity. As these actors are particularly afraid of the negative consequences of failure, then should encounters still go wrong, with the presented image falling below a desired standard, these consequences may be viewed as particularly embarrassing by the actor concerned.

(c) Self-consciousness

While the two factors referred to above (desire for social approval and fear of negative evaluation) are particularly important concerns over approval and disapproval, a crucial role in activating concern about one's identity appears to be the part played by self-consciousness. As mentioned, this is the disposition to be self-attentive as distinct from the manipulated state of self-awareness discussed previously.

As with self-awareness one can be either privately self-conscious and/or publicly self-conscious, the former referring to awareness of one's unobservable thoughts and feelings, and the latter to the awareness of one's observable actions and behaviours. Cheek and Briggs (1982) found that public self-consciousness was significantly related to the importance that subjects attached to self aspects contributing to 'social' identity, e.g. 'My gestures and mannerisms—the ways I express myself', 'Memberships that I have in various groups', and 'My physical features—height, weight, shape of my body, etc?'

In the same way then that audiences can cause people to attend to one's social facets some people are particularly disposed to be self-attentive. It seems reasonable to suggest that chronically attending to facets of one's social self would engender particular concern with the kind of impression created for others. Being thus concerned they may be more inclined to adopt a protective style of presentation even under conditions of minimum threat. People who are chronically high in public self-consciousness may be more likely to entertain doubts about their self-presentation abilities across a wide variety of situations. Further, should an event occur which discredits in some way the identity image they are presenting, they are likely to be more aware that a discrepancy exists between their current state and their desired standard for presentation, or to envisage the discrepancy as being considerably larger that it in fact is. For someone who is chronically predisposed to be self-attentive, behavioural standards are more likely to be salient, leading to active comparison between the standard and one's present behaviour or state.

> A major consequence of self-consciousness is an increased concern with the presentation of self and the reactions of others to that presentation. (Fenigstein, 1979, p. 75).

The suggestion that public self-consciousness plays a central role in the experience of embarrassment gains some support from the findings that public self-consciousness is positively related to a number of aspects of social anxiety. It is thus positively related to measures of shyness (Cheek and Buss, 1981), interaction-anxiousness and audience-anxiousness (Leary, 1983b), social reticence (Jones and Russell, 1982), self-reports of shyness (Pilkonis, 1977) as well as with general measures of social anxiety (Fenigstein, Scheier and Buss, 1975; Fenigstein, 1979; Buss, 1980). The relationship between public self-consciousness and embarrassibility is reviewed in Chapter 6.

As Fenigstein (1979) suggests, public self-consciousness may be a necessary, but not sufficient, precondition of social anxiety; concern with how others evaluate us can lead to concern that we either guard against failure if possible (adopt a protective style) or risk the negative consequences and embarrassment of failure. Both audiences, especially high-status, expert, evaluative audiences, novel and ambiguous situations, etc., can lead us to chronically attend to the public aspect of ourselves, i.e. over-concern with how others present are evaluating us. In addition, some individuals are chronically predisposed to be publicly self-conscious.

(d) Self-monitoring

Goffman's concept of self-presentation assumed that we fill the various roles in our life in a manner similar to the manner in which actors adopt roles on stage. There are thus likely to be variations in the extent to which we are aware of and regulate social affects and/or behaviour. Mark Snyder (1979) has brought attention to individual differences that exist in the ability to monitor and control one's expressive behaviours, proposing that people differ in their self-monitoring ability.

> The prototypic high self-monitoring individual is one who out of concern for the situational and interpersonal appropriateness of his or her social behaviour, is particularly sensitive to the expression and self-presentation of relevant others in social situations and uses these cues for monitoring (that is regulating and controlling) his or her own verbal and nonverbal self-presentation. (Snyder, 1979, p. 89).

It has recently been suggested (Carver and Scheier, 1981, p. 325) that while the self-consciousness scale was specifically intended to assess attentional focus, the self-monitoring scale assesses the more general orientation to the use of private or public information for behavioural regulation. Self-monitoring differences may then predict where the subject will look to determine behavioural regulation, while self-consciousness differences should predict the degree to which those standards are used.

Snyder (1974) has developed a scale to measure self-monitoring; high self-monitors seem to possess both the ability to successfully control their expressive behaviours and the motivation to seek out and use cues that indicate what is socially appropriate. As far as ability is concerned, it has been found that high self-monitors are better able to communicate emotions accurately on demand even when they don't feel in a particular way (Snyder, 1974). Thus a high self-monitor can more easily feign being angry, and, happy, etc. As far as motivation is concerned, high self-monitors are more attentive to social comparison information, they look to audiences to provide cues about what they should do in a particular situation (Snyder, 1974).

Failure to monitor and control one's responses is likely to result in the projection of an identity image that others deem undesirable, resulting in negative evaluations from others. Low self-monitors, not being so capable of controlling the impressions others form of them, may attempt to manage their impressions less often than high self-monitors. They may be less competent at gauging which cues from the environment to use to select an appropriate self-presentation style. It is not difficult to speculate that larger, higher-status, evaluative audiences or novel and ambiguous situations would present greater difficulty for low self-monitors than for high self-monitors; difficulty selecting appropriate cues may well lead to the presentation of an undesirable identity image with the resulting negative consequences and embarrassment.

One problem for analysing the relationship between self-monitoring, embarrassibility and other constructs of relevance is the fact that self-monitoring refers to a set of psychological characteristics. Recent investigations have in fact suggested that the scale used to measure self-monitoring is multidimensional with only a relatively stable factor structure. This issue will be taken up in some detail in Chapter 6. Suffice it to say at this point that self-monitoring ability is closely related to impression management skills. As Snyder (1981) comments:

> The self developed impression management skills of high self-monitors give them the flexibility and adaptiveness to cope quickly and effectively with a wide variety of social roles. They can choose with skill and grace the self-presentation and social behaviour appropriate to a wide variety of social situations. (p. 102).

Those who doubt their ability to seek out cues indicating what is socially appropriate (i.e. low self-monitors) may well guard against failure by adopting a protective self-presentation style. These people may be particularly fearful of the negative and potentially embarrassing consequences of failure.

E. SUMMARY

Embarrassment then has to do with a failure to present a desired image to others whom we regard as evaluating our performance. This failure can occur in both face-to-face interaction with acquaintances as well as the more structured presentation before groups. Given that we have our own standards of presentation based upon assumptions of the identity image that we feel is most appropriate in a given situation, any disrupting or discrediting event can have negative consequences. Given also our desire to present ourselves in a way which is at the very least not unfavourable, there are certain factors which can influence our desire to protect our image before others. Thus larger, more competent audiences, novel or ambiguous interaction contexts or facets of one's own personality can influence our desire to be more or less protective of our identity image. These are all factors which can increase the negative consequences of failure and the likelihood that embarrassment will occur. One assumption, however, is that we have prior knowledge of the rules of conduct and deem these rules to be appropriate for determining our standards for presentation. It is only when our knowledge of, and motivation to concur with, these rules exists that embarrassment, is a consequence of our failure. The types of situation which can give rise to embarrassment and the remedial tactics used to explain away undesirable conduct are evaluated in the following chapter.

CHAPTER 3

Social Predicaments and Embarrassment

Embarrassing events are generally assumed to involve a *faux pas*, impropriety, accident or transgression which results in the actor's projected image creating an undesired impression. As suggested, however, the actor may experience anxiety and trepidation in social encounters simply because he/she has certain expectations about his/her performance. That is, actors believe they *will* behave in a way which is embarrassing in the social encounter. Whether one is discussing an embarrassing 'event' which has occurred, or the fear that an 'event' might occur, an implicit assumption is that such 'events' are indeed definable by both the actor and the observer as 'embarrassing'. That is, we should be able to identify and perhaps categorize the types of antecedent events which are likely to result in our projected image creating an undesired impression.

Further implicit assumptions are that (1) we are all aware of these antecedent events and hence which behaviour is appropriate and inappropriate in social situations; and (2) that we are generally motivated to behave in a way which is 'appropriate'. Should an event occur which suggests that our behaviour is indeed inappropriate, and that we have projected an undesired impression of ourselves, then we may use a number of strategies to restore our desired image.

A central part of any discussion of embarrassment must therefore address itself to the precise nature of the antecedent events which give rise to the experience of embarrassment. How do we become aware of the way we are expected to behave in social encounters? Which categories of social events give rise to the experience of embarrassment? What strategies do we use to explain away our behaviour should an undesired event occur? These questions form the central themes of this chapter, which outlines the links between social rule transgression and embarrassment.

A. THE RULES OF CONDUCT

1. Knowledge of social rules

Embarrassment is systematically built into our social system. As Goffman (1955) has stated:

societies everywhere, if they are to be societies, must mobilise their members as self-regulating participants in social encounters. One way of mobilising the individual for this purpose is through ritual; he is taught to be perceptive, to have feelings attached to self and a self expressed through face, to have pride, honour, and dignity, to have considerateness, to have tact and a certain amount of poise. (p. 131).

People interact in a variety of social situations and settings, generally with some aim or goal in mind, although this need not be clearly specified. In order that this aim or goal might be effectively attained, however, certain constraints on our behaviour, or rituals, develop. Societies everywhere have rules which regulate everyday behaviour, including that between participants in social encounters. These rules have been defined by Argyle, Furnham and Graham (1981) as 'behaviour which members of a group believe should or should not, or may not be, performed in some situations or range of situations'. They further point out that there are several different types of rule: some are prescriptive, others are proscriptive; some are categorical, others are guides to behaviour; there are laws, morals, etiquette and conventions; some rules are laid down by authority, others emerge from the group; some are stated in words, others have never been put into words.

Social rules are by their very nature unwritten rules, so that stating what is meant by 'knowing' a social rule becomes a complex question. Many rules which we are aware of are actually difficult to articulate although we may be aware when they have been broken. Collett (1977) has suggested four senses in which an individual can be said to know a rule. It is only in one sense that knowing a rule involves being able to articulate some recognizable formulation of the rule. The etiquette books which provided Goffman (1963) with lists of rules provide one such example. The second involves being able to recognize infringements of the rule, either by observing that a particular act is inappropriate, or observing a nonverbal display (possibly of embarrassment) which reveals that an infringement has occurred. Thus it is possible to verify the existence of a possible rule by finding out what happens when it is broken; the resulting sanctions can be observed and/or those present could be asked if they disapprove of what has happened. Garfinkel (1963), who experimented with various ways of breaking unwritten social rules (students behaving towards their parents as if they were lodgers; trying to buy articles of clothing from other customers in a shop, etc.), found reactions ranging from consternation to embarrassment and anger.

The third way of knowing a social rule involves the application of sanctions when the rule has been broken. In the above example, if the student had felt it appropriate to behave as a lodger, the error of his judgement may have been revealed by the actions of the other participant in the encounter; this may have involved laughter, apparent disregard, or even an 'embarrassed reaction' by the observer to the rule-breaking.

The fourth and final sense of knowing a social rule would occur where an inference about the operation of a rule was made purely on the basis of some observed behavioural regularity. Experimental studies of conformity often reveal very dramatically the operation of various social rules. It is only when there is nonconformity that the rules become more explicit and apparent. Thus Milgram (1974) observed the reactions of passengers to requests by confederates acting as other passengers, to allow them to sit in their seats. While all the passengers who were asked looked disturbed or angry a number voluntarily vacated their seats. It seems that not only do we dislike disruptions to our everyday expectations—such disruptions can also give rise to discomfort and embarrassment until the old balance is restored. As Modigliani (1971) has commented:

> The tendency to conform to blatantly erroneous judgments (Asch, 1956) and the reluctance of bystanders to intervene in emergencies (Latané and Darley, 1968) can be attributed, at least in part, to people's unwillingness to risk appearing foolish or stupid before others. Even Milgram's (1965) staggering findings on obedience to authority can be viewed in the light of embarrassment aversion. (p. 15).

This would suggest that the aversive consequences of embarrassment are so extreme that one reason for our tendency to follow the rules, conventions and behaviours adopted and expected by others is our fear of the possibly embarrassing consequences of not so doing. The extent to which our behaviour in emergencies may be constrained by fear of embarrassment will be discussed in detail in Chapter 7.

In assuming then that we can describe social rules, either because they can be articulated or because they are recognized by reactions to infringements, we must also acknowledge that any given individual may or may not know the appropriate rule and yet be prone to embarrassment. Assuming that we know the appropriate rule and our behaviour accords with it then no problems should be encountered. Similarly, even if we do not know the rule but our behaviour is nevertheless appropriate then no problems should occur. In any instance where our behaviour does not accord with the rule, however, embarrassment is a possible outcome. If we know the rule but behave in an untoward fashion then we are likely to be aware of our error. If we do not know the rule while behaving in an untoward fashion we may well be made aware that something is amiss from the actions of others (i.e. the negative sanctions of laughter, being ignored or even others' embarrassment).

It should be noted, however, that it is only in situations where we are actually motivated to behave in a way which accords with the social rules that embarrassment may be the outcome.

The way in which prevailing rules act to constrain our behaviour, with transgressions resulting in embarrassment, is vividly illustrated in a participant observation study in a nudist colony conducted in conjunction with an interview and questionnaire study (Weinberg, 1968). Weinberg suggests that nudists are resocialized to view heterosexual nudity in a special way. He suggests four 'offical rules': (a) nudism and sexuality are unrelated; (b) there is nothing shameful about exposing the naked body; (c) the abandonment of clothes can lead to a feeling of freedom; and (d) nude activities, especially full exposure to the sun, lead to a feeling of physical, mental, and spiritual well-being. He further suggests that the fact that these definitions of the situation are sustained, precludes embarrassment as an emotion relevant to nudity. The new set of rules take over and a new definition of the situation is established—it is then unintentional transgressions of the new social order that can give rise to embarrassment.

This is clearly illustrated by the following examples from Weinberg's work. A rule of nudist camps is to remove one's clothes, so that inadvertently leaving on a sock or bra becomes embarrassing. Weinberg illustrates this with the following remark made by a woman: 'I took all of my clothes off but my bra. I forgot to take it off. . . . [Everyone] laughed . . . I thought I'd just die.' As mentioned, it is also inappropriate in a nudist colony to equate nudity with sexuality—to do so can result in embarrassment as illustrated in another example by Weinberg: 'A guy who was a soldier got . . . [an erection] down at the lake. It was the first time he had been to camp. I got embarrassed and looked away.' The likelihood that embarrassment will occur is thus heavily dependent upon the way in which the social context is defined and the rules which serve to govern the social situation in which the interactants find themselves.

2. Degree of intent

Of particular relevance to the issue of social rules and embarrassment is the issue of intentionality on the part of the actor to follow or transgress a particular rule. In a study of Ginsburg, *et al.* (1981), subjects were presented with written scenarios of two events in which various features were varied including whether the central character broke a rule deliberately or accidentally, and whether the action was precipitated by a male or female. The two scenarios were as follows:

1. P deliberately (or by accident) coughs a mouthful of potatoes back onto his own plate, or into the serving dish.
2. P wittingly decided to shop (or unwittingly lost track of the time) and was late for the theatre where friends were waiting. P was so late that they almost missed the start of the play.

Subjects were then asked to rate whether the episode was odd, rude, funny, irritating, understandable, insulting or embarrassing, and whether they would laugh, be angry or embarrassed. As predicted, deliberate actions by the perpetrator were seen as being ruder and more difficult to comprehend, and as more likely to generate anger from those present. The author's prediction that accidental rule-breaking would lead to embarrassment was not, however, supported by the results. This latter finding is somewhat surprising and contrary to the authors' own expectations. There are, however, a number of difficulties associated with the study cited which suggest that the results should be treated with some caution. Thus, it is probably wrong to assume that *all* accidental rule-breaking is potentially embarrassing while all deliberate rule-breaking is not. Accidental rule-breaking may be *more likely* to provoke embarrassment for the actor concerned; deliberate rule-breaking may be *more likely* to provoke embarrassment for an observer to the event. Of further importance is the degree to which the observer interprets an event as accidental. Thus, unwittingly losing track of time before attending a theatre implies active engagement in another activity—the action may thus not have been regarded as entirely accidental.

The study illustrates most vividly the difficulties of defining embarrassment purely on the basis of the rule-breaking episode concerned. Of equal (or perhaps greater) importance are the expectations of both the actor and the observer and the way in which they interpret the situation. The nature of the rule-breaking episode is just one part of the story.

In a further study, Manstead and Semin (1981) examined subjects' perceptions of vignettes depicting transgressions that were either low or relatively high in apparent intent. The two low-intent vignettes involved:

1. dropping an object on display in a store while examining it, and
2. spilling some drink over strangers while in a pub.

The two 'high-intent' vignettes involved:

1. having a discussion at a party and criticizing the inhabitants of a country in front of someone who turns out to be from that country, and
2. being discovered at a library checkout point with an unstamped library book in one's bag.

Subjects were asked to rate the situation, either as themselves as the central character or as the observer, on 10. seven-point bipolar 'dispositional' rating scales. These scales had end points labelled 'cautious–reckless, sociable–unsociable, unpleasant–pleasant, tolerant–intolerant, insincere–sincere, friendly–unfriendly, cold–warm, reliable–unreliable, unpopular–popular, and likeable–unlikeable'. As predicted, dispositional attributions to the actor were more negative when the transgression was relatively high in intent rather than low in aparent intent.

The two studies referred to above thus suggest that intentional rule-breaking may engender rather more by way of negative attributions. We are more likely to respond with anger and negative feelings toward an actor who deliberately breaks a social rule. Whether we view an actor who accidentally breaks a social rule as behaving in an embarrassing way is, however, not supported by the empirical results, although this hypothesis is suggested by analyses of rule-breaking episodes (Argyle, Furham and Graham, 1981).

Before dismissing the notion that accidental rule-breaking is more likely to result in embarrassment, more research is clearly needed. Both the actors' and observers' interpretations of, and reactions to, the rule-breaking clearly need to be taken into account. Embarrassment is clearly bound up with our knowledge of, and desire to follow, social rules and conventions. As Armstrong (1974) points out, occasionally persons may cross a socially defined boundary and fail to take on a new role appropriate to the situation in which they find themselves. Embarrassment may then ensue. Armstrong further suggests that embarrassment indicates that individuals acknowledge (by their embarrassment) that their behaviour has been deviant and if they fail to come back into line they will either be excluded from the interaction or the interaction will disintegrate. In order to test this suggestion, Armstrong used a group discussion task designed to investigate the speed of time it took to reach a unanimous decision recommending a desired course of action. One of the group was a confederate of the experimenter, whose job it was to hinder the group from reaching a speedy decision in such a way that embarrassment occurred. By pressing buttons the members of the group could produce a red light indicating that they felt a particular person (i.e. the confederate) had spoken enough. If the confederate was embarrassed (i.e. acknowledged his/her deviant behaviour), the pressing stopped more abruptly than if the confederate was not embarrassed.

In a similar vein, Modigliani (1966) suggests that 'embarrassment plays an important part in social control and social influence' (p. 41). He emphasizes the importance of others' reactions to our rule-breaking, so that once a person becomes aware that others perceive him/her as deficient, embarrassment may be inevitable. Hence the view that since one would rather avoid appearing deficient, embarrassment can act as a social control mechanism. The issue of embarrassment and social control is discussed in some detail in Chapter 7 where the social implications of embarrassment are discussed.

Embarrassment then results from our concern with social rules, and our desire to avoid behaving in a manner which is inconsistent with the way in which we would have wished to behave. Both intentionally and unintentionally transgressing social rules can occasion embarrassment, at least for the observer to the event, although in the former circumstances the perpetrator may be seen in a more negative light.

The question of what categories of event cause embarrassment has tended to look both at the type of rule-breaking episodes that give rise to embarrassment as well as the behaviour of the perpetrator within the situation. How to classify the type of rule-breaking episodes which give rise to embarrassment is, however, fraught with difficulties. We could, for example, look for the amount of, or lack of, rule-based knowledge displayed in the event and whether the actor and/or observer possesses this knowledge, i.e. the actor knew the rule and transgressed it; or did not know the rule, transgressed it and was made aware of the transgression by the observer. We could perhaps add to this a dimension of intentional versus accidental. The majority of studies, however, have attempted to classify embarrassing events into categories on the basis of actions or situations as causes of embarrassment. These studies will be reviewed in the following section.

B. CATEGORIES OF PREDICAMENT

A number of authors have attempted to systematically categorize different classes of embarrassing incidents (Buss, 1980; Gross and Stone, 1964; Argyle, 1969; Modigliani, 1966; Sattler, 1965; Edelmann, 1985b). These tend to represent different clusters of causes with a common explanatory thread encompassing them all. Each cause in some way reflects rule-breaking—albeit unintentional—and each results in the projecting of an image which is discrepant from the one we would have wished to present. A self-presentation which reveals a discrepancy between our ongoing behaviour and our standard for self-presentation, leading to activation of concern about our identity image and the generation of negative affect. By pooling the recollections of people to embarrassing events, we can attempt to systematically categorize different subsets.

One of the first attempts to do this was by Gross and Stone (1964), who collected over 1000 instances of embarrassing events from 880 students. In order to investigate the content of the descriptions they began by classifying them into categories which remained as close to the originals as possible. Seventy-four categories were developed in this way, including public mistakes, misnaming, forgetting names, uncontrollable laughter, drunkenness in the presence of sobriety (or vice-versa), loss of visceral control and the sudden recognition of wounds or other stigmata.

They suggest that further inspection of the categories enabled them to be grouped into three main clusters:

1. inappropriate identity,
2. loss of poise,
3. disturbance of the assumptions persons make about one another in social transactions.

The first category refers to instances:

> When one is 'not himself' in the presence of others who expect him to be just that, as in cases where his mood carries him away either by spontaneous seizure (uncontrollable laughter or tears) or by induced seizure (drunkenness). (Gross and Stone, 1964, p. 2).

Other instances of embarrassment involving inappropriate identity may include those where our behaviours are inconsistent with our role (Gross and Stone give the example of a professor whose transactions with female students emphasize the sexual rather than the professorial) or when we enter a setting reserved for members of the opposite sex. (Gross and Stone refer to this situation as one in which one literally has no identity).

The second category, loss of poise, refers to all those events in which the actor's control over self and situation are disturbed or incapacitated. Spilling food, stumbling over the furniture, slips of the tongue or sudden dumbness, exposure of undergarments, fainting and flatulence are all included within this category. Five subcategories can be identified. First, some social accidents are really failures of motor skill—tripping over furniture or stumbling on a rug are instances of loss of physical poise. Second, some accidents are due to failure to control bodily behaviour (flatulence, fainting). Third, an interactor may forget another's name, introduce him with the wrong name, forget important facts about him/her, etc. Fourth, a harmless question or line of conversation may unexpectedly embarrass another, particularly if the topic is one which he hoped to avoid. Finally, an interactor may simply not know how to proceed; there is no social technique available in his repertoire to deal with this problem.

The final category, disturbance of assumptions, refers to those instances when we mistakenly identify a co-actor or assume something about the context which is patently false. Denegerating a product to the manufacturer, a research topic to the researcher, a book to the author, etc., without realizing that there is a connection between the topic and the person with whom one is conversing, are all instances of this category of embarrassing events. In one of our own experimental studies we used this method of inducing embarrassment (Edelmann and Hampson, 1979). An interviewer revealed something unexpected about himself during the course of the interview. Thus the intervieweees had a set of expectations about the person with whom they were conversing, only to discover that their assumptions about the person were in fact incorrect. This study is described in full in Chapter 4.

Gross and Stone's latter two categories (loss of poise and disturbance of assumptions) have been referred to by Argyle (1969) as 'failure of social skill' and 'failure of meshing'. The first implies a failure of social graces or the failure in skilled performance where there is an interruption in the smooth flow of the actor's performance. The latter refers to disagreement over the definition of the situation or failure to agree on the roles played by those present. Garfinkel (1963), as mentioned, has carried out some intriguing demonstrations of the way we react when someone behaves in an unexpected manner. The reactions of customers in a shop treated as salesmen (i.e. treating the other in an inappropriate role) and when a competitor moved his opponent's pieces in a game of chess, are examples. Each of these behaviours created embarrassment, and in some cases anger and withdrawal from the situation. In everyday encounters, similar results may occur. If the pattern of interaction established on the basis of earlier assumptions suddenly becomes inappropriate, interaction may be brought to a sudden and embarrassing halt. Examples of this type of situation are: when an interactor suddenly realizes that the other person is more important than he/she assumed; has a deformity he had not noticed; or reveals something unexpected about himself.

In a further study investigating recollections of embarrassing events, Sattler (1965) collected data from four groups: adolescents, college students, normal adults, and chronic schizophrenics. The 50 from each subgroup (25 male and 25 female) who wrote the greatest number of written situations within each group were selected for further analysis; this gave a total of 3067 descriptions. It was found that 39 categories were required to encompass all the possibilities expressed by the subjects, which could then be subdivided into five general categories (a sixth category was used for unclassifiable descriptions).

The first category describes incidents when the subject places major emphasis on his/her personal feelings or actions. He/she is the one who initiates the action and the embarrassing event is one in which he/she is directly involved. Thus, being concerned about blemishes or bodily appearance, feeling inappropriately dressed, or displaying or losing control of one's feelings are all examples of this category.

The second category contains incidents when the subject places another person in an awkward or improper position. This was only rarely reported in Sattler's study and includes cases where one refuses invitations from a member of the opposite sex or turns down gifts.

The third category describes incidents where another person performs or does something to the subject. This includes all those situations where one is made to feel conspicuous either by criticism, rejection, or praise, or when someone invades our privacy either by approaching too close or seeing parts of our body we wish to conceal.

The fourth category describes situations in which the subject is in the position of an observer and is affected by the actions of another person or persons since they may reflect on him. Being embarrassed when one's children act up in front of others, if a pet misbehaves, or when other people argue or are intimate in public are examples of this category.

The fifth category describes situations in which the subject is in the position of an observer and is affected by the situation in which another person is involved. Being embarrassed for a close friend or relative would be included in this category.

Some interesting points emerge from Sattler's study with regard to similarities and differences between the groups investigated. Fewer adults report concern about the opposite sex compared with adolescents, the latter also emphasizing 'ungraceful' behaviour. Sex differences within each group were minimal, although schizophrenic women had a cluster of categories that were concerned with status and emotional control. The issue of gender, age and personality differences in the experience of embarrassment will be discussed in detail in Chapter 6.

The five categories used by Sattler are almost identical to those used by

Modigliani (1966, 1968), although the wording is slightly different. Thus the five classes of embarrassing events used by Modigliani are:

1. Situations in which the person discredits his/her own self-presentation through some inadvertent foolishness or impropriety. This includes tripping and falling in a public place, or wearing clothes inappropriate to the occasion.
2. Situations in which the person finds himself/herself unable to respond adequately to an unexpected event which threatens to impede the smooth flow of the interaction, e.g. having attention drawn to some physical stigma of a co-actor or to one's own failings.
3. Situations in which the actor loses control over his/her self-presentation without having any well-defined role. This includes occasions when we open gifts in public view of the people who have given them to us, are the recipients of Happy Birthday wishes or when we are introduced to a large group of people.
4. Situations involving empathic embarrassment where the person observes another person who is in a seemingly embarrassing situation. Typical examples include watching a play or show in which the actor forgets his lines or fails to evoke the desired reaction from the audience, or where someone who we are with behaves inappropriately.
5. Situations in which the individual is involved in an incident having inappropriate sexual connotations, such as walking into a bathroom occupied by a member of the opposite sex, having one's clothing in disarray, or being complimented by a member of the opposite sex.

A major difference between the Gross and Stone/Sattler categories and those derived by Modigliani is the fact that while the former rely upon categorization of collected episodes, the latter are derived from factor analysis of a 26-item embarrassibility questionnaire. In the former case clusters are based either upon visual inspection or upon theoretical predictions, while in the latter case categorization is based upon statistical procedures. Different categories of embarrassing events have been produced both within and between these differing approaches.

A further set of categories are referred to by Buss (1980), who describes Sattler's (1965) clusters of embarrassing events, but introduces two additional categories: breaches of privacy, and overpraise. Breaches of privacy refer to: (1) exposure of taboo parts of the body; (2) touching or coming too close to another; (3) leakage of feelings (as revealed by sentiments that one wished to hide), or bodily noises. As is clear, this extra category could well fit into the category 'loss of poise/failure of social skill' used by Gross and Stone, and Argyle, and could be subsumed by categories 1 and 5 in Modigliani's system.

Buss's second additional category, 'overpraise', refers to discomfort occasioned by excessive compliments: Buss suggests that in our society children are socialized to be modest, and overpraise results in a desire to hide any immodest feelings. Again, however, this description has a great deal in common with Gross and Stone's description of inappropriate identity (i.e. 'I am capable but not brilliant'), and Sattler's first category concerned with displaying or losing control of one's feelings, or Modigliani's third category concerned with being the undeserving centre of attention.

While the various categories seem to differ between studies, in reality there is a great deal of overlap. Any differences perhaps reflect alternative approaches rather than a radical difference in the descriptions of embarrassing events obtained. Thus Sattler's categories tend to reflect a Heider-type interpersonal situations approach (Heider, 1958), i.e. descriptions based upon the notion of the central character in the description as the agent, recipient or observer of the embarrassing event. Gross and Stone, and Argyle's categories, on the other hand, reflect the properties of social trans-actions, particularly role requirements and performance. The latter categories thus perhaps reflect rather more clearly a classification of the antecedent event to the embarrassment experienced, while the former is rather more a description of what is embarrassing to whom (agent, recipient, or observer). Modigliani's categories, as mentioned, are again based upon a different methodology, using 26 preselected embarrassing items and by factor analytic procedures examining the way these descriptors might be grouped. In an attempt to resolve the above conflicts, it was recently suggested (Edelmann, 1981a, b) that the studies referred to can be used to identify six discernible categories:

1. inappropriate identity;
2. loss of poise or loss of social skill—including loss of bodily and visceral control;
3. disagreement over the definition of the situation/failure of meshing;
4. breaches of privacy;
5. overpraise;
6. vicarious embarrassment.

It is clear, however, that this category system also does not present an ultimate solution, a fact which was illustrated in our own study (Edelmann, 1985b).

We asked 100 undergraduate psychology students (37 and 63 female) to try to recall an embarrassing experience which had occurred within the past few weeks. The frequencies of descriptions of the antecedent categories are given in Table 3.1. Whilst it is possible to recode some categories to fit the six classes of embarrassing events referred to previously, this is not possible in all cases. Thus, categories 1 and 2 in Table 3.1 involve loss of poise; categories 11, 12 and 16 involve breaches of privacy; and categories 6 and 10 involve being the undeserving centre of attention. The main factor to emerge is perhaps the richness and variety of different situations which can occasion embarrassment.

Table 3.1 Antecedents of embarrassment
($N = 100$; frequency = both number of responses and percentage response in each category)

	Category	Frequency
1	Loss of physical control	13
2	Loss of control of bodily functions	8
3	Failing a test	2
4	Not knowing the rules of behaviour	1
5	Making an error of judgment (e.g. entering wrong room)	18
6	Being on stage/speaking in public	3
7	Talking behind someone's back, who overhears	8
8	Meeting/talking to someone one wished to avoid	3
9	Contacting a neglected friend	1
10	Being singled out by other's criticism/laughter	19
11	Interaction having sexual overtones	6
12	Buying personal objects	1
13	Pet behaving badly	1
14	Visiting someone who does not expect us	4
15	Being seen naked/semi-naked	5
16	Inadvertently revealing information about self	1
17	Causing traffic chaos	1

The most predominant categories were: (1) 'Being singled out by others' criticism, laughter, scorn and Happy Birthday wishes' with 19 per cent—clearly comparable with Modigliani's third category; (2) 'Making an error of judgment such as greeting someone in error, giving a wrong answer to a question, or entering a wrong room', with 18 per cent which while having elements of loss of poise does not fit clearly into any of the previously suggested categories; and (3) 'Loss of physical control', such as falling through a door and dropping luggage, with 13 per cent—the consistently recognized 'loss of poise' category.

Typical situations in the 'being singled out' category were:

Claiming meal-rebate, reprimanded for having forgotten ID card.

A couple of weeks ago I unintentionally jumped the queue at a bus stop and at least three people told me off with many words, attracting everybody's attention.

Getting verbally and physically attacked by a group of about 12 who resented me criticizing Doris Stokes (the spirit medium) during question time at one of her shows.

Typical situations in the 'error of judgment' category were:

Misunderstanding a question asked to me and giving a totally different answer to that expected.

Walking into the wrong room for a tutorial.

I sat down at the dinner table opposite someone I thought I knew and said 'Hello' very loudly; it turned out I didn't know the person after all.

Typical situations in the 'loss of physical control' category were:

I was walking up to a door while turning round and talking to a friend. As I approached, someone opened the door from the outside and I fell through.

I fell flat on my bum and skidded along on my bum, feet outstretched.

When I stood up to get off the bus my bag was undone and everything fell onto the floor of the bus. No-one helped, they just sat and commented on what I'd had in my bag.

In terms of the circumstances surrounding the events, 76 per cent of the subjects were with one or more people known to them personally, although only one person reported being embarrassed while on his/her own. Forty-eight per cent of the subjects saw themselves as being responsible for causing their own embarrassment, but on a scale of 1 (= not at all) to 5 (= extremely) rated what others present were thinking about them as being moderately important ($\bar{X} = 29$). Thirty per cent of the events occurred in the university environment'; 30 per cent in a public place such as a shop or restaurant, and 17 per cent in the subject's own home.

There are then certain situations which regularly occur in surveys of embarrassing events—particularly being singled out by others and losing poise. What becomes clear is that there is certainly a rich array of circumstances which are potentially embarrassing, and no author has reported difficulty eliciting recollections of embarrassing events from subjects. What does create difficulty is deciding on a clear rationale for subdividing the collected descriptions into meaningful categories. Thus neither content descriptions (e.g. loss of poise) or factor labels (e.g. inadvertent foolishness) really convey a clear picture of the *nature* of the embarrassing events. Sattler's (1958) attempt to label the events in terms of attributions of responsibility is perhaps a more useful alternative, although this fails to bring into the picture the relationship between the event and the rules of behaviour surrounding the event. What is required is a classification system taking into account both the nature of the rule-breaking episode and the actor's and observer's interpretation of this event. Orthogonal dimensions of rules known–rules not known; intentional action–accidental action; actor responsible–observer responsible; could provide a useful starting point. This would obviously necessitate eliciting from the subject rather more than just a description of the event, but would also provide a more meaningful classification system.

What is evident from the studies cited, however, is the fact that, regardless of the event or how it is classified, there is a common thread running through all the situations. Each involves a transgression of a social rule—as pointed out in the first part of this chapter, embarrassment may only occur if the actor's behaviour does not accord with the rule assuming that he/she either knows the rule, or is made aware of his/her transgression. Thus, it is an unwritten rule that we do not fall over in public, or forget the answer to a question. In each situation we are attempting to control our image, to present a desired image toward our audience; should we fail to behave appropriately the result will be the projection of an undesired image. It is then the discrepancy between this projected image and our own standard for self-presentation which gives rise to our focusing of attention on the public aspects of ourselves with embarrassment as a possible consequence. As discussed in the preceding chapter, it is our desire to present ourselves in a favourable light which leads both to attempts to protect this image when it might be under threat (hence protective self-presentation styles) and to our subsequent attempts to remedy the situation and re-establish a more acceptable image. This latter phase in which we are attempting to redress the balance has been referred to as face-saving (Goffman, 1955) or remedial explanations (Edelmann, 1985a) or impression management strategies (Tedeschi and Riess, 1981b; Tedeschi et al., 1983). We are in effect attempting to account for or explain our conduct.

C. EXPLANATIONS FOR CONDUCT

> Accounts are the ordinary-language explanations actors offer when the course of interaction is disrupted and they are faced with predicaments. Accounts are remedial explanations meant to restore the identity that the actor puts forth to mitigate a negative or unwanted identity fostered by some behaviour. (Tedeschi and Riess, 1981b, p. 280).

As with attempts to classify the situations that give rise to embarrassment, there have also been a number of attempts to classify the verbal accounting strategies that might be used by the actor to mitigate the negative circumstances associated with the embarrassing event. Generally, however, there is far less disagreement over the categories used, apologies, excuses and justifications emerging consistently from the literature (Scott and Lyman, 1968; Austin 1970; Tedeschi and Riess, 1981b; Tedeschi et al., 1983; Schlenker, 1980, 1982; Semin and Manstead, 1983). Each variety of remedial tactic can be regarded as an attempt to reinstate a more positive image, hence reducing the discrepancy between one's present behaviour and one's desired behaviour. In some cases the attempt will not just be to reduce the discrepancy but actually to redress the balance—to present an image which is positive enough to outweigh the previous negative one. Schlenker (1980) has defined remedial tactics as:

> Impression management activities that attempt to deal with the predicament, offering the audience—real or imagined, an explanation of it or an apology for it that can place the actor and the event in a different perspective. By so doing, the actor attempts to minimise the negative repercussions of the predicament. (p. 136).

1. Varieties of remedial tactics

(a) Apologies

An apology is an acknowledgment of blameworthiness, an acceptance of responsibility for the embarrassing event. By apologizing, the actor is admitting that a norm or rule has been violated, that the behaviour displayed is inappropriate while at the same time seeking a pardon, implying that the transgression will not recur. According to Schlenker (1980) an apology asserts that:

> the undesirable event is not a fair representation of what the actor is really like as a person. The current good self is split off from the past bad self, the part that is guilty is split off from the part that dissociates itself from the offense and affirms a belief in the offended rule. The bad self is left behind, discredited and vilified by the actor. Thus the actor evidences rehabilitation. (p. 154).

Goffman (1971) has listed the essential elements of apologies (also cited by Schlenker, 1980; Tedeschi and Riess, 1981; Semin and Manstead, 1983).

1. an expression of responsibility and blame for one's actions by expressions of guilt, remorse, or embarrassment;
2. an indication by the actor that he/she knows what the appropriate behaviour is in the situation and believes the application of negative sanctions for such rule violation to be appropriate;
3. rejection of the inappropriate behaviour with playing down of the 'bad' self which misbehaved;
4. an acknowledgment that 'correct' behaviour will occur in the future, the performance of an act of penance or the offering of restitution.

It is important to note that the first element—expression of guilt, remorse or embarrassment—is seen as actually being the link in the chain of an apology. The act of being embarrassed, as the first part of an apology, needs to be disentangled from the process of embarrassment.

Consider the following situation. You start a conversation at a party with someone whom you recognize, but you cannot quite place where you have seen her before. During the conversation you ask if she recalls X, with whom you think she is associated, in order to help you pinpoint where you first met. She retorts that she should recall X, her ex-husband, who had had an affair with a relative of yours.

What would a comment of 'I'm sorry' achieve in this situation? As outlined above, an apology acknowledges blame for causing an upset; it acknowledges that we have asked something inappropriate and that we know what the appropriate action should be. On its own, however, without an expression of something else, this apology is likely to fall on deaf ears. This something else could well be an expression of embarrassment; a visible sign that we have committed an undesirable act. In this sense the very act of being embarrassed can be seen as part of the apology. It is wholly desirable and appropriate.

It may well be the case that a show of embarrassment as an apology, or in conjunction with an apology, is in certain cases image-enhancing rather than damaging to one's image. These situations are likely to be those in which the undesired behaviour may have occasioned discomfort to someone else who was present. That is, those situations referred to in the previous section of this chapter as reflecting a disagreement over the definition of the situation or a failure of meshing. As Tedeschi and Riess (1981b) comment:

> Embarrassment itself as an emotional reaction thus plays a role in restoring the identity in question. (p. 299).

That embarrassment is indeed seen as a desirable reaction in certain circumstances is illustrated in one of our own studies (Edelmann, 1982). During a role-played interview subjects were required to inform a confederate of the experimenter that he had performed badly on a task. The confederate responded to this in one of three ways: (a) a defiant stare; (b) gaze aversion and fidgeting; (c) gaze aversion with both fidgeting and laughing. The latter two reactions were intended to be variations of a display of embarrassment, i.e. an acknowledgment that the information had indeed shown the confederate in a bad light and that there was a discrepancy between his current behaviour (failure) and his own standard for behaviour. In the second condition the comfederate was seen as being most embarrassed but he was also seen as being more likeable and causing the other interactor less discomfort than in the first condition (defiant stare). ('Liking for the confederate' and 'degree of comfort' were most when laughter was present.) In this case then a display of embarrassment was perhaps seen as appropriate, and may indeed have served as an apology in its own right.

It is almost as if an apology is used in a ritualistic way to allow minor indiscretions to be passed over quickly and forgotten by the interactants. The offending event is of such little consequence that it is best to resolve it as rapidly and with as little effort as possible–'I accept that it was all my fault, but who cares anyway?'.

It seems then that apologies are most likely to be used by actors when: (1) they do not mind accepting responsibility for the event because any repercussions which might occur are going to be trivial; or (2) independently of the importance of the event, in situations where it is unlikely that the actor will be able to avoid being seen as responsible for the event.

In sum, an apology, whether verbal or in conjunction with a display of embarrassment, allows the actor to accept responsibility for the event while at the same time reducing the likelihood of negative repercussions. Displaying just the right amount of 'self-castigation' can indeed turn the event into one in which the audience in turn feel compelled to play down the need for an apology. The embarrassing event can thus be left behind and the new restored identity of the actor presented to the audience.

It is often the case, however, that an apology is either inappropriate or is at least inappropriate if offered in isolation. We may also wish to account for or explain why we have committed the undesirable, discrepant and embarrassing behaviour.

(b) Accounts

> An account is a linguistic device employed whenever an action is subjected to evaluative enquiry. . . . By an account, then, we mean a statement made by a social actor to explain unanticipated or untoward behaviour. (Scott and Lyman, 1968, p. 46).

Numerous authors (Austin, 1961; Scott and Lyman, 1968; Tedeschi and Riess, 1981b; Schlenker, 1980; Schonbach, 1980; Semin and Manstead, 1983) have suggested that accounts consist of excuses and justifications, each of which has several further subcategories. An excuse is an attempt to play down the importance of, and minimize one's responsibility for, the embarrassing event, while at the same time admitting that the behaviour was wrong, bad or inappropriate. A justification, while admitting that the embarrassing event has occurred and that the actor was at least partly responsible for it, at the same time denies that it has negative qualities attached to it. It is not the intention of this chapter to discuss the various taxonomies of account offered by the above authors—an excellent analysis is provided by Semin and Manstead (1983). It is important to note that embarrassing events are just one class of predicament (i.e. a situation in which a person is held to be responsible for his/her negative behaviour) so that within each taxonomy only a selection of strategies will be appropriate as remedial tactics for dealing with embarrassing events. The aim of this section then is to evaluate accounting tactics in order to gain an impression of which ones are most suitable for dealing with embarrassing events.

(i) Excuses

In their analysis of excuses, Scott and Lyman (1968) distinguish four main categories: appeal to accidents, appeal to defeasibility, appeal to biological drives, and scapegoating. To illustrate how each of these might be used to deal with embarrassing experiences, consider the following very basic and common embarrassing event: falling on a slippery floor (i.e. loss of poise). An excuse claiming an accident as the reason for the untoward behaviour, diminishes responsibility by highlighting recognizable environmental hazards. Thus one can actually comment on the slippery nature of the floor or point out that it is impossible to walk on such surfaces.

An excuse appealing to defeasability or interference with 'free will' highlights one's lack of intent in performing the untoward behaviour or one's lack of awareness concerning possible negative consequences of one's actions.

Comments such as 'I did not think I would fall over' or 'I did not realize the floor had just been washed' are encompassed by this category.

An excuse invoking biological drives is a plea that all behaviour is determined by biological factors, so that one can claim that an act is part of one's nature, because of one's gender or because of one's bodily shape, etc. Comments such as 'tall people find it more difficult to keep their balance' would be encompassed by this category.

Finally, scapegoating locates the cause of failure in the actions of someone else. Comments such as 'the cleaners are always trying to catch us out' would fit into this category. The use of one embarrassing event to illustrate these types of excuse perhaps demonstrates that some excuses are more appropriate than others in certain situations, a point which will be returned to later in this chapter.

Schonbach's (1980) modification of Scott and Lyman's typology lies more in the expansion of categories than in any marked alteration of specific categories themselves. The first category (appeal to own human shortcomings, whether through knowledge, skill or will impairment) corresponds to Scott and Lyman's appeal to defeasability category. The second category (reasons for the appeal to one's own shortcomings) consists of a number of subcategories of incident which might temporarily cause an unwanted or negative event to occur. These include illness, provocation, duress, biological factors, or external circumstances. Many of these subcategories can be encompassed by Scott and Lyman's appeals to accidents or appeal to biological drives categories. The third category (appeal to own effort and care before and during the failure event) overlaps to some extent with Scott and Lyman's excuse type (appeals to defeasability). Both are concerned with knowledge or intent behind the act. Schonbach's fourth excuse (appeal to shortcomings or misdeeds of other persons as frame of reference for the evaluation of the failure event) as well as his final excuse subdivision (appeal to the participation of other persons in the failure event) could both be regarded as variants of Scott and Lyman's scapegoating excuse.

Schlenker (1980) also offers a variation of Scott and Lyman's original category system. He distinguishes between unforeseen consequences and extenuating circumstances. The former include explanations that the event was an accident or mistake (cf. Scott and Lyman category 1) or that one behaved through ignorance and carelessness (cf. Scott and Lyman category 2). Extenuating circumstances involve attempts by the actor to shift responsibility for the event from himself/herself to factors which may have influenced his/her behaviour. These factors might include alcohol, illness, stress, etc. (cf. Scott and Lyman category 3) or the action of others (cf. Scott and Lyman category 4).

Tedeschi and Riess (1981b) have also modified and expanded Scott and Lyman's (1968) typology of accounts. They identify three major subcategories of excuse: denial of intention, lack of volition and denial of agency.

Within the denial of intention subcategory they distinguish four types:

namely accidents (cf. Scott and Lyman), pleas of ignorance as a result of such factors as a lack of information, poor judgment, distraction by others or a mistake; cases of mistaken identity or lack of capacity. Within the denial of volition subcategory, Tedeschi and Riess distinguish three types of excuse: those involving physical causes (drugs, alcohol, illness, exhaustion), psychological factors (insanity, brainwashing, hypnotism) or through a lack of authority to perform the action that would have prevented the embarrassing event. Within the denial of agency subscategory, Tedeschi and Riess distinguish between mistaken identity and amnesia/fugue state.

It is not difficult to see that both Scott and Lyman's, and Sconbach's, categories can be readily accommodated within Tedeschi and Riess's typology with the exception of those looking to the role played by persons other than the actor as an excuse. In view of this, Semin and Manstead (1983) present a modified version of Tedeschi and Riess's typology of excuses with a fourth category (appeal to mitigating circumstances) added to Tedeschi and Riess's three main categories of excuse: denial of intent, denial of volition, and denial of agency. This is shown in Table 3.2, below.

Given that there is rough agreement amongst theorists about the categories of excuses that one might use as remedial tactics, it is useful to examine the use of excuses following embarrassing events. There is, however, little research on embarrassment and remedial tactics which makes any discussion largely speculative. In our own study (Edelmann, 1985b) we asked people to record what they said in their attempts to deal with embarrassment. These were later coded into nine categories, one of which dealt with excuses. Forty-nine per cent of the subjects reported that they would say something, of these 17 per cent could be coded as using an excuse. As this represented only eight out of 100 subjects further subdivision would not have been very meaningful. This low figure suggests that an excuse may be the most appropriate response to an embarrassing event in relatively few instances. One possibility is that excuses are only used under conditions of extreme embarrassment where it is not suitable to brush aside the event with an apology.

The only other study to look at remedial tactics and embarrassment was Modigliani's (1966, 1971) study in which he constructed a 'facework' index. This contained any statements made by the subject intended to improve his image in the eyes of the confederate, and included items which introduced information excusing the performance. Modigliani did not separate out the individual types of 'facework' used.

There are nevertheless clear links between the categories of embarrassing events referred to previously and the categories of excuse referred to in Table 3.2. Instances of inappropriate identity (where our behaviours are inconsistent with our role) could well be excused by either denial of intent (accident or lack of skill) or more likely by denial of volition (that would not have happened if I had not been ill, deafened, coerced, drunk, etc.). Instances of loss of poise could similarly be excused by resorting to denial of intent (accident) or denial of volition (ill, drunk, etc.) but could also be excused by an appeal to mitigating circumstances ('I was pushed'; 'Everyone was looking at me', etc.). Instances where a disagreement over the definition of the situation occurs (e.g. wrongly identifying a co-actor) may be excused by resorting to denial of agency if the mistake refers to past encounters ('I don't think it was me you met') or perhaps denial of intent (accident) or in a few cases by resorting to denial of volition.

Breaches of privacy, overpraise and vicarious embarrassment are much more difficult to excuse than the previous categories. An apology is most likely in cases of a breach of privacy, although denial of intent/denial of volition may also be used—perhaps in conjunction with an apology. It is indeed rather difficult to talk one's way out of, or excuse oneself in, situations involving overpraise or vicarious embarrassment.

At the present time no research has been conducted to bear out the above suggestions, and it is likely that wide variations will occur, both as a function of individual differences and as a function of factors giving rise to the embarrassing event.

(ii) Justifications

As with excuses, justifications allow the actor to admit some responsibility for the embarrassing event. While an excuse is an attempt to explain the event away, a justification is an attempt to minimize or deny its undesirability. In their analysis of justifications, Scott and Lyman (1968) distinguish six main categories: denial of injury, denial of victim, condemnation of condemners, appeal to loyalties, sad tales, and self-fulfilment.

In denying injury the actor acknowledges that he has performed a particular act but justifies it on the grounds that no-one was injured by it. In denial of the victim the actor expresses the position that the action was permissible since the victim deserved the injury. In condemnation of the condemner the actor admits performing an untoward act but justifies it on the grounds that others would get away with this and worse. In an appeal to loyalties the actor justifies his/her action by pointing out that it served someone else to whom the actor is committed. Sad tales are attempts by the actor to use unfortunate past experience to explain his/her present state. Finally, self-fulfilment justifies the action on the grounds that it leads to some form of enlightenment.

Schonman's (1980) modification of this typology contains only two categories which cannot be subsumed by Scott and Lyman's scheme: minimizing damage and appealing to positive intentions. Schlenker (1980) also offers a variation of Scott and Lyman's original category system. He distinguishes between direct minimization, justification through comparison and justification through higher goals. In the first type of justification, actors attempt directly to minimize the importance of the event. Schlenker gives the examples of a business person describing an embarrassing *faux pas* as a minor fluff not worthy of comment, and a disappointed Romeo who derogates his date's intelligence and explains that he did not like her anyway. This does not fit clearly into any of Scott and Lyman's categories.

Schlenker's second category (justification through comparison) allows an actor to try to minimize the undesirability of the event by comparing his/her own behaviour with that of others who go unpunished (c.f. Scott and Lyman condemnation of the condemner). Finally, justifications through higher goals such as god, government or more important rules is a further category not covered by Scott and Lyman.

Tedeschi and Riess's (1981b) typology of justification is in effect a combination of those referred to above. They suggest that there are ten major categories of justification, each of which can be subdivided. Of these, 'self-fulfilment' and 'appeal to loyalties' have direct counterparts with Scott and Lyman's categories, while 'denial of victim', 'denial of injury' and 'condemnation of condemners' overlap with Tedeschi and Riess's effect misrepresented, appeal to norm of justice, and social comparison respectively.

Of Tedeschi and Riess's remaining five categories, 'appeals to higher authorities' and 'appeals to ideology' overlap with Schlenker's category 'justification through higher goals'. 'Appeals to norms of self-defence' is perhaps self-explanatory; 'reputation-building' seeks to justify the act by presenting it as one which was necessary to maintain a positive public image or reputation, and finally 'appeals to humanistic values' such as love, peace, truth, etc. seek to present the act as one which promotes these values.

Semin and Manstead (1983) present a slightly revised version of Tedeschi and Riess's typology which is presented in Table 3.2. Their first category (claim that effect has been misrepresented) is similar to Tedeschi and Riess's category 'effect misrepresented'. Their second category, 'appeals to principal of retribution', overlaps with Tedeschi and Riess's category 'appeal to norms of self-defence'. The third category, 'social comparison', is equivalent to Tedeschi and Riess's category of the same name. Both the fourth and fifth categories, 'appeal to higher authority' and self-fulfilment' are similar to Tedeschi and Riess's categories of the same name, while the sixth category derives in part from Tedeschi and Riess's 'appeal to norms of justice'. Category 7, 'appeal to values', incorporates three categories in Tedeschi and Riess's typology, namely 'appeal to ideology', 'appeal to loyalties' and 'appeal to humanistic values'. Finally, category 8, 'appeal to need for facework', reflects the content of Tedeschi and Riess's 'reputation-building' category.

As with excuses, then, there is rough agreement about the categories of justification that one might use as remedial tactics. In which way do these various categories link with the categories of causes of embarrassment discussed in the previous section? Again, there is little research on embarrassment and remedial tactics which makes any discussion largely speculative. In our own study (Edelmann, 1985b) asking people to record what they said in their attempts to deal with embarrassment, only 6 per cent of the 49 per cent of subjects who reported that they would actually say something could be coded as justifications. As this represented only three out of 100 subjects,

Table 3.2 A synthetic typology of accounts (*Reproduced by permission of Academic Press from Semin and Manstead, 1983*)

A	**Excuses**

A1 *Denial of intent* ('I did not intend to produce these results')
Accident
Unforeseen consequences, due to:
    lack of knowledge
    lack of skill or ability
    lack of effort or motivation
    environmental conditions
Identity of target person mistaken

A2 *Denial of volition* (I did not want to perform this act')

Physical causes
    temporary (e.g. fatigue, drugs, illness, arousal)
    semi-permanent (e.g. paralysis, blindness, deafness)

Psychological causes originating in:
    self (e.g. insanity, overpowering emotion)
    others (e.g. coercion, hypnotism, brainwashing)
Lack of authority ('I would like to help you, but I do not have the authority to do so').

A3 *Denial of agency*

Mistaken identity ('It wasn't me, honest')
Amnesia ('I can't remember anything about it')
Joint production ('It wasn't only me who did it')

A4 *Appeal to mitigating circumstances* ('I am not entirely to blame)

Scapegoating—behaviour in question was a response to the behaviour or attitudes of another or others
Sad tales—selected arrangement of facts highlighting dismal past

B	**Justifications**

B1 *Claim that effect has been misrepresented*

Denial of injury (no harm done)
Minimization of injury (consequence only trivially harmful)

B2 *Appeal to principle of retribution*

Reciprocity (victim deserving of injury because of his/her actions)
Derogation (victim deserving of injury because of his/her qualities)

B3 *Social comparison*

(Others do same or worse but go unnoticed, unpunished or even praised)

B4 *Appeal to higher authority*

Powerful person(s) commanded
High-status person(s) commanded
Institutional rules stipulated

Table 3.2 Continued

B5   *Self-fulfilment*

Self-maintenance (catharsis, psychological or physical health)
Self-development (personal growth, mind expansion)
Conscience (acted in accordance with)

B6   *Appeal to principle of utilitarianism*

Law and order
Self-defence
Benefits outweigh harm

B7   *Appeal to values*

Political (e.g. democracy, socialism, nationalism)
Moral (e.g. loyalty, freedom, justice, equality)
Religious (e.g. charity, love, faith in deity)

B8   *Appeal to need for facework*

Face maintenance ('If I hadn't acted like that I would have lost credibility)
Reputation-building ('I did that because I wanted to look tough')

---

further subdivision would not have been very meaningful. This low figure suggests that the use of justifications may, as with excuses, be the most appropriate response to embarrassment in relatively few instances. Again it is possible that justifications are only appropriate under conditions of extreme embarrassment where it is not possible to brush aside the event with an apology.

The only other study looking at remedial tactics and embarrassment is the study by Modigliani (1966, 1971) concerned with the facework index. Subjects used verbal strategies to introduce redeeming or self-enhancing information that might compensate for their failure such as: 'I'm usually much better at these types of tasks.' They also used verbal comments to look for reassurance, and defensively changed the subject. It was found that the more embarrassed the subjects were the more of these accounting techniques they used. There was no attempt, however, to look at which particular techniques were actually used.

As with the various categories of excuse, however, it is possible to speculate about which categories of justification are most likely to occur with which cause of embarrassment, and indeed whether some of the attempts to justify one's behaviour are in fact appropriate for embarrassing events. It seems clear that many of the categories cited are in fact rather too strong for dealing with minor transgressions and attempts at justifying one's actions may in fact only serve to prolong, heighten, and add to the implications of the embarrassing event. As mentioned, this may be the reason why so few cases were coded into this category in our own study. It is possible that the categories of 'social comparison', 'appeal to a higher authority', and 'appeal to values' may be used in some cases but this is likely to be the exception rather than the rule. This raises two important issues. First, it is unlikely that an excuse or justification will be used in isolation; there is certainly a degree of overlap between the two tactics and each may be used together with an apology. The second related point concerns which tactic to use and when. What factors affect the selection of a particular explanation for one's conduct?

2. Selecting explanations

Scott and Lyman (1968) suggest three criteria which are implicated in making an explanation successful. First, it must be acceptable; that is it must fit the prevailing ideas and beliefs in a particular society or subgroup. Blaming one's behaviour upon witchcraft is likely to be dismissed or treated as a joke in Western society while being accepted as the 'truth' in other cultures. Second, an explanation must be reasonable; that is it must fit the facts that are known about the event by the audience. Stating that 'I was not aware it was a formal dinner' might work if a verbal invitation had been given, but might be less appropriate if dress style had been specifically mentioned on the invitation. As Schlenker (1983) suggests:

> Accounts can only be pushed so far before the concepts they contain no longer fit the accepted facts, and they are rejected by the audience. (p. 152).

Third, explanations must be adequate; that is they must be appropriate to the offensiveness of the act in question. As the offensiveness of the situation increases it is likely that different types of explanation become appropriate. It seems unlikely that very offensive acts are likely to be passed over by denial or attempts at justification, although excuses may just be successful. However, excuses too are likely to become unacceptable if the predicament is too offensive. Thus, as Schlenker (1983) points out (p. 150), stating 'I forgot what time it was' may be an appropriate excuse for arriving embarrassingly late at a party, but would not work for a doctor whose patient died in the emergency room while waiting for the doctor to arrive. Similarly, the justification 'It did not matter' might be appropriate if a plant pot falls out of a window, but might be less appropriate if one accidentally allows one's child to fall from a window with the same degree of oversight. People are expected to take certain offences more seriously than others and therefore to take extra precautions to prevent them.

It is thus possible to construct a hierarchy of explanations ranging from serious to nonserious events—as the event becomes more serious the more likely it is that an excuse or justification will be added to an existing apology. In the most serious events, however, no amount of excuses and justifications for one's behaviour may be adequate, whilst in the least serious predicaments attempts at justification may be too extreme. Explanations need to be acceptable, reasonable, and adequate. This may explain why in our own study (Edelmann, 1985b) we found that of the 49 people who made a verbal response as an attempt to deal with their embarrassment, 18 of them used an excuse, an apology or an excuse/apology combination, while only three attempted to justify their behaviour. Apologizing for causing embarrassment or for one's embarrassing behaviour may be more appropriate than attempting to excuse or justify one's actions. This suggestion in fact receives some support from a study by Schlenker and Darby (1981). They examined the use of different types of apology, an excuse or a justification by asking subjects to imagine themselves as the central character in a scenario in which they inadvertently bumped into another person in a public place. The vignettes describing the incident were manipulated to vary the actor's responsibility for the incident (high or low) and the amount of harm done to the victim (high, medium, or low). Subjects were asked to imagine themselves in the place of the central character and to reflect on how they might have acted in the circumstances specified.

The questions which followed assessed how likely the subjects were to use each of six elements of apologetic behaviour, two types of nonapologetic responses and two types of accounts to deal with the event. The apology types were as follows: (1) say 'Pardon me' to the other person and then walk away without doing or saying anything else; (2) say 'I'm sorry'; (3) express feelings of remorse about the situation (e.g. you might say 'I'm very sad about this' or 'I feel so badly about this'); (4) offer to help the other person in some way; (5) do or say something to get the other person to forgive you; and (6) say something to castigate yourself (put yourself down) about the situation (e.g. you might say 'How stupid of me' or 'How clumsy of me' or 'I feel foolish'). The two nonapologetic items asked subjects how likely they were to (a) say or do nothing with regard to the other person, and (b) acknowledge the other person's presence through some nonverbal behaviour (e.g. making eye contact, smiling, or making some other facial expression) but not saying anything to the other person. The two accounting tactics included how likely subjects were to (a) use an excuse, that is 'do or say something that might decrease your responsibility for the situation' (e.g. you might say, 'I didn't notice you standing there' or 'I tripped' or 'someone bumped into me and I fell into you', and (b) use a justification, that is, do or say something that might try to minimize the amount of harm that was done (e.g. you might say 'no harm done' or 'it doesn't look as if you're hurt too badly', or something similar).

Responses to these questions indicated that subjects were unlikely simply to walk away from the incident without doing anything. Acknowledging the other's presence by nonverbal behaviour was considered more likely, but only in the low-consequence condition. Excuses were more likely to be used when responsibility was low rather than high. There was no significant variation across conditions in the use of justifications. Both excuses and justifications had only intermediate likelihoods of use.

With regard to the variations in apology type, the most likely one to be used was saying 'I'm sorry', which was especially likely to be used when the consequences were described as medium or high as opposed to low. The 'pardon me' type of apology was more likely to be used when the consequences were low rather than medium or high, and was especially likely to be used when consequences were low and responsibility was high. Expressions of remorse and offers of help were judged to be more likely where the consequences were medium or high, rather than low. Requesting forgiveness and self-blame were more likely to occur when both responsibility and consequences were high.

Schlenker and Darby's study thus suggests that as in our own study (Edelmann, 1985b) apologies are the most favoured way of handling an embarrassing event, unless responsibility is low, in which case an excuse may be used. As the actor's responsibility and the consequences of the event increase, so the type of apology offered becomes more elaborate and self-blaming. Neither justifications nor excuses are used with any great frequency.

As a final point, it is worth noting that the type of explanation offered, whether an apology, excuse, justification or a combination of these, may be offered by the audience rather than by the actor (Scott and Lyman, 1968; Schlenker, 1982). For example, an observer to an embarrassing event (e.g. when an actor trips and falls or drops his/her shopping), might try to help the actor by making light of the event by commenting 'that's the sort of thing I always seem to do'. The observer is thus notifying the actor that he/she does not regard the event as being particularly undesirable. The actor's identity is thus preserved and the interaction can proceed without any untoward disruption. As with the previous suggestions, as the predicament becomes more severe the likelihood that the observer will offer help is likely to decrease.

D. SUMMARY

In summary then embarrassment is likely to be experienced following the public violation of a social rule. This assumes (1) that the actor either knows the rule that he/she has violated or is made aware of it by the observer's reactions;. and (2) that the actor wishes to behave in a way which is consistent with that rule. A number of attempts to classify the type of event which gives rise to embarrassment have been outlined in this chapter. Most of these are based upon category systems reflecting the situation in which the event occurs rather than reflecting factors surrounding the event such as intentionality, knowledge of social rules and attributions of responsibility for the event. Once an actor has transgressed a social rule and hence increased the likelihood that he/she will present him/herself in a way which is discrepant from their desired image, attempts will be made to remedy the situation by using various explanations for their conduct. A number of attempts to classify the types of remedial strategies were outlined, and strategies which might be appropriate for dealing with embarrassing events were discussed. It seems that apologies are the most favoured way of handling an embarrassing event, unless responsibility is low, in which case an excuse is used. As the actor's responsibility for, and the consequence of, the event increases, so the type of apology offered becomes more elaborate and self-blaming.

CHAPTER 4

Physiological and Behavioural Concomitants of Embarrassment

Having examined theoretical explanations and antecedents we can turn our attention to the outward signs and behaviours that accompany embarrassment. As anyone who has ever been embarrassed (and that means almost everyone) will testify, the signs of embarrassment often serve to heighten the experience of embarrassment. Behaviours which we find difficult to control give the game away.

In a survey we conducted into the antecedents and consequences of embarrassing events (Edelmann, 1985b), the specific reaction of embarrassment was characterized by blushing, rising in temperature, increased heart rate, muscle tension, grinning, smiling or laughing, avoidance of eye contact and self-touching (see Table 4.1). While a number of these behaviours have been produced in laboratory-based studies, there have also been contradictory findings, e.g. laboratory studies suggest that embarrassment results in a heart rate deceleration. There have also been a number of suggestions as to the possible functions these behaviours might serve within embarrassing episodes. This chapter explores our current knowledge of the occurrence and functions of both the physiological reaction (blushing, temperature and heart rate change) and nonverbal behaviours (reduced eye contact, increased body motion and speech disturbances) and the presence of smiling and laughter in embarrassing situations.

A. PHYSIOLOGICAL REACTIONS

1. Blushing

Blushing has been described by Buss (1980) as the hallmark of embarrassment although, as will be discussed later, it is possible to be embarrassed without blushing and to blush without being embarrassed. Blushing and

Table 4.1 Physiological and nonverbal reactions to embarrassment. (The total reaction for voice, face, eyes and body refers to those mentioning at least one of the components of each reaction.) (Items occurring with greatest frequency, i.e. > 15, are italicized.) (N = 100; frequency = both number of responses and percentage response in each category.)

Physiological response	Frequency	Specific response
Temperature	79	*Blush 52; heat 17*, sweat 3, warmth 3
Mouth	1	Dry
Heart	44	*Faster 35*; slower 8
Stomach	1	'Butterflies'
Muscles	24	*Tension 21;* trembling 3
Nonverbal reaction		
Voice	35	Quieter voice 11; pitch change 10; louder voice 8; quality change 5; changed voice, type unspecified 8
Facial expression	53	*Grin/smile 28; laughing 17;* biting lips 2; raised eyebrows 1; face change, type unspecified 8
Eyes	53	*Avoid eye contact 44;* seeking eye contact 4; closing one's eyes 2; staring 1; changed eye contact, type unspecified 2
Body	34	*Self-touching 20*; increased movement 13; controlled movement 7; normal movement 2
Motor behaviour	7	Leaving situation 7
Posture	15	Head down 5; shifting 5; collapsed 2
Global description of sensations	6	Pleasant
	22	Unpleasant

embarrassment have, however, been inextricably linked by a number of authors for many years.

Charles Darwin, writing more than a century ago, commented:

> Blushing is the most peculiar and most human of human expressions. Monkeys redden from passion but it would take an overwhelming amount of evidence to make us believe that any animal can blush. (1873, p. 309).

Using his own and others' observations, Darwin also noted that:

> The young blush more freely than the old but not during infancy
>
> The blind do not escape.
>
> The tendency to blush is inherited
>
> In most cases the face, ears and neck are the sole parts which redden.

Darwin also concluded that blushing is universal, and although it is easier to discern in people with light skin, even dark-skinned people blush:

> Several trustworthy observers have assured me that they have seen on the faces of negroes appearances resembling a blush, under circumstances which would

have excited one in us, though their skins were an ebony-black tint. Some describe it as blushing brown, but most say that the blackness becomes more intense. (1873, p. 318).

It is perhaps somewhat surprising to note that little more is known about the association of embarrassment and blushing than Charles Darwin knew 100 years ago, although there are number of speculative comments that can be made. First, however, we need to consider the physiological facts. Cutaneous (or peripheral) vasodilation, although not quite synonymous with blushing, refers to the physiological response. As is well known, running, or indeed any form of exercise, results in an increase in blood temperature, causing the bed of capillaries close to the skin to fill with blood. In this way heat loss can occur and our body is prevented from overheating. In other words, the blood vessels beneath the skin regulate our temperature, explaining why we redden from activity, and also a number of facts associated with blushing and embarrassment.

The thermoregulatory skin areas in humans include the face, hands and feet. Reddening is more visible in the facial region, because the skin is finer in this region. This explains why blushing in most people is limited to the face, neck and ears, as Darwin had noted.

The association of blushing and the experience of embarrassment is, however, rather more puzzling than reddening as a result of other forms of activity. Many animals have the physiological capacity to redden (monkeys, as has been noted, redden from rage or when sexually aroused), but whether they redden under other, perhaps embarrassing, circumstances would be rather more difficult to accept. Perhaps more contentious is the suggestion by Buss (1980) that the severely mentally retarded and young infants do not blush with embarrassment although they redden with anger.

What seems to be clear is that reddening of certain areas of the body, whether in certain members of the animal kingdom or in humans, is the direct result of an increase in blood temperature. Activities or emotions that increase blood temperature are thus likely to result in reddening of those same areas of the body. The question then becomes 'Why does embarrassment result in an increase in blood temperature and why do only humans (and certain humans at that) experience embarrassment?'

The latter point has been hinted at in previous chapters. Our desire to present ourselves in a particular way, to appear competent and able to control identity-relevant information before others, requires a certain degree of social sophistication. It would not be implausible to assume that animals other than humans as well as socially unsophisticated humans (perhaps the very young, retarded or certain psychiatric patients) do not possess that degree of sophistication, thus they would neither be fully aware of how to control their identity nor would they recognize discrepant identity presentation. It is thus possible that the groups referred to do not experience embarrassment and hence would not blush in the situations which we, as observers, would define as embarrassing. (The probability that embarrassment can be both a private feeling and a social act is examined in the following chapter, and the development of embarrassment is discussed in Chapter 6.)

Assuming then that most adult humans experience embarrassment, why should the experience of embarrassment result in increased blood temperature and blushing? Although we can trace back the physiological reaction to embarrassing situations as one involving an increase in heart rate (although this may not be the case, as discussed in the following section) and hence an increase in body temperature, we are still left with the problem of why embarrassment leads to an increase in heart rate and whether blushing serves any function other than to decrease body temperature. Blushing certainly serves to communicate our embarrassment to others, and as embarrassment is a state that generally we wish to hide, blushing can hardly help us in our efforts at concealment. This is particularly true for fair-haired, thin-skinned individuals, whose blushing is particularly visible. It may be the case that embarrassment is always associated with changes in skin temperature, but that the associated blush is only visible in those with thinner skin. What is required is a carefully conducted study assessing subjectively reported embarrassment, heart rate, and skin temperature changes together with observer ratings and subjective ratings of degree of blushing present. Unfortunately such a study does not exist to date. There are also very few empirical studies which have investigated the precise physiological reaction accompanying embarrassment. These are discussed in the following section.

2. Skin conductance and heart rate

We have already noted that temperature and heart rate changes were reported by a number of subjects in our study as being typical reactions that they experienced during embarrassment (Edelmann, 1985b). This reported experience does not however tie in with experimental findings, although there is only one empirical study looking specifically at the physiology of embarrassment (Buck, Parke, and Buck, 1970; Buck and Parke, 1972).

The 120 male subjects in this study were divided into two groups—a fear group and an embarrassment group. Upon arrival at the laboratory, subjects were told that the purpose of the experiment was to assess the subject's physiological response to different kinds of stimulation. The subject was left alone for a 5-minute adaptation period followed by a 2-minute base-line period. The subject's heart rate and skin conductance were recorded continuously during the 2-minute base-line period. At the end of the 2-minute base-line period the experimenter entered the experimental room to deliver the stress manipulation.

In the fear condition an electrode was attached to the subject's arm and subjects were told that they would receive completely safe, but intense and painful, electric shocks. In the embarrassment condition, the subjects were given the following instructions:

'What I will ask you to do is very simple. Here are a number of objects, namely a baby bottle, a breast shield, a pacifier, and a couple of nipples. In a few minutes I'd like you to take each of these objects in your mouth and suck on it for a few seconds. This will allow us' to gauge your physiological sensitivity to such oral stimulation.'

In both conditions the subjects waited for a further 2 minutes while physiological measures were recorded, and then the experiment ended. No-one was actually shocked or required to suck the objects.

As well as the physiological measures, subjects rated their mood before and after the experiment along the dimensions of calm–tense, unpleasant–pleasant and embarrassed–not embarrassed. Perhaps, surprisingly, there were no differences between the fear and embarrassment groups on any of these self-report items. It would seem that facing the possibility of sucking certain objects did not induce embarrassment in the subjects, at least from their own subjective experience of the situation.

As an empirical investigation of the physiology of embarrassment one must thus treat the findings of this study with a certain amount of caution. The study necessitates the assumption that subjects did in fact experience embarrassment but did not wish to report it. If indeed that was the case the findings are of some interest. The level of skin conductance rose higher during fear than during embarrassment, suggesting that the fear subjects were more aroused. Heart rate acceleration was nonsignificant in the fear condition, while the embarrassment condition led to a significant heart rate deceleration. Assuming that the subjects were in fact embarrassed (and as mentioned previously this is open to doubt), two important questions need to be answered:

1. Why does embarrassment lead to a deceleration in heart rate?
2. Why do subjects typically report heart rate increases associated with embarrassment, with a pounding or racing heart being frequent subjective reports?

On the first point, Buck and his colleagues draw on the research of Lacey (1959) and Lacey *et al.* (1963) for explanation. The latter researchers found a heart rate deceleration and skin conductance decrease to tasks which seemed to demand that subjects pay attention to environmental stimuli. As embarrassment entails self-evaluation in the presence of real or imagined others, it is possible that when experiencing embarrassment we both expect, and look for, the reeactions of others. It should again be emphasized, however, that the need for this explanation is based on the assumption that embarrassment does in fact lead to a heart rate deceleration. On the basis of one study, in which subjects may not have even experienced embarrassment, the evidence is rather flimsy.

Assuming though that embarrassment does lead to a heart rate decleration, why do subjects report experiencing a heart rate acceleration? Two plausible explanations can be offered for this occurrence. First, any deceleration that occurs may be fairly transitory—a momentary orienting response—followed by a heart rate acceleration. As the latter would be longer-lasting it is more likely to be reported by the subject. A second explanation lies in the possibility that tensing of the muscles during embarrassment gives the subject the impression that his heart is actually beating faster, when that is not in fact the case.

Whatever the explanation, it is clear that further research is required in which the embarrassment manipulation gives rise to a clearly reported experience of embarrassment on the part of the subject. It is only in this way that one can verify whether heart rate deceleration or acceleration is associated with embarrassment.

One difficulty involves the problem of inducing embarrassment under laboratory conditions, although a useful technique has been suggested by Strom and Buck (1979). They investigated arousal in relation to staring, which induced significantly more embarrassment on the part of the subejcts than a non-staring condition. Unfortunately they only measured skin conductance in this study, and not heart rate. Unlike the previous study where the embarrassment manipulation did not give rise to an increase in skin conductance, staring gave rise both to more embarrassment and skin conductance deflections than the 'no-stare' condition. It can only be emphasized that carefully conducted studies are required in order to evaluate the total physiological response to embarrassing events. The relationship between skin temperature, heart rate and blushing still remains to be adequately investigated. Perhaps better understood and researched is the nonverbal reaction with accompanies embarrassment, as detailed in the following section.

B. NONVERBAL REACTION

1. Eye contact, body motion and speech disturbances

The association of certain behaviours during embarrassing events has already been noted. Three of these behaviours will be discussed in this section, the fourth (smiling and laughing) will be discussed separately. The reasons for this are two-fold: first, because laboratory studies have tended to concentrate upon changes in eye contact together with body motion and speech disturbances, rather than looking at the presence of smiling; and second, because changes in eye contact, body motion and speech disturbance might serve separate functions from smiling and/or laughter.

As with blushing, Charles Darwin (1873) was one of the first authors to comment that people who are ashamed (which he appears to use as a synonym for embarrassment) appear to cast their eyes downwards, use particular gestures and suffer from speech disturbances. Thus he states:

> An ashamed person can hardly endure to meet the gaze of those present so that he almost invariably casts his eyes downwards or looks askant. (p. 340)

> Under a keen sense of shame there is a strong desire for concealment. We turn the whole body, more especially the face which we endeavour in some manner to hide. (p. 340)

> Persons in this condition lose their presence of mind, and utter singularly inappropriate remarks. They are often much distressed, stammer and make awkward movements or strange grimaces. (p. 342)

Indeed, the existence of these behaviours has received a great deal of empirical support. One of the first empirical investigations of the relationship between eye contact and embarrassment was a study by Exline, Gray, and Schuette (1965). Different degrees of embarrassment were induced by a continuously gazing confederate who varied the nature of the questions put to the subjects. One group of subjects was asked about very personal matters—for example their fears, desires, needs, and impulses. The remaining subjects were asked about their recreational interests, preferred films, books, sports, and so on. The personal nature of the questions for the first group was assumed to create a more embarrassing situation for the subject than the relatively innocuous questions for the second, although there was no independent validation of this assumption.

As predicted, the amount of looking while speaking for the subjects was significantly more for the recreational interview topic (49.8 per cent) than for the personal interview topic (39.3 per cent). It may be the case that subjects were embarrassed by the personal nature of the questions and avoided eye contact in order to conceal this embarrassment. It may be the case, however, that the subjects were experiencing surprise, disgust or some other emotion, and clearly a subjective assessment by the subject of his/her state is required as well as an objective measure. In a further study on the relationship of eye contact to embarrassment (Modigliani, 1971), subjects were caused to succeed or fail in public or private on their portion of a group task. In the public condition subjects were either praised for success, or criticized for failure, by a continually staring confederate. As predicted, the public failure subjects reported more embarrassment than the public success subjects. Embarrassment was assessed by a self-report measure consisting of four bi-polar nine-point scale (at ease–self-conscious, poised–awkward, free–constrained, not embarrassed–embarrassed) averaged together to create a scale of felt embarrassment with a range of 1–9. Eye contact for the public failure group occurred in 18 per cent of the interaction, and for the public success group, in 30 per cent, although there was no correlation within conditions between gaze aversion and reported embarrassment. While it is possible that the reduction in eye contact was caused by embarrassment, it is also possible (as Modigliani himself suggests) that the reduction in eye contact was a result of dislike for the confederate who was assessing eye contact. Ellsworth and Carlsmith (1968) have suggested that people are particularly prone to dislike someone who criticizes them while looking directly into their line of regard. In Modigliani' study this is exactly what the confederate did.

The relationship between body motion and embarrassment has only been investigated empirically in our own studies in conjunction with changes in eye contact and speech disturbances. Some examples of gestures suggested from the literature as indicating embarrassment include putting the finger to the lip (Krout, 1954), shuffling the feet (Birdwhistell, 1952) and the various face-touching gestures which are also associated with shame and other negative attitudes toward the self (Ekman and Friesen, 1969, 1972).

Again, apart from our own studies looking at the constellation of nonverbal behaviours associated with embarrassment, there is only one study looking directly at speech disturbances and embarrassment. This was an investigation by Cook (1969) designed ostensibly to investigate anxiety, speech disturbances and speech rate. Subjects participated in a three-stage interview—during the first and last part of the interview a subject was asked to talk about various topics, usually his or her interests, sports, theatre, cinema, etc. During the middle part of the interview subjects were asked to talk about work and sex. During this phase of the interview the 'interviewer followed up any line of questions that appeared to embarrass or worry the subject' (p. 16). During this phase of the interview there was a marked increase in speech errors.

Finally, in our own studies we were interested in studying the range of nonverbal behaviours occurring during embarrassing episodes. In the first of two studies (Edelmann and Hampson, 1979), embarrassment was induced in a videotaped interview when an interviewer revealed something unexpected about himself. This was designed to embarrass the interviewees. (Subjects were criticizing a painting to an interviewer when he revealed that he was the artist of the picture they were criticizing.) Embarrassment was assessed at the end of the interview by asking subjects to rate on a five-point scale (where 1 indicated 'did not experience' and 5 indicated 'experienced strongly') which emotions they could recall experiencing from a list of 19 emotions. These ratings were then compared with ratings for two similarly worded but non-embarrassing control questions asked during the interview. Fifteen of the 22 subjects reported embarrassment at the interviewer's revelation. The level of eye contact for these subjects decreased significantly at this point in the interview relative to preceding and subsequent levels, whereas body motion and speech disturbances increased. The seven non-embarrassed subjects showed a significant increase in eye contact at this stage of the interview but no change in body motion or speech disturbances.

These latter findings may have been due to a number of factors. Firstly, the unembarrassed subjects may have been generally more at ease; secondly, the unembarrassed subjects might have been trying to dominate the situation for, as Argyle and Cook (1976) suggest, this is one factor which causes people to look more at others; alternatively, they may have actually felt embarrassed but tried to conceal it both by looking more and then by denying it during the embarrassment assessment. One of the major difficulties in research of a negative state such as embarrassment is that subjects may deny that they have experienced the emotion even when this is not in fact the case. Possible explanations for the changes in nonverbal behaviour which occurred for the embarrassed group will be discussed later in this chapter.

In the second study (Edelmann and Hampson, 1981b), subject pairs took part in an alternating question-and-answer session and were assigned to one of two conditions. For the embarrassment manipulation, subjects used questions which increased in their intimacy content, while the control group had only non-intimate questions. Degree of embarrassment experienced was assessed retrospectively for three points in the interview using the scale described for our previous study. Topic intimacy resulted in increased embarrassment, decreased eye contact, increased gestural activity and speech disturbances and also increased smiling.

It would appear then from self-reports, a number of comments from the literature and a number of empirical studies, that embarrassment results in a fairly well-defined constellation of behaviours. The question remains as to what possible function these behaviours serve. One possibility is that the functions of the behavioural display associated with embarrassment are similar to the functions of the behavioural display of social anxiety suggested by Schlenker and Leary (1982), and Leary (1982, 1983a). That is, nervous responses, disaffiliative behaviours and image-protection responses (the latter refers mainly to the presence of smiling and laughter and will be dealt with in the following section).

Nervous responses refer to manipulative gestures (such as fingering one's clothes, hair or surrounding objects), turning one's body away, and stammering. These behaviours make up the increases in body motion and speech disturbances referred to previously. As well as being present in embarrassment these behaviours also occur in other forms of social anxiety (Cheek and Buss, 1982; Pilkonis, 1977; Zimbardo, 1977). Leary (1982) suggests that:

> Arousal-mediated responses are merely side effects of the activation of the sympathetic nervous system that accompanies all arousal states, but they serve no useful social function for the individual. (p. 110)

When the sympathetic 'flight or fright' reaction is activated by perceived threat, general arousal and muscular tension increase with accompanying behavioural reactions. In social settings flight is not possible following an embarrassing event, leaving the behaviours as a residue of prevented flight. (It should be noted that this suggestion is in direct contrast to Buss's (1980) view that deceleration of heart rate suggested by Buck and Parke's (1972) study indicates that in embarrassment the parasympathetic division is dominant.)

The occurrence of speech disturbances as nervous responses has a number of possible explanations. Leary (1983a) suggest three possible mechanisms by which anxiety can interfere with speaking: first, preoccupation with the source of threat which makes it difficult for the individual to pay sufficient attention to what he or she is saying; second, anxiety may operate in the opposite way by making people pay too much attention to what they are saying; and third, arousal may interfere with normal breathing so that with shorter, faster respiration people may have difficulty speaking. Of the three explanations the second seems to be most plausible in the case of embarrassment. Embarrassment has to do with public self-attention and a preoccupation with oneself, and stuttering may result from paying too much attention to what one is saying (Kamhi and McOsker, 1982). The relationship between embarrassing and stuttering then would not be suprising.

Disaffiliative behaviours refer to behaviours that serve to decrease our contact with others. Reducing eye contact, covering one's eyes, turning away or simply not saying anything, all serve to increase our psychological distance from others. Thus Exline, Gray and Schuette (1965) suggest:

> The visual reactions to embarrassment would seem to be most reasonably interpreted as suggesting that individuals whose composure is threatened by the nature of the interaction with another, may, perhaps unconsciously, signal a desire to maintain psychological distance from the other b avoiding eye contact with him. (p. 209).

A common feeling when experiencing embarrassment is a desire to disappear, sink through the floor, or leave the situation in some way. Generally speaking this is not possible, so that the nonverbal behaviours may be a signal of this desire, translated into a more socially acceptable framework.

A number of studies have in fact indicated that embarrassment causes people to avoid affiliative behaviour. Sarnoff and Zimbardo (1961) found that when subjects were about to perform an embarrassing task such as sucking on nipples, baby bottees, etc.—labelled by the authors as highly 'anxiety' arousing—they preferred to affiliate less with similar-state others than did persons in the low-anxiety control condition.

Teichman (1973) has suggested that the situation in which the subjects found themselves in Sarnoff and Zimbardo's study was highly specific and could be regarded as causing feelings of embarrassment. She thus extended and replicated their study but took specific measures of anxiety and embarrassment. The latter was measured on a 0–100 scale with subjects asked to indicate their feelings of embarrassment, shame, or being absurd. In her study she compared reactions to general and specific emotional arousal. High general anxiety was induced by telling subjects that they would be exposed to an extreme self-disclosure situation with two complete strangers. In the high specific arousal condition subjects were led to believe that they would perform the oral manipulation utilized by Sarnoff and Zimbardo (1961). These conditions were compared with a low general and low specific arousal condition. Teichman found that general arousal increased affiliation while specific arousal (i.e. embarrassment) decreased it. It would seem then that the specific arousal induced in these studies, which seems to be equivalent to embarrassment, played a role in the decision to avoid affiliation. One possibility suggested by Fish, Karabenick and Heath (1978) is that apprehension about revealing embarrassment to others may cause the desire for social isolation.

They thus assessed the influence of anticipated experimenter surveillance during the performance of a painful or potentially embarrassing act on affiliative preferences before engaging in that act. The procedure was again similar to that used by Sarnoff and Zimbardo (1981), but before the affiliation choice was made, subjects were shown a series of slides appropriate to each experimental conditon, the intention being to reinforce the subjects' differential expectations of the nature of the stimulus situation. Subjects were also asked to estimate their feelings of fear, anxiety, and embarrassment by circling the word(s) 'not of all', 'slightly', 'moderately', or 'very' that described the extent to which the emotion was felt. As they predicted, there was an overall preference for isolation when the act to be performed was embarrassing, and there was an increase in this tendency with anticipated surveillance. Subjects who are about to be embarrassed avoid company. This suggestion has important implications for the link between embarrassment and social anxiety introduced in Chapter 1 and dealt with in detail in Chapters 8 and 9. If subjects who are about to be embarrassed avoid company it may well be the case that those who fear that they will behave in a way which is embarrassing will also avoid company (i.e. fear of embarrassment may result in avoidance of social situations or occasion distress when, of necessity, one engages in social encounters). This issue is discussed in detail in later chapters.

In a further study of affiliation and embarrassment, Ellsworth *et al.* (1978) also present a conceptual replication and extension of the Sarnoff and Zimbardo study. Subjects were motivated to seek (fear arousal) or to avoid (embarrassment arousal) social comparison. They were then required to affiliate with another person who either encouraged social comparison by gazing directly at the subject or discouraged it by averting his gaze. For social comparison purposes the other person was either an appropriate reference person (i.e. one who was assumed to be in the same state as the subject) or an irrelevant comparison person. Pre- and post-experimental self-report measures included ratings of fear, embarrassment, and other relevant and irrelevant emotional dimensions. In line with the previous research cited, fear subjects liked a companion who looked at them and felt less tense in his presence, while embarrassed subjects preferred people who looked away. This tends to support the idea first raised by Darwin, in connection with shame, that gaze aversion occurs because the person wants to disappear from sight and thinks that if he cannot see the other then he cannot be seen himself.

A second suggestion raised by Argyle and Cook (1976) is that people may look away when embarrassed to avoid seeing the signs of rejection on the faces of another. The payoffs from any post-embarrassment interaction are not likely to be high for the embarrassed person, hence the desire to withdraw from the interaction. Embarrassment may well be regarded by the subjects in all the studies cited as a negative and unacceptable state. Brooding on the unacceptability of one's own feelings may lead a person to assume that social comparison will prove his inferiority. Others present may also be able to guess the 'bad' acts or feelings that have produced the embarrassment. The scrutiny of others may thus serve to reinforce the assumptions of the subjects about their 'unacceptable' feelings and bad actions, and hence increase their embarrassment. It seems that embarrassed subjects actively seek to avoid company.

While the presence of speech errors and gestures may signal 'nervousness' and the occurrence of reduced eye contact, turning away and reduced speech may signal a desire to disaffiliate—they may also serve at least one further function; they may act as cues for recognizing embarrassment in others.

2. The recognition of embarrassment

In view of the signs of emotionality discussed above, embarrassment should be a clearly recognizable emotion. In two of our studies (Edelmann and Hampson, 1981a) we thus investigated the ability of an onlooker to recognize embarrassment in others and the cues that they used in this recognition process.

In the first study subjects were assigned at random to one of three viewing conditions, being shown either the face, or the rest of the body, or the face and body together. Within each condition each subject saw three videotaped displays of amusement, three displays of embarrassment, and three 'distractor tapes', all of which were between 25 and 34 seconds in length. The results indicated that while amusement was recognizable from a facial display, embarrassment was recognizable from films of facial and bodily cues together, but on less than a third of the occasions from either the face or body alone. The mean values for correct recognition of the two emotions for each condition of visibility are given in Table 4.2. It was also found that embarrassment was often mistakenly identified as amusement when the facial display alone was seen. The average values for an incorrect judgment of amusement for the three embarrassed encoders at each level of visibility are given in Table 4.3. The maximum accuracy score for each condition was 3.

Table 4.2 Mean accuracy scores for recognition of embarrassment and amusement

	Face and body	Face	Body
Embarrassment	2.18	0.91	1.00
Amusement	1.82	1.55	0.18

Table 4.3 Mean scores for incorrect judgment of amusement for displayed embarrassment

Face and body	Face	Body
0.45	1.55	0.36

In the second experiment, subjects only viewed the face plus body condition, but were asked to indicate on a schematic drawing of a person which part they were utilizing to make their judgments. The frequencies with which different parts of the person were used when making a correct judgment of amusement or embarrassment are shown schematically in Figure 4.1.

For a correct judgment of embarrassment the eyes, hands, mouth, and lower legs all provided important cues. While body cues are thus important indicators of embarrassment, this is only when they are seen in conjunction with facial ones—particularly the eyes and mouth. In fact the facial expression, which is viewed as indicating amusement when seen in isolation, is actually seen as indicating embarrassment under normal viewing conditions. Thus, when the apparently amused expression occurs in conjunction with downcast eyes and nervous hand and leg movements, it is interpreted by observers as a display of 'embarrassed laughter' and not as a mask of amusement. One possible explanation for the *apparently* amused component of embarrassment follows Ekman and Friesen's suggestion (1975) that a smile is frequently added as a comment after the expression of a negative emotion. Thus a more general display of amusement, occurring at the same time as the negative emotion, might serve the function of telling the observer how seriously the situation is viewed by the actor. Thus, far from concealing embarrassment, one possible interpretation of the display of apparent amusement associated with embarrassment is that it makes the embarrassed person feel better, because he is able to communicate to the other interactor not to take the embarrassment too seriously. The occurrence of smiling and laughter during embarrassing episodes has been extensively noted in the literature, and requires detailed attention. The questions of when and why smiling and/or laughter occurs in conjunction with embarrassment are thus considered in the following section:

3. Smiling and laughter

That smiling and laughter can be initiated during embarrassing events has been recognized by a number of authors. As mentioned previously, in one of our own empirical studies (Edelmann and Hampson, 1981b), increased embarrassment, induced by varying the intimacy of topics that subjects were asked to discuss, resulted in increased amounts of smiling. In a more recent study (Edelmann, 1985b), in which subjects were asked to record their

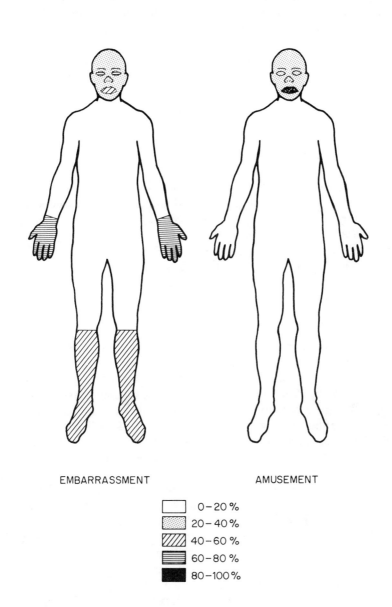

EMBARRASSMENT   AMUSEMENT

0-20 %
20-40 %
40-60 %
60-80 %
80-100%

Figure 4.1   The percentage frequency with which different parts of
the face and body are used to make a correct judgment of
embarrassment or amusement

nonverbal reaction to embarrassing events, grinning and smiling were referred to by 28 per cent of the subjects, while laughing was mentioned by a further 17 per cent (see Table 4.1). As Chapman (1983) has commented:

> We know that laughter can erupt in association with any of the emotions; certainly it can be witnessed in fear, embarrassment, contempt and grief. (p. 151)

As mentioned in the preceding section, one function of both smiling and laughter in embarrassing events is that they are often used in conjunction with other nonverbal cues as indicators of embarrassment. This suggests the existence of a discernible 'embarrassed smile' or 'embarrassed laugh'. Thus Birdwhistell (1970) has noted: 'A smile in one society portrays friendliness, in another embarrassment' (p. 35). A recent empirical study (Asendorpf, 1985) does in fact suggest that embarrassed and non-embarrassed smiles are clearly distinguishable. Thus for 85 per cent of embarrassed smiles, gaze aversion occurred before the apex of the smile ended, while only 23 per cent of smiles judged as non-embarrassed showed this type of gaze. It seems that people avert their gaze during embarrassed smiles in the most communicative part of smiling: between the beginning of the smile and the end of its apex. This seems to be the reason why embarrassed smiles carry a flavour of ambivalence: approach (smiling) and avoidance (gaze aversion) at the same time.

Asendorpf offers two explanations for the presence of this ambivalence. The first explanation is based upon the suggestion that gaze aversion is a natural concomitant of embarrassment while attempts to cope with embarrassment are indicated by smiling. The second explanation is based on the suggestion that gaze aversion is actually a response to smiling. In the latter case, smiling tends to conflict with our desire to avoid our interactional partners because it increases the intimacy of the situation; therefore an attempt is made to reduce the level of intimacy by averting one's gaze.

In relation to both the above explanations it is important to recognize that a number of further issues are likely to be involved. First, both smiling *and* laughter can occur during embarrassment and the relationship between smiling and laughter is far from clear. Berlyne (1972) has suggested that, though they are distinct, the smile and the laugh are not independent. This matter remains an issue of contention, and smiling and laughter may well serve differing functions within the experience of embarrassment. Second, embarrassment rather than being a precise event is constructed or built up over time, a factor which is discussed in detail in Chapter 5. In particular, embarrassment, as discussed previously, consists of a recognizable display of nonverbal cues with smiling playing an important part in this display. In addition, a social transgression or accident giving rise to embarrassment provokes attempts by the individual to regain lost social approval and restore his/her public image. As with an initial display of embarrassment these coping attempts may also be associated with smiling and laughter. Smiling and laughter associated with these phases of embarrassment are thus likely to serve very different functions.

In the earlier stages of embarrassment the incongruity/arousal–safety model (Berlyne, 1969; Rothbart, 1976) of laughter provides a useful explanation for the presence of laughter in embarrassing situations (Edelmann, 1985c). The starting point for this view is the notion that laughter can result when there is a dissimilarity or discrepancy in the stimulus variable present. In the case of embarrassment it could be argued that the discrepancy between one's actual self-presentation caused by the embarrassing event and one's standard or normal self-presentation *is* the incongruity. While the perception of an incongruous or unexpected event may lead to laughter from an observer it is possible that the self-perception of one's own incongruous behaviour could also generate laughter. As Rothbart (1976) points out, there are a number of situational conditions which are necessary to differentiate laughter from distress as responses to the perception of incongruous stimuli. Sudden, tense, highly incongruous stimuli judged to be dangerous are unlikely to provoke laughter. Thus, stumbling in front of your boss/professor at the top of a flight of stairs may be embarrassing but not laughter-provoking, whilst stumbling in front of acquaintances and spilling a plate of food may be both embarrassing and laughter-provoking. This leads to a range of testable predictions about the association of embarrassment with smiling and/or laughter. Thus, laughter is *less* likely to occur if

1. the experience of embarrassment is intense (e.g. in front of high-status others);
2. the self-presentation displayed is so discrepant from one's standard for self-presentation as to be unthinkable;
3. the event could be construed as being potentially dangerous.

Evidence that the first of these predictions is correct comes from a study by Fink and Walker (1977). In this study 60 subjects engaged in an embarrassing interaction with an experimenter by telephone. Examples of the embarrassing questions asked were: 'Describe in detail the most embarrassing situation you have been in'; 'Describe your most positive traits for attracting the opposite sex'; and 'Describe your most negative traits for turning off the opposite sex'. Two trained coders listened to the interview on extension telephones and rated laughter, verbal humour, speech loss, anxiety, the openness of the subject, avoidance of the issues in the conversation, and embarrassment. Subjects were told by the interviewer either to anticipate meeting with her in future or not to anticipate meeting her. Independently of this manipulation, the interviewer introduced herself as either a college professor (higher status), an undergraduate (equal status) or a high school student (lower status).

Of central importance to our present discussion was the fact that although embarrassment as perceived by the coders was relatively high throughout, more laughter occurred between status equals than between persons of unequal status.

While there is no direct evaluation of the second of the two predictions referred to above (that degree of discrepancy between one's self-presentation and one's standard for self-presentation is inversely related to the amount of laughter), this supposition would seem to imply that degree of embarrassment experienced should be inversely related to amount of laughter and/or smiling. In one of our studies (Edelmann and Hampson, 1981b) we found that as the intimacy of the topic on which subjects were asked to speak increased, so did the degree of embarrassment experienced and the amount of smiling which occurred. One possibility is that smiling increases until an optimal level is reached, at which point the experience of embarrassment becomes too distressing. This would link directly with the third supposition—that smiling does not occur when the embarrassing event is potentially dangerous. Smiling may always be present as an integral part of displayed embarrassment, serving a possible communicative function; in extreme cases of embarrassment smiling may cease.

Indeed, during certain embarrassing experiences laughter may be viewed by observers as being the most appropriate response. In a study by Edelmann (1982) referred to previously, subjects were required to inform a confederate of the experimenter during a role-played interview that he had performed badly on a task. The confederate responded to this by reacting in one of three ways: (a) a defiant stare; (b) a typical nonverbal reaction to embarrassment described previously, i.e. reduced eye contact and an increase in body motion and speech disturbances but without smiling; and (c) with smiling in addition to the nonverbal behaviours listed in condition (b). Subjects experienced most discomfort when the confederate just stared, and also liked him least in this condition. When he smiled, looked away, and fidgeted the confederate was evaluated most favourably and caused least discomfort to the subject. In sum then, smiling and laughter are likely to occur as an integral part of displayed embarrassment serving a communicative function with, in some circumstances, their occurrence being seen as highly appropriate and image-enhancing.

In addition to being part of displayed embarrassment, however, laughter may also occur as part of the attempt made by the actor to restore his/her public image once the embarrassing event has occurred. This may or may not be used in conjunction with attempts to introduce humour into the situation as an attempt to reduce the importance of the event giving rise to the predicament. This issue is discussed in the following section.

4. Laughter as a coping response

When an embarrassing event has occurred, the actor may use a number of strategies in an attempt to restore his/her public image. Various attempts to minimize, explain away, or excuse the behaviour which has caused the embarrassing incident were discussed in the previous chapter. A further face-saving device that helps to preserve a person's identity after an embarrassing incident is humour (Kane, Suls, and Tedeschi, 1977). Dixon (1980) has cogently argued that humour may have evolved as a uniquely human strategy for coping with stress, while Martin and Lefcourt (1983) have illustrated empirically that humour reduces the impact of stress.

A number of further reports, mainly from within medical settings, illustrate the way in which humour can be used to cope with embarrassing situations. During medical examinations or treatment, rules about social behaviour and social conduct regarding our bodies, bodily functions and intimate behaviours are often violated or ignored. In fact, the rules of the game are that neither the patient nor the professional is to show embarrassment. Rather, each is expected to show an air of detachment and nonchalance. Emerson (1970) discusses the use of humour as a strategy for neutralizing embarrassment during gynaecological examinations. She found that it was usually the staff, most often the male doctor, who initiated the humour. The joking seemed to be a method used by the staff to persuade patients to put up with embarrassing affronts to their dignity.

Robinson (1983), writing about health and humour, also reports that jokes about bedpans, bodily functions, and sex are frequently used as a way of coping with or forestalling embarrassment.

Humour then may be used by both the observer and/or the actor as a face-saving mechanism or as a method of coping with possible anxiety engendered by the embarrassing event. It is important in this context to note that the audience can assist the actors by 'playing along' with them, either by initiating or maintaining the potentially 'humorous' nature of the situation.

Thus, laughter and humour can be initiated by either the actor and/or the observer and responded to by either the actor and/or the observer. The result can be either a reciprocal or a mismatched response. That this situation can occur was illustrated graphically in a recent study (Edelmann, 1985b). Subjects were asked to record nonverbal reactions they used to cover or hide their embarrassment (they were also asked to record verbal responses they used to deal with embarrassment, as referred to in Chapter 3). In addition, they were asked to record the verbal and nonverbal reactions of observers to the event. Thirty-six per cent of the actors reported using smiling and laughter to cover their embarrassing (which, as has been discussed, is unlikely to have been successful in view of the fact that smiling and laughter are often used as signs of embarrassment). In contrast it was reported that 55 per cent of the observers smiled or laughed in response to the embarrassing event (see Tables 4.4 and 4.5). There was thus a mismatch between the number of observers and actors who laughed and joked. It would seem that observers are slightly more inclined to make light of the event, perhaps in an attempt to help the actor out of their predicament, than actors are inclined to use laughter/humour as a face-saving strategy. By not joining in with the observer in his/her attempts to help, the actor is likely to become the butt of the joke.

Table 4.4 Nonverbal reactions as attempts to cover or hide embarrassment. The total reaction for face, eyes and body refers to those mentioning at least one of the components of each reaction. Nonverbal reactions as attempts to cover or hide embarrassment. (Items occurring with greatest frequency, i.e. 15, are italicized). ($N = 100$; frequency equals both number of responses and percentage response in each category.)

Nonverbal reaction	Frequency	Specific response
Facial expression	47	*Smile/grin 22*; laugh 14; no smile 5; controlled face 8; clenched teeth 2; raised eyebrows 1
Eyes	48	*Avoiding eye contact 35*; seeking eye contact 4; controlled gaze 5; changed eye contact, type unspecified 4
Body	19	Self-touching 7; controlled movement 8; increased movement 3; normal movement 1
Motor	15	Leaving the situation 9; turning away 6
Posture	8	Head down 6; collapsed 2; lean back 1; erect 1

Table 4.5 Observers' nonverbal reactions to actor's embarrassment. The total reaction for face, eyes, and body refers to those mentioning at least one of the components for each reaction. (Items occurring with greatest frequency, i.e. > 15 are italicized. ($N = 100$; frequency equals both number of responses and percentage response in each category.)

Nonverbal reaction	Frequency	Specific response
Facial expression	66	*Laugh 33; smile/grin 22;* raised eyebrows 3; expression changed; type unspecified 11
Eyes	27	Avoid eye contact 6; see eye contact 5; stare 5; eye contact changed, type unspecified 11
Body	11	Ojbect touching 2; movement changed, type unspecified 9
Motor	5	Approaching 2; leaving 3
Posture	5	Lean forward 3; lean back 1; head down 1

In summary then, laughter and humour can be used as purposeful strategies by either the victim of the embarrassing event or the observer to the event in order to change the meaning and focus of the situation. By diminishing the importance of the event the identity 'victim' can be transformed to 'co-actor' and the label 'embarrassing' transformed to 'humorous'. It is clear that effective coping will involve careful appraisal of the situation in order to determine the appropriateness of laughter or humour, as well as an ability to adequately effect the use of humour as a coping strategy.

Overall, while smiling, laughter, and humour form an intrinsic part of the experience of embarrassment, it seems that they fulfil different functions depending upon when they occur within the experience of the embarrassment.

Laughter which occurs during the later phases of the experience of embarrassment may be invoked by the individual as remedial or face-saving strategies. Laughter and/or smiling during the initial stages of embarrassment is much more likely to be an intrinsic part of the nonverbal display of embarrassment with its occurrence dependent upon a number of factors. These include the intensity of the embarrassment experienced, the danger involved in the situation, and the extent of the discrepancy between one's self-presentation and one's standard for self-presentation.

C. SUMMARY

In the preceding sections of this chapter the various physiological and behavioural responses to embarrassment have been described and possible functions that these displays might serve have been discussed. The overlap between the functions of the behavioural display of embarrassment and functions of the behavioural display of social anxiety referred to by Schlenker and Leary (1982), and Leary (1982, 1983b) was noted. As mentioned, they group the behaviours into three functional classes: nervous responses, disaffiliative behaviours, and image protection. In the case of embarrassment, fidgeting and stammering could be regarded as nervous responses; avoiding eye contact or covering one's face could be viewed as behaviours that decrease social contact with others and hence are disaffiliative, whilst smiling may in some cases be an attempt to protect one's image following a disruption of social routine.

While it is likely that the behaviours mentioned function in the way described, it seems that they may also serve at least one other function. They act as cues for recognizing embarrassment in others. The presence of smiling and laughter as behavioural responses to embarrassing events also suggests that it may be appropriate to regard embarrassment as an experience which varies as a function of time. Thus smiling and/or laughter may be part of an intrinsic behavioural display of embarrassment, while laughter alone is more likely to be introduced as a coping response at a later stage in the experience of embarrassment.

As well as the functions of nonverbal behaviours discussed in this chapter, a recent suggestion (Edelmann, 1985a) is that one's own overt embarrassment can be perceived and labelled as such by using information from one's own facial expression and other expressive behaviours as well as physiological responses including blushing and memory from past experience. The issues of (1) embarrassment as an emotion which is constructed or built up over time rather than being a discrete event, and (2) the use of nonverbal and physiological reactions to label the state as embarrassment, form the central aspects of Chapter 5.

CHAPTER 5

Embarrassment: Private Feeling or Social Act?

Three aspects of embarrassment have been emphasized in the chapters forming the first part of this book. The first major issue discussed was the involvement of self-presentational difficulties in the experience of embarrassment. The second major issue was the way in which our knowledge of social rules, and the extent to which we deem them to be appropriate, determine our standard for behavioural presentation. The third major theme was the way in which our behavioural and physiological responses can be affected when self-presentations fail should we inadvertently transgress our own standards for social performance.

As was pointed out in the first chapter, and as has been emphasized by a number of authors adopting a self-presentational approach to embarrassment, it is clear that the experience of embarrassment is likely to involve a sequence of events rather than being a single definable state. The experience of embarrassment necessitates the actor making appraisals of the social event (i.e. the social setting, expected behaviours, expectations of others, the rules of conduct), the physiological and behavioural consequences of that event (i.e. the behaviours associated with the negative consequences of failure to follow the rules of conduct), as well as the behaviours associated with consequent attempts to rectify the situation once a negative event has occurred. The label 'embarrassment' may then be assigned as a result of the subjective experience of the actor and/or based upon an evaluation of the event which precipitated the experience and/or based upon an evaluation of the behavioural display which results from this event.

The present chapter forms a pivot around which the book is structured. One side of the pivot—the factors giving rise to the experience of embarrassment—has been outlined in detail in the first half of the book. The other side of the pivot forms the second half of the book and looks at ways in which the experience of embarrassment affects our everyday lives. This involves: (1) the way in which we may differ with regard to age and personality in our susceptibility to the experience of embarrassment; (2) the way embarrassment can affect how we behave in certain settings; and (3) the way in which fear of embarrassment can inhibit our social behaviour. Ways of rectifying these inhibited thoughts and behaviours are also discussed. The pivot itself consists of an analysis of embarrassment as a process or chain of events, some aspects of which may be more salient to some individuals than others.

A. EMBARRASSMENT AS AN EMOTION

A cursory glance at the historical and recent literature on emotions is all that is required to reveal the wide variety of views and traditions that have developed. Four broad classes of theory can be recognized. In the first group, derived from the writing of William James (1884), the experience of an emotion is regarded as being the result of a particular pattern of autonomic activity. Thus, whether one *feels* embarrassed would be viewed as being the result of some specific physiological change—perhaps blushing. The issue of which comes first, the feeling of the emotion or the physiological change which is assocated with it, is far from resolved and is the centre of an ongoing debate.

In the second group of theories the experience of the emotion is the product of the combination of undifferentiated autonomic feedback with a congition, i.e. a thought, perception or idea (e.g. Schachter, 1964). Thus the physiological arousal associated with an emotion labelled 'embarrassment', may be the same as that for sadness, surprise, fear, etc., with the differentiating factor being the way in which the individual perceives the situation. Cognitive appraisal of the antecedent event thus becomes central in labelling the experience as embarrassment. This may involve recognizing that a disruption of social routine, such as a *faux pas*, impropriety, accident, or transgression has occurred.

The third group of theories, the neurological tradition, is identified with the writings of Walter Cannon (1929). The emphasis here is on the notion that emotion is constructed from the interaction of specific 'emotion' sites in the central nervous system. On this basis it should thus be possible to map the various areas of the brain associated with emotional reactions. The evidence linking the experience of embarrassment to specific sites of the brain is particularly scanty. As the emotional experience of embarrassment is thought to be restricted to humans, the only available evidence can be derived from reactions to brain trauma or seizures. A case of a 40-year-old male physician reported by Devinsky, Hafler, and Victor (1982) is of relevance here. At the age of 38 this man experienced a nocturnal grand mal seizure, although subsequent neurological examination showed the EEG and CT to be normal. Six months later the patient had two episodes in which he was awakened from sleep by a seizure characterized by hyperextension and external rotation of the left arm. After a further 6 months the patient experienced the first of many stereotyped episodes beginning with a 15-second aura that he described as 'the feeling of extreme embarrassment, as though I had made a very foolish remark'. Devinsky *et al*. report that the episodes occurred at social gatherings, during consultations with patients, and while alone. They also suggest that the episodes did not appear to be triggered by events in the environment (e.g. situations that might have been labelled 'embarrassing') and were not accompanied by automatic changes such as facial flushing. A further CT evaluation, which included coronal sections, revealed a tumour deep within the medial aspect of the right frontal lobe, extending into the genu of the corpus callosum and frontal horn. The seizure focus thus appeared to be in the frontal lobes (although the original focus might have been in the limbic system) so that an electrical discharge in this area might be responsible for producing embarrassment. This is consistent with the frequent observation that lesions in the prefrontal areas result in a behavioural syndrome characterized by some combination of apathy, indifference, incontinence, irritability, impulsivity, and a failure to act appropriately in social situations (Blumer and Benson, 1975). This lack of social grace stands out as a prominent feature of the frontal lobe personality disorder. Actions that are normally embarrassing are performed by patients with frontal lobe disease without hesitation, as though the capacity for embarrassment were absent. It may well be the case then that the specific 'emotion' site in the central nervous system in the case of embarrassment is located in the frontal lobes. This site may well function in an evaluation capacity allowing us to make sense of the antecedent event, and the physiological and behavioural reactions.

The fourth group of theories may be characterized as the evolutionary tradition, and are identified with the writings of Charles Darwin (1873). He suggested a basic continuity of emotional expressions from lower animals to humans. Emotions thus increase the animals' chances of survival by being appropriate reactions to emergency events in the environment and by acting as signals for future intentions or actions. A number of theorists have taken up this notion to build up 'process' theories of emotion (Izard, 1971, 1977; Leventhal, 1979, 1980; Leventhal and Mosbach, 1983; Plutchic, 1980, 1984; Scherer, 1982, 1984; Tomkins, 1962, 1980). Although these theorists tend to accept the notion that emotion depends upon specific 'emotion centres' of the central nervous system they have also emphasized the importance of feedback from the face as having an important role in creating the specific emotional experience. The question then arises as to whether the expression comes before the experience of the emotion (i.e. blushing occurs and then the emotion is labelled as embarrassment) or whether the expression is just a consequence of the activation of the central emotional processes.

In view of the contrasting views on the starting point for the experience of an emotion (physiological, neurological, cognitive), it is perhaps not surprising that over the years the question of 'what comes first' has developed into an ever more vigorous debate. Thus, issues of (1) whether cognitive appraisal of the event precedes the affective or feeling component, (2) whether facial activity is necessary for an emotion to be experienced, (3) whether an emotion can be elicited without an antecedent event, are central debates which have emerged over the years. With reference to the experience of embarrassment these central questions become:

1. Is it necessary for a specific antecedent even to occur before embarrassment can be experienced?
2. Rather than a specific event occurring, is it the way in which the situation is perceived which is central?
3. Can embarrassment occur in the absence of nonverbal and physiological responses associated with embarrassment but in situations which are perceived as embarrassing?
4. Does the nonverbal and physiological reaction associated with embarrassment precede or follow the subjective experience of embarrassment?
5. If the former is the case, can the experience of embarrassment be labelled as such purely on the basis of the nonverbal and physiological reaction (i.e. can blushing cause embarrassment?)

In view of the complexities of the issues involved it is perhaps not surprising that many researchers have taken the view that emotions are best regarded as being made up of several aspects and components, the salience of which can vary, that is emotions including embarrassment are built up or constructed over time.

B. EMOTION AS A PROCESS

The word 'emotion' refers to a wide variety of behaviours, subjective, expressive (facial, postural) and autonomic and any theory that tries to account for these behaviours will necessarily be complex. We believe that such a theory must conceptualise emotion as a multicomponent, hierarchical set of mediating mechanisms that function as a unified system. (Leventhal and Mosbach, 1983, p. 353).

An emotion is an inferred complex sequence of reactions to a stimulus and includes cognitive evaluations, subjective changes, autonomic and neural arousal, impulses to action, and behaviour designed to have an effect upon the stimulus that initiated the complex sequence. (Plutchic, 1984, p. 217).

As the two recent quotes above indicate, there tends to be some agreement that the term 'emotion' is best treated as a psychological construct consisting of several aspects or components. As mentioned, a number of emotion theorists have tended to agree that the concept of emotion should be used to refer to a whole syndrome of different components of the psychological states referred to.

Scherer (1982) suggests five components for any emotion: (1) precognitive and cognitive evaluation; (2) physiological reactions; (3) motivational components and components of preparation for action; (4) motor expression; and (5) the subjective emotional state. Scherer's starting point is to describe a series of stimulus evaluation checks (SEC) which he regards as being minimally necessary for adequately evaluating or appraising the emotion-producing stimuli (Scherer, 1982, 1984). The first SEC, which involves an evaluation of the novelty or unexpectedness of the stimuli, is a fairly rapid and perhaps reflex reaction. The second SEC involves an evaluation of the inherent pleasantness or unpleasantness of the stimuli; that is, the likelihood that the stimuli will induce pleasure or distress independently of higher cortical appraisal. The third SEC has to do with an evaluation of the goal-relevance of the stimulus; that is, the extent to which the introduction of the stimulus will further or hinder the attainment of a specific goal. The fourth SEC, involving more complex information processing on the part of the organism, is concerned with an evaluation of the extent to which it is capable of coping with the stimulus; that is, whether the organism can control the stimulus or can change, avoid, or adjust the outcome. While the first four SECs are likely to be present in many species of animals, the fifth and final SEC is likely to be specific to humans. This SEC consists of a comparison of stimuli as well as the behaviours resulting from one's own actions or the actions of others with social norms and various aspects of self-concept. As Scherer (1982) points out, 'If one's own behaviour does not conform to social norms or if it is not compatible with one's self concept, shame or guilt may result' (p. 560). Much of this last SEC will obviously be relevant to any comprehensive model of embarrassment. A major SEC in the case of embarrassment is the evaluation of one's behaviour in relation to standards of behaviour and rules for conduct. Both an external check (i.e. 'What is the appropriate way in which to present myself in this particular setting?') and an internal check (i.e. 'What is my own personal standard for presentation?') could be postulated.

As Scherer points out, if more advanced processing capacities are required for later, more sophisticated checks, then emotions for which such checks are central are more likely to occur in humans as opposed to other animal species, and are more likely to occur at a later stage in human development (perhaps later than 2/3 years). The issue of developmental differences in the experience of embarrassment is taken up in the following chapter.

The response to the stimulus evaluations checks, i.e. the expressive behaviours, the physiological substratum, and the subjective experience, make up the different components of the emotion. Each of these components is obviously interlinked in some rather complex manner. As embarrassment is an emotion which results from the most advanced SECs, the human, subjective element may be of particular importance. This may not only involve a check on personal standards, but also a check on behavioural and physiological reactions. These latter reactions, and possibly nonverbal behaviours, in particular, may then play an important part in constructing the experience of embarrassment.

1. The role of nonverbal behaviour

The fact the embarrassment is characterized by a fairly well-defined behavioural display has been outlined in the preceding chapter. The occurrence of reduced eye contact, increased body motion, and speech disturbances and the likely occurrence of blushing has been described, as well as possible functions for these behaviours (nervous responses, disaffiliative behaviours, image protection). While it is likely that the behaviours referred to function in the way described, embarrassment has a number of added complexities which need to be explained:

1. It is possible to become embarrassed (or at least to elicit the behavioural display of embarrassment) by informing an interactant that he/she looks embarrassed even if this is not the case and/or the situation itself is not defined as embarrassing.
2. The experience of embarrassment (or at least the behavioural display) can be increased by making the actor aware that he/she is embarrassed (either by verbal comment or nonverbally).
3. It is possible to become embarrassed as a result of perceiving the fact that one is blushing even in a situation which is not deemed by others present or the actor him/herself to be intrinsically embarrassing.

In order to account for these issues, Asendorpf (1984) has introduced the notion of primary and secondary embarrassment. Primary embarrassment refers to the immediate response to the embarrassing event, whereas secondary embarrassment is a response to one's own overt embarrassment. This suggestion tends to assume that the subjective experience of embarrassment is initially triggered by a definable external antecedent event. An alternative viewpoint (Edelmann, 1985a) is that one's own overt embarrassment can be perceived and labelled as such by using information from one's own facial expression and other expressive behaviours (body motion, smiling, speech patterns) as well as visceral cues (alerting to environmental events) and memory from past experience (knowledge of social rules and other's reactions to rule-breaking episodes). The latter two components are likely to form an important element in Scherer's sequence of stimulus evaluation checks.

The notion that feedback from one's facial expressive behaviours gives rise to the experience of the emotion has had a long and checkered history. Darwin was one of the first to suggest that:

> The free expression of the outward signs of emotion intensifies it. On the other hand the repression of all outward signs softens our emotion. (1873, p. 22).

Similarly, James (1884/1968) has argued that peripheral bodily changes are essential to add an emotional quality to the perception of an event:

> Bodily changes follow directly the *perception* of the exciting fact, and . . . our feeling of these same changes as they occur *is* the emotion. . . . Without the bodily states following on the perception, the latter would be purely cognitive in form, pale, colourless, destitute of emotional warmth. (p. 19, italics in the original)

The present argument with respect to embarrassment is that:

1. The outward sign of embarrassment can cause embarrassment to be experienced even in the absence of an external eliciting stimuli (i.e. a social predicament, or the appraisal of an external event which calls the actor's competence into question, does not have to occur for embarrassment to be experienced).
2. In the presence of an event which is appraised as one likely to elicit embarrassment, the presence of nonverbal signs of embarrassment can intensify the experience of embarrassment.
3. Embarrassment can be experienced in the complete absence of nonverbal signs of embarrassment if the situation is one which is labelled by the actors present as one in which embarrassment is likely to occur.

The argument then is that embarrassment can be elicited by the situation and/or the display, with the display intensifying the experience of embarrassment (i.e. via facial feedback). The evidence for the facial feedback hypothesis is, however, contradictory while the implication of nonverbal reactivity in the experience of embarrassment is speculative; it nevertheless provides a useful account for all the nuances involved.

Two procedures have been used to test the feedback hypothesis directly: (1) direct manipulations of facial expressions, and (2) instructions to reveal or hide expressive reactions. These have been referred to by Kraut (1982) as the dynamic facial pose paradigm and the static facial pose paradigm respectively. The former offers a strong version of the facial feedback hypothesis stating that facial feedback is sufficient to induce and specify an emotion. The latter offers a weak version of the facial feedback hypothesis stating that proprioceptive and cutaneous feedback from facial muscles and the skin modify the intensity of the ongoing emotion. Both kinds of investigation assume that expressive changes mediate subjective feeling. According to the stronger version of the theory, manipulations of facial expressions result in the subject reporting feeling that emotion in the absence of an eliciting stimulus, whilst hiding an emotion should produce the opposite effect.

In an early study (Pasquarelli and Bull, 1951), subjects in a hypnotic trance were asked to contract specific facial muscles as the experimenter touched them with a pointer. The subjects were then instructed to feel an emotion (but not make an expression) that required an expressive display which was either opposite or similar to that in which the subject had been locked. Unless their expression changed, none of the subjects felt the suggested emotion if the pattern for this second emotion was opposite to that first formed under hypnosis; that is, the formed expression blocked the emergence of the suggested emotion. This study answered half the question—expression can block emotions dissimilar to the expression—but did not answer the question of whether expression could create feeling.

In a study by Laird (1974), which set the pattern for later feedback experiments using the static pose paradigm, subjects were asked to contract particular facial muscles (avoiding the use of such words as smile or frown) thus producing, presumably without the subjects being aware of the fact, happy or frowning expressions. These expressions were then held while the subject was exposed to pictures with affective contents that were or were not related to the pose. The face manipulation had a small though significant effect, when compared with the effect of the slides, on the subject's reported feelings.

A further study (Tourangeau and Ellsworth, 1979), however, failed in an attempt to show that subjects induced to adopt facial expressions of emotion would then report feeling these emotions. Like the previous studies referred to, they claimed to have manipulated facial expression without alerting subjects to the emotional meanings of these expressions. Subjects made either fear or sad expressions, or a grimace unrelated to emotion. They then watched either a fear, sad or neutral film and reported their emotional feelings. The experiment revealed no effect of facial expression on self-report, either for producing a corresponding feeling or for inhibiting other feelings aroused by the film. Nor did the investigators find a correlation between observers' ratings of the intensity of expression and self-reports of feelings. The complexity of the issues involved in studying facial feedback can perhaps be gauged from the comments generated by this article. Tomkins (1981) and Izard (1981) both wrote replies in large measure disowning this empirical form of the facial feedback hypothesis on grounds that feeling required more than such simple facial movement. Tomkins (1981) explained that the experiment had nothing to do with his theory of emotion because artificial expressions are not related to emotional feelings in the same way as spontaneous expressions. Izard (1981) also suggested that artificial expression should not be expected to produce emotional feelings although extreme voluntary movements can increase emotional experience. Hager and Ekman (1981), on the same issue, argued on methodological grounds that the experimental hypothesis would not be expected to be confirmed. Ellsworth and Tourageau (1981) then found themselves defending their attack on 'this authorless hypothesis' and their 'failure to confirm what nobody ever said' (p. 363). A recent study (Rutledge and Hupka, 1985), however, convincingly demonstrated the effects of facial feedback for static poses of joy and anger with 142 male undergraduate students. This study replicated the original study by Laird (1974) but 'improved on his basic procedure with the benefit of a decade of hindsight' (p. 221). The facial feedback effect obtained in this study was constant and uniform, across different poses and emotions. In a review of available studies, Laird (1984) suggests that Tourangeau and

Ellsworth's study is the only published study which failed to show an effect of the muscle-by-muscle procedure on emotional experience. In summarizing this form of study, Laird comments that 'the box score favours the facial feedback hypothesis, 10 to 1 on published articles, and probably by the same margin among unpublished articles' (p. 909).

The second set of experiments which have attempted to test the facial feedback hypothesis are those asking the subjects to exaggerate or minimize their expressive reactions, usually to deceive a purported observer. In a series of experimental studies by Lanzetta, Kleck and colleagues (Lanzetta, Cartwright-Smith, and Kleck, 1976; Kleck *et al.*, 1976; Colby, Lanzetta, and Kleck, 1977) the effect of overt facial expression on the intensity of emotional arousal produced by shock was investigated. Ratings were taken of painfulness of electric shock across experimental conditions of varying shock intensity and across conditions where subjects were encouraged to express or control their expressions of pain. Attempts to conceal the facial signs of pain consistently led to decreases in both skin conductance and subjective ratings of pain, whereas posing the expression of intense shock significantly increased both measures of arousal. When subjects were told they were being observed by another person, they showed less intense facial expressions and correspondingly decreased autonomic responses and subjective ratings of pain, even though they received no instructions to inhibit their responses (Kleck *et al.*, 1976). In reviewing the available studies on the exaggerate/minimize paradigm, Laird (1984) suggests that box scores favour the facial feedback hypothesis by 6 to 1.

In spite of this evidence, however, there are a number of writers who remain unconvinced. Leventhal (1980) points out that even if the results of these studies are accepted, a number of cautions are necessary. First, one might argue that the studies do not test the hypothesis that facial feedback is necessary for subjective feeling (i.e. it may add to or attenuate it but not cause it). Second, it might be the case that the facial motor system is important for creating feelings but its operation is more complex than a simple feedback mechanism would allow.

A further issue raised by Buck (1980) is the need to distinguish between two versions of the hypothesis that feedback from facial expression underlies the feelings of emotion. The 'between-subject version' specifies individual differences in emotion (e.g. less expressive people have less intense emotions) and the 'within-subjects version' specifies that, for any given person, the degree of expressiveness is positively related to intensity of emotion. Looking at the evidence for each version separately, Buck rejects the between-subjects version based on evidence showing an inverse rather than a positive relation between facial expression and physiological arousal.

As can be seen, there are those who support (or who claim that the evidence supports) some version of the facial feedback hypothesis and those who are less convinced by the available evidence. As Ekman and Oster (1982) note, the numerous methodological problems involved in experimental studies of the facial feedback hypothesis lead to contradictory findings which are difficult to evaluate. It seems clear, however, that while it may be difficult to conclude that facial expression is the emotion, it can almost certainly add to or accentuate emotional experience. This is presumably in conjunction with cognitive appraisal of the external eliciting circumstances, or, in the absence of such external circumstances, then on the basis of the emotional expression itself. As Leventhal (1979, 1980) points out some form of expressive-motor mechanism is likely to be central in the generation of affect, even if this takes the form of intensifying and sustaining emotional experience rather than causing it. Thus, subjects can experience emotion in the absence of outward signs of expression (as in the case of facial diplegia—absence of expressive motor movements—cited by Leventhal, 1980, p. 166) or can burst into intense laughter or crying without an appropriate accompanying affect (as in the case of double hemiplegia cited by Leventhal, 1980, p. 166).

In spite of the controversy surrounding the facial feedback hypothesis, the present line of reasoning holds that feedback from facial and bodily signs of emotion plays a central part in the experience of embarrassment. Two lines of reasoning lend some support to this hypothesis.

First, anecdotal reports suggest that those who blush more readily are more easily embarrassed. This receives some support from the clinical literature on chronic blushing. Timms (1980), for example, refers to a client who comments, 'I come on all red . . . as red as that pencil . . . people associate redness with embarrassment, and when I'm red I think people think I must be embarrassed and then I do get embarrassed, but I'm not embarrassed to start with' (p. 59). It is important to note here the sequence of events that involves blushing followed by the client's own subjective evaluation of that blushing. The situation may only be salient because it is associated with blushing and not because it is intrinsically embarrassing in its own right (as viewed by others). When the situation or the expression is most salient in determining the experience of embarrassment is of course a central issue, and is discussed below.

The second line of reasoning involves the mediating function of self-directed attention in the experience of embarrassment. As Carver and Scheier (1981) point out: 'The flushing face of embarrassment is an important internal state monitor in the process of self-attention' (p. 37). This suggestion would seem to tie in which Tomkins's (1981) updated theory of affect. As he points out:

> I have now come to regard the skin in general, and the skin of the face in particular, as of the greatest importance in producing the feeling of affect. (p. 386).

He further adds that:

> Changes in hotness, coldness, and warmth would undoubtedly be involved but there may well be other, as yet unknown, specific receptors, which yield varieties of experience peculiar to the affect mechanism. (p. 389)

As Tomkins suggests, contemporary experimentation with the feedback from voluntary simulated facial muscle response would be an inadequate test of such a mechanism. More precise measures such as thermography may herald major new avenues for investigation.

It is thus possible that skin temperature changes associated with blushing play a part in producing the experience of embarrassment. As mentioned in the previous chapter, it remains to be seen whether changes in skin temperature are related to changes in the intensity of reported embarrassment. It is a further inferential leap to assume that the facial flush leads directly to the experience of embarrassment. Whether other aspects of facial expression and body movement serve a similar function is also a matter of speculation. Tomkins (1981) reports that lowering the tonus of all facial muscles and lowering the head via a reduction in tonus of the neck muscles occurs during shame. Unfortunately he refers to shame, shyness, and guilt as identical affects, which is clearly not the case, and the shame response he describes appears to resemble a typical embarrassment reaction. The feedback function of these changes could have an additive effect to the feedback function of changes in skin temperature. If, however, shame, shyness, and guilt are regarded as similarly expressed affects one most question again whether feedback from expressive behaviour *is* the emotion. Clearly feedback does not appear to tell the whole story, although expressive behaviour is likely to play an important part in the generation of embarrassment. What needs to be considered is whether feedback from expressive behaviour is automatic in determining the emotion (which seems unlikely) or whether the subject makes use of the expressive content in some way to label the emotion, and that the facial feedback effect (used in the loosest sense) is not equally strong for all people. Of central importance, is likely to be the part played by congitive factors in evaluating the bodily and situational cues available, and perhaps creating the emotion from these factors.

2. Cognitions and embarrassment

In contrast to theories that emphasize the idea that feelings of emotions, including embarrassment, arise from characteristic bodily changes are theories that emphasize cognitive or inferential decisions as the source of emotional feelings. Schachter and Singer (1962) suggested one of the first cognitive social theories of emotion in a widely cited experiment. In their theory, the important determinants of the quality of emotional feeling are our cognitions about physiological arousal. Arousal, with no apparent explanation, has to be labelled in emotion terms, with situational or social cues providing a basis for inferring an appropriate category of emotion. It is then this decision which underlies the qualitative differences in emotional feeling, rather than the arousal itself which may be the same across emotions.

The experience of emotion in this sense is thus strongly influenced by three elements: the existence of some perceptible internal state that differs from one's baseline level; the focusing of sufficient attention on the internal state to result in awareness of its existence; and the use of some knowledge structure to interpret the state. Although there have been numerous disagreements with, and alterations to, the original theory there is nevertheless general agreement about the nature of the existence of the above three factors.

In determining feelings of embarrassment, autonomic arousal and cognitive interpretation thus undoubtedly play an important part. Interpretation of arousal may well determine the quality and character of the experience. Facial expressions may also play a role in this process. Mandler (1975) has suggested that facial expressions may be biologically tied to certain events or situations which, in turn, have a high probability of eliciting certain cognitions about emotion. Also, expressions may generate automatic cognitions which contribute to the interpretative process. Rather than expressions having an inherent, direct link to feelings, these automatic cognitions depend on cognitive interpretation to influence emotional feelings. In this sense emotional feelings will be dependent upon cognitive appraisal of the situation and/or our bodily state.

A further theory linking emotional feelings to inferences based on behavioural cues is Bem's self-perception theory (1967, 1972). Bem suggests that we are in the same position as any observer who must infer our current state from observing our actions and the circumstances in which we act. Like the observer we can only know something about ourselves by observing what we do and say. Bem (1967), for example, argued that we infer our attitudes from our speech and self-descriptions of attitudes. From the perspective of self-perception theory the relation between facial expression and emotional experience is a particular case of the general relation between behaviours and affective state. One possibility is that there are general differences between people in the kinds of information they use in identifying their own emotional state. One kind of information is likely to arise from our actions, such as expressive behaviours, bodily activities including arousal, and instrumental action. The other kind of cue is likely to consist of situational information—that is, normative information from the situation and knowledge of, and memory for, the way in which anyone in the situation should or probably would feel. The salience of cues may be determined by their relative 'strength' or impact upon the individual concerned. Thus situational or personal cues may differ in their importance on separate occasions (a major *faux pas* may be hard to ignore in the absence of excessive blushing, or alternatively excessive blushing may be hard to ignore in the absence of a very mild *faux pas*). In addition, there may well be individual differences in the processing of information so that perception of internal states and/or situational cues may have a lower threshold for some individuals than others.

Those factors, which are likely to be important in determining whether subjects are more or less likely to attend to personal as opposed to situational cues, are those referred to in an earlier chapter as determining the adopting of a protective as opposed to an acquisitive self-presentational style. That is, individuals who are high in need for approval, fear negative evaluation, are self-conscious, and high self-monitors are most likely to attend to their own behavioural cues for feedback on their emotional state while underplaying environmental cues. This tendency to direct attention towards oneself is present in situationally induced improprieties as discussed previously, but may also explain why chronic blushers experience such distress. They may, by nature, be predisposed to attend to bodily cues for information, thus setting in motion a cycle of mild blush, attend to and appraise the blush, moderate blush, attend to and appraise the blush, severe blush. This sequence occurs relatively independently of any environmental cues.

In fact it may well be the case that subjects become to feel the way they are expected to feel (i.e. 'I am blushing, others must think I am embarrassed, therefore I feel embarrassed'). Indeed this possibility has been tested empirically by Baumeister and Cooper (1981). In this study subjects were to perform a singing task, and were expressly told that they should expect to feel inhibited. This expectancy was presented as based either on the subject's description of his personality, on the past performance of others with similar interests to those of the subject, or on the past performance of others with the same birth order position as the subject. Subjects then sang a piece, without accompaniment, into a tape-recorder, ostensibly providing data about the effects of inhibition on the physical properties of the human voice. Subjects expected to be paid proportionally to the duration of their singing. The expectancies based on self-descriptions and on others with similar interests elicited faster singing than for the non-expectancy control group. This implies that the two experimental groups were willing to sacrifice financial rewards in order to end an embarrassing situation. One explanation for these results is that subjects' attention was directed towards a specific aspect of themselves (i.e. your personality is such that you will be inhibited in this situation; or others like you have been inhibited in this situation), rather than wholly towards the task.

One assumption that is often noted in the literature is that we have a relatively fixed amount of attention to allocate to our object of focus (whether ourselves or the environment) (Duval and Wicklund, 1972; Scheier, Carver, and Matthews, 1983). This suggests that a 'mutual antagonism' may exist between focus on the self and focus on the environment. Assuming that a person has only a limited amount of attention to allocate to a particular stimulus, then increasing the salience or input from one source of information will of necessity decrease the salience or input from other sources. Thus, as attention inward to the self increases, then attention outward to others or the environment will decrease.

One possibility (Scheier, Carver, and Matthews, 1983; Hull and Levy, 1979) is that our attention is shifting between ourselves and environmental cues on a continual, but non-random basis. Thus:

> When we attend to the self, we are often examining an aspect of the self that
> has been suggested by some cue in the environment. And analogously, when we
> look outward, we are often examining a part of the external world that has been
> suggested by some cue from within. (Scheier *et al.*, 1983, p. 515).

For example, if a social predicament has occurred (such as those outlined in
Chapter 3) and the situation has been labelled as embarrassing, an inward
focus of attention might be guided specifically to those aspects of the self
that are presumed to be associated with the experience of embarrassment
(e.g. blushing, trembling, stammering, averted gaze). Following appraisal of
these sensations, focus on the environment may then be guided by a search
for the reactions and/or evaluations of others to one's state. One way of
interpreting the data in an acceptable manner is to view the process as one
involving an element of subjective appraisal in parallel, but linked with an
appraisal of possible eliciting stimuli. This subjective appraisal, alternating
with environmental appraisal, allows us to evaluate our response, whether
clearly evoked by the stimulus or not. This alternating of focus from self
to environment may also serve to increase the subjective experience of
embarrassment.

There is indeed some evidence that attending to, or focusing on, our own
state can make that experience subjectively more intense while distraction
can alleviate the feeling. As self-attention seems to play a central role in the
experience of embarrassment any factor which increases self-attention in a
person who is already embarrassed would be likely to enhance that state.
This may include personality differences (i.e. self-attention) as reviewed in
the following chapter, or facets of the situation (e.g. the audience) or the
individuals themselves (e.g. physiological reactivity). Thus laboratory
manipulations of self-focus or individual differences in the tendency to focus
on aspects of oneself may well serve to increase a subject's emotional
experience.

3. Self-focus and the perception of bodily states

The possibility that self-focus increases emotional intensity, while distraction
decreases it, has been tested in a number of studies. In one experiment,
Scheier (1976) exposed half the subjects to an anger provocation. Subjects
were later asked to report their moods, including self-rating of anger level.
Among subjects in the provocation condition significantly more intense anger
was reported by subjects who had been self-attentive than by those who were
less self-attentive. This in turn led to significant differences in aggressive
behaviour.

In a subsequent study, Scheier and Carver (1977) tested this intensification
effect in a wider variety of emotional states. In one experiment, male subjects
were shown a series of slides of nude women, under conditions of experimentally enhanced self-focus (in the presence of a mirror) or with no manipulation. Subjects were asked to rate the attractiveness of the women in the

slides according to the degree of bodily responses they were experiencing. Subjects in whom self-focus had been increased by the mirror manipulation made reliably more favourable ratings than did subjects with less self-focus. As well as the manipulation of self-focus, Scheier and Carver (1977) investigated differences in emotional response using subjects who varied in their levels of dispositional private self- consciousness. The emotional state investigated was that of repulsion, subjects being asked to view slides of mutilated bodies. Significantly greater repulsion was expressed by persons high in private self-consciousness than by those lower in private self-consciousness. A replication of these effects concerning fear has been reported by Carver, Blaney, and Scheier (1979). It seems then that situationally induced self-focus or individual differences in tendency to be self-attentive can affect the extent to which we experience an emotional state.

In two further studies, Scheier and Carver (1977) investigated the effect of induced pleasant mood states in some subjects and depressed moods in others, using differences in self-focus (mirror-induced) or individual differences in private self-consciousness. Among those given the depression induction, reliably greater depression was reported by self-focused subjects than by those who were less self-attentive, although the comparable tendency among subjects in the elation condition did not reach significance. These findings were replicated using individual differences in private self-consciousness.

An extension of the facial feedback notion to Scheier and Carver's results requires the assumption that the presence of a mirror increases facial expressive activity and/or alters skin temperature, which in turn increases the intensity of emotional experience. Unfortunately this tends not to be borne out by the experimental results. Thus Lanzetta, Biernat, and Kleck (1982) showed subjects attractive and repulsive slides and videotaped subjects' facial expressiveness when viewing each slide. Self-focus was manipulated by the presence/absence of a mirror. Unexpectedly their data failed to replicate the earlier findings that mirror presence would cause self-reports of more intense affect. In fact they found a reversal of that effect, both in self-rated affect and facial expressiveness. Kleck *et al.* (1976) report similar results when an 'observer' was present. One possible explanation for these unexpected results is offered by Carver and Scheier (1981) and Scheier, Carver, and Matthews (1983). They point out that subjects may well have been aware that they were being videotaped. It is commonly noted that people try to suppress public expression of their feelings. Enhanced self-focus in a situation in which the display of emotion was public may have led to increased suppression of facial movements. This, in turn, may have resulted in less reported affect.

This latter point is particularly important to the experience of embarrassment. As has been discussed, embarrassment is a state which is difficult to conceal in the presence of an observer. Attempts to do so invariably meet with failure, with recognition from both the observer and the actor that a failure has occurred. The observer then acts like a mirror, reflecting back to us the consequences of our actions. As has been suggested, a mirror tends to increase subjective experience of an emotion—reflecting back from an observer may increase arousal perhaps via an increase in the amount of blushing, fidgeting, and other outward signs of embarrassment discussed previously. Whether the experience of embarrassment actually results from the behaviours themselves (i.e. the behaviours are the emotion) or cognitions about one's state (i.e. the thoughts are the emotion) is difficult to resolve empirically. In the case of social anxiety, rather than embarrassment as such, there is indeed some evidence that some socially anxious persons are overattentive to the internal feedback associated with somatic changes. McEwan and Devins (1983) divided socially anxious subjects into 2 groups (high and low levels of concomitant somatic symptoms) on the basis of a self-report measure of the intensity of 7 somatic anxiety symptoms (palpitations, perspiration, difficulty breathing, trembling, nausea, urinary urgency, bowel sensations). It was found that socially anxious individuals with elevated somatic symptoms believed that they displayed a greater number of visible signs of anxiety, as measured via a behavioural checklist, than were actually noticed by their peers. The authors comment that:

> It may be . . . that highly socially anxious people rely on internal arousal to the exclusion of other valid indicants in estimating the salience of their anxiety. (McEwan and Devine, 1983, p. 420).

In a further study, Öst, Jerremalm, and Johansson (1981) found it possible to divide socially anxious subjects into 'behavioural reactors' or 'physiological reactors' on the basis of standardized scores derived from behavioural and physiological measures. It may well be the case that these two groups of subjects rely on different cues to indicate the salience of their anxiety.

In the case of embarrassment it may also be the case that the three systems of behaviours, cognitions, and arousal operate to some extent in parallel, with cue salience varying as a function of both the situation and individual differences. Any comprehensive account of the phenomenon of embarrassment must thus be able to account for all these possibilities.

C. TOWARDS A MODEL OF EMBARRASSMENT

In an attempt to conceptualize the events which constitute the experience of embarrassment, a component-process model has been developed (Edelmann, 1985a). This model assumes a collection of events including cognitions, arousal, and behaviour which together constitute the experience of embarrassment. The issues raised in both the preceding chapters and the present chapter are encompassed by this model. These include the situation and its appraisal, attentional focus, behavioural cues and coping attempts. The main theme of the model can be summarized as follows:

1. In social situations individuals attempt to control images of self, or identity-relevant information before real or imagined audiences. This presupposes:
   (a) that the actor is aware of (or is made aware of) a particular goal or standard;
   (b) that the actor is concerned with avoiding significant *losses* in social approval.
2. Given the above standard, a disruption of social routine, such as *faux pas*, impropriety, accident or transgression, will result in the actor's projected image creating an undesired impression.
3. Awareness of a discrepancy between present state and standard leads to the focus of attention on the self.
4. The presence of an audience, whether real or imagined, directs attention to the public rather than the private self.
5. A number of behavioural consequences are associated with heightened public self-attention resulting from an observed disruption of social routine (Edelmann and Hampson, 1979, 1981a, 1981b). Self-focus on specific aspects of this display can have the effect of intensifying the experience of embarrassment.
6. As a result of the identity-threatening situation, a number of impression-management strategies can be invoked by the individual to deal with his or her predicament (Goffman, 1959, 1971; Modigliani, 1971; Schlenker, 1980; Tedeschi and Reiss, 1981; Semin and Manstead, 1983).

While it is undoubtedly the case that all these events may be present, and in the sequence described, within the experience of embarrassment it is also possible for an emotion to be labelled as embarrassment in spite of gaps or variations in the process outlined above. All emotions are complex experiences; embarrassment as an emotion specific to humans may be even more complex. It may thus be necessary to operationalize a rather more detailed interactive model to account for the whole experience of embarrassment. Leventhal's perceptual-motor theory of emotion (Leventhal, 1979, 1980; Leventhal and Mosbach, 1983) offers a number of pointers to a comprehensive model of embarrassment. As he suggests:

> Emotions are constructed by a hierarchical processing system which is parallel to and partially independent of nonemotional (perceptual and cognitive)processes. (Leventhal and Mosbach, 1983, p. 354).

Any comprehensive model of embarrassment must account for the fact that situations labelled as embarrassing do not necessarily evoke the emotional experience to the same extent in all individuals, while it is also possible to experience embarrassment in situations which are not necessarily labelled as embarrassing. A summary model of the salient features involved in the process of embarrassment is presented in Figure 5.1.

The starting point for the revised model of embarrassment is the stimulus

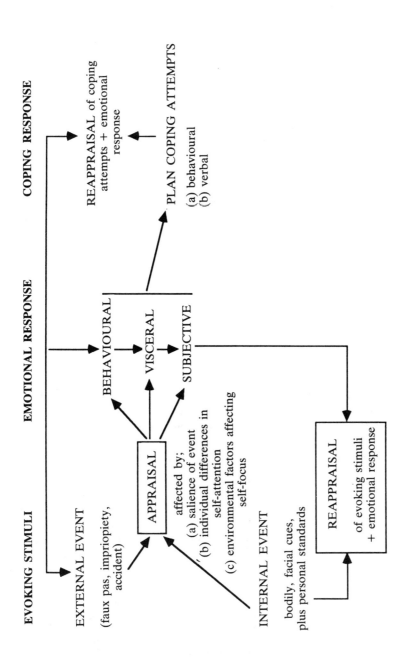

Figure 5.1 A component process model of embarrassment

evaluation check suggested by Scherer (1982, 1984). As mentioned, this may be both an external check ('What is the appropriate way in which to present myself in this particular social setting?') and/or an internal check ('What is my personal standard for presentation and/or what is my current behavioural display?'). As a result of this cognitive appraisal a number of consequences are possible ranging from no response to physiological, behavioural, and subjective experience of embarrassment. The salience of external versus internal appraisal will depend upon features of the environment likely to enhance self-focus (i.e. a mirror or an audience) or upon individual differences in self-attention (i.e. high public self-attention). Thus features of the environment which enhance self-focus or a predisposition to be self-attentive will lead to an increase in the salience of internal cues. For some people ('chronic blushers'), attending to internal cues may be sufficient to generate the subjective experience of embarrassment.

In line with both Leventhal's model and suggestions by Scheier, Carver, and their colleagues which have been referred to, attention alternates between environmental and self-focus (cf. Leventhal and Mosbach's feed-forward and feedback system, 1983, p. 376). This can lead both to reactions from the environment (i.e. the reactions of others) and feedback from one's own behaviour (i.e. facial expressions, blushing, body movements, etc.) modifying initial perceptions of the stimulus. If the initial evoking stimulus is internal (i.e. 'I am blushing'), subsequent appraisal will involve both an evaluation of external reactions to this event (i.e. 'Have others noticed?' 'How are they reacting?' etc.) as well as an appraisal of one's own subsequent reaction (visceral arousal, bodily reaction, and so on).

If the initial evoking stimulus is external (i.e. a social transgression) subsequent appraisal will involve both an evaluation of one's initial internal state plus an ongoing evaluation of changes which might occur.

One important aspect to note is that the appraisals themselves may not be 'accurate'. Thus, in evaluating the evoking stimuli there is likely to be a tendency to concentrate on aspects of particular salience to the individual concerned, who assumes them to be of equal importance to observers. In fact these cues may not be salient to the observer, so for people with high personal standards for self-presentation or a particular proneness to blushing (both internal evoking stimuli), the cause of any resultant embarrassment may be evident only to the actors themselves. The part played by cognitions in the experience of embarrassment is of particular importance in clinical intervention, and will be discussed in detail in Chapters 8 and 9.

A further factor of importance involves the use of strategies for coping with embarrassment, which may well be invoked following an initial reappraisal of the evoking stimuli and one's own reaction to these events. The various verbal and nonverbal strategies have been discussed in previous chapters. Several points are of importance here: it is likely that the use of coping strategies will be dependent upon a wide range of factors including the initial evoking stimuli and the initial reaction to this event. An initial external evoking stimulus may be easier to deal with than an internal event; coping with a mild event easier than a major event; coping for certain individuals more difficult than for others (i.e. those prone to be self-attentive).

In contrast to earlier models of embarrassment the present attempt is to view embarrassment as a complex interaction of events and appraisals of these events, rather than being a clear sequence of events. The emotional response may well be innate but the evoking stimuli, subsequent appraisals, and coping attempts are undoubtedly learnt aspects. A number of features of the model are thus central to the remainder of the book.

1. Assuming certain aspects of the experience of embarrassment are learnt, at what ages do which features become salient and why?
2. Assuming individual differences in the tendency to attend to self-relevant information, what personality characteristics are salient to the experience of embarrassment?
3. Assuming that external events and/or personal standards are central to the experience of embarrassment, do we in fact avoid certain acts in order to avoid embarrassment?
4. Assuming that internal events can be responsible for giving rise to embarrassment there are likely to be individuals who experience embarrassment in the absence of a definable external evoking stimuli.
5. Assuming that appraisals of external and/or internal events may be inaccurate, faulty cognitions may play an important part in the experience of embarrassment.

These five aspects are dealt with in the final four chapters of the book, and involve respectively developmental and individual differences; social implications of embarrassment; and cognitive, physiological, and behavioural aspects of embarrassment and their importance in clinical intervention.

CHAPTER 6

Developmental and Individual Differences

> The young blush much more freely than the old but not during infancy, which is remarkable, as we know that infants at a very early age redden from passion. (Darwin, 1873, p. 329).

> Adolescence is the peak period of private and public self-consciousness and of social anxiety. (Buss, 1980, p. 244).

It is frequently noted, as the two above quotes illustrate, that feelings of embarrassing are unlikely to occur in early childhood, but that their frequency gradually increases until they reach a peak during adolescence. The first part of this chapter will examine the scanty research evidence which looks at changes in the experience of embarrassment during childhood and adolescence, possible explanations for any changes which might occur, and the way in which the very experience of embarrassment might be used as a means of teaching children to behave in a socially acceptable manner.

A. AGE AND EMBARRASSMENT

In one of the few developmental studies of embarrassment, Buss, Iscoe, and Buss (1979) sent a questionnaire to the parents of children in three preschool nurseries and four elementary schools. The questionnaire inquired about blushing or other signs of embarrassment that parents had noted in their children during the past 6 months. The authors point out that any definition of embarrassment was deliberately avoided so that parents would not feel constrained by someone else's definition. Of a total of 1414 parents contacted, 355 responded.

Buss and his colleagues found that there were too few reports to yield reliable data for children below 3 years or above 12 years. For the age groups within this boundary, embarrassment was reported in roughly one in four children in the 3- and 4-year-olds. This proportion jumped to three out of five of the 5-year-olds and stayed at this proportion or more for the remaining age groups. The authors conclude that:

> embarrassment begins for most children at five years of age. A minority of

children show embarrassment earlier, a precocity analogous to the early development of walking or talking.

Is this conclusion reasonable? There are obviously several difficulties inherent in a study of this type. Buss himself points to the problem of possible errors by the parents of young children in their interpretation of when an event was embarrassing; parents may be more likely to label the same experience as embarrassing for older than for younger children. A further problem involves the small sample size in the study (only 35 of the respondents had children aged less than 5 years (Buss, 1980, p. 240), and the low percentage response rate to the questionnaires. The 25 per cent who responded may have been a selection of those parents who had specifically noted signs of embarrassment in their children, and were thus motivated to take part in the study. It is clear that far more research is needed on the question of when embarrassment first appears.

In a further study Horowitz (1962) investigated the reported embarrassment memories of 100 elementary school, 100 high school and 100 college students. Each subject completed the Embarrassment Questionnaire, consisting of 46 items concerning embarrassing experiences. These items had been derived from a preliminary study in which subjects were asked to record their most recent embarrassing experience and the earliest embarrassing experience they could remember. In the subsequent study the subjects were asked to indicate, for each of the 46 items, if they could recall ever having experienced the particular incident, regardless of whether they had been embarrassed by it. Subjects then reported the degree of embarrassment they had actually experienced in each situation. For each individual a proportion of reported embarrassment memories was obtained by dividing the number of reported embarrassment memories by the total number of memories.

A number of Horowitz's findings are of interest. First, within each educational group (elementary, secondary, college) it was found that the older the subject the later the reported age of earliest remembered embarrassing experience. It seems that the older the individual the greater the tendency to 'forget' early experiences of embarrassment. The second and most important finding (bearing in mind the suggestions made at the beginning of this chapter) was that for both the high school and college sample a greater proportion of embarrassment memories were reported for the period that they were 11 to 15 than for the period that they were 2 to 7.

There are obviously several methodological problems with this study. Firstly, it is obviously questionable whether memories are reliable; the use of retrospective reports is not the most suitable methodology for studying age differences in embarrassment; second, whether the definition of embarrassment is the same for the different age groups is also questionable. Nevertheless this study does hint at two important points. First, the youngest subjects (who were already 11 years old) seemed to be clearly embarrassible; secondly, it seems that embarrassing events have more importance attached to them during adolescence. Obviously these suggestions need to be treated with considerable caution considering the methodological problems referred to above.

In a final unpublished study, Modigliani and Rosenfeld (1979) talked with teachers and children and observed children from the ages of 6 to 15. They also collected essay responses from 15/16-year-olds to the questions: 'What was the most embarrassing thing that ever happened to you?', 'Why was it embarrassing?', 'What were you thinking?' 'What were the other people thinking?'

They suggest that there was little indication of embarrassment in the youngest children, with clear indication of its presence in the older ones. The responses of the latter to the question, 'What was the most embarrassing experience you ever had?' could be grouped into four categories:

1. Incompetence: a variety of lapses in mental or physical coordination that led to appearing inept in the classroom or on the playground.
2. Impropriety: defined as any situation in which the person's demeanour violates existing norms. (The most frequent cases in this category involved 'indecent exposure' or inappropriate body display.)
3. Ridicule: that is, any situation in which the person is publicly degraded, laughed at, or made fun of, irrespective of whether he/she has acted incompetently or properly.
4. Excess attention: defined as any situation in which the person is receiving more attention than is warranted by the quality of his/her performance.

These categories match quite closely those referred to in Chapter 3, suggesting little difference in the type of situation found to be embarrassing by adults and adolescents. The difference may well be one of intensity and the likelihood that at different ages different types of event become more embarrassing than others.

What then can be concluded from the limited data available on developmental changes in embarrassment? It would seem that only tentative suggestions can be made at this stage and clearly more research is required. It is difficult to assess whether any conclusions drawn from the studies are simply tailored to our previous expectations. It would seem, though, that:

1. embarrassment is unlikely to occur with any great frequency in very young children;
2. there is an increasing likelihood that embarrassment will be experienced by older children;
3. there seems to be little difference between adolescents and adults in the type of event that can give rise to embarrassment;
4. adults are more likely to recall embarrassing events which occur during their adolescent years.

Whether there are differences in the intensity of the experience, as well as in the likelihood that embarrassment will be experienced at all, is, however, less clear. If we are to assume that there are indeed developmental differences in the likelihood that embarrassment will be experienced, what then are the likely explanations? Three areas need to be considered which relate to the issues raised in earlier chapters:

1. whether they are differences in self-presentation with age;
2. whether there are changes in self-consciousness with age; and
3. whether knowledge of social rules differs with age.

1. Age and self-presentation

Self-presentation was defined in Chapter 2 as 'the attempt to control identity-relevant information before real or imagined audiences'. Each individual strives to convey the most positive aspect of self, or at least seeks to protect him/herself from self-presentation failures. It is clear that children, even at a relatively young age, often attempt to embellish their basic behaviour pattern with imitations or acts, perhaps mimicking teachers, parents, or other targets of identification. In playing games children will readily enact various fictional characters, fire imaginary weapons, play with imaginary objects, or attempt to be like the character they are portraying. In these actions it is clear that children are concerned with realistic enactments; they wish to portray the character in a way that *they* consider to be 'real'. It is also clear that children at a fairly young age have a repertoire of actions, sounds, and routines which are displayed for an audience. Whether this enacting is the same as clearly coordinated attempts at impression management is, however, open to some degree of doubt. It would seem that the child is rather more concerned with the degree to which his/her actions are right for him/her at that particular moment, and not whether they will actually evoke a positive response from the audience. The latter is, of course, important in encouraging the child to continue; it is not surprising, however, for a child to respond by saying 'It *is* right and anyway I don't care', when told that his/her portrayal of Batman is wrong. He/she may be concerned with giving a correct portrayal, but may not be aware of how to achieve this goal and may be motivated more by what appears to be right to him/her than by what appears to be right to the audience. As research on peer group pressure and conformity shows, conformity is at its height during early adolescence but then diminishes significantly from about 14 or 15 onwards (Coleman, 1980). The desire to win approval from others becomes more important during adolscence. The need to wear the correct clothes, have the right interests and appropriate skills, replaces the desire to just 'join in the fun'.

Studies of children's wishes seem to support the notion that need for approval increases as children reach adolescence. Thus, Ables (1972) suggests that while young children wish for pets or possessions, older children more often wish for attributes that bring them popularity and prestige in the eyes of their peers. At some stage there appears to be a change both in one's desire to present a clearly coordinated impression to an audience and in one's desire to present an impression which is correct in the eyes of the observer. When and how this process occurs is open to speculation, although Modigliani and Blumenfeld (1979) have suggested a tentative sequence of thee overlapping stages.

The first stage, referred to as the S-R stage, lasts from approximately 3 to 7 years. During this stage the child does not wish to portray a *particular* image but merely wishes to perform a sensory-motor sequence which avoids disapproval and sanctions. The second stage, referred to as the 'impression-flashing' stage, lasts from approximately 4 to 9 years, overlapping with and running concurrently with the first stage. During this stage the child is much more concerned with behaving in a way that is consistent with the person or object being portrayed, rather than merely watching to see what actions are right or wrong. Thus, accurately imitating the routines of admired characters gradually assumes importance. At first the actions are primarily for the child's benefit but gradually the salience of the audiences' reactions takes on a greater significance. This is particularly true during the third, or impression management stage, which occurs after about 8 years of age. During this time the child becomes more concerned about conveying a certain image of him/herself to the audience. Unlike the impression-flashing stage, where the aim is largely for self-enhancement, in this later stage the purpose is to create an appearance that fits the occasion and is evaluated positively.

If the desire to manage the impressions of ourselves conveyed to others becomes salient at about 8 years of age, this might represent an important milestone for the development of embarrassment. As the child's concern to present himself/herself in a way which avoids blame and social disapproval increases, the likelihood that the experience of embarrassment will become salient also increases. It is important in this context to note how difficult it is to ascertain whether or not children have experienced embarrassment. The studies referred to previously were concerned with the views of parents or older children; it is far more difficult to ascertain from younger children whether they have experienced embarrassment. Situations which adults might define as embarrassing may not be perceived that way by younger children. Younger children are also likely to have difficulty conceptualizing the meaning of the term 'embarrassment'. Blushing or embarrassed behaviours thus become important in assessing the presence of embarrassment, assuming that a behavioural display of embarrassment is the same in young children as with older children and adults. Testing the stage model of self-presentation referred to above could be conducted in this way.

Ability to manage the impression created towards others is thus important in determining the onset of embarrassment. This, however, implicates other aspects of the self referred to in Chapter 2. Thus, Buss (1980) comments:

Self-presenters tend to play roles, each role specific to a particular situation. Knowing what is expected or desired they arrange their social selves to conform. Such conformity requires not only the ability to read social cues (or know generalised expectations) but also the ability to monitor and alter one's style of behaviour. Self-monitoring requires an advanced cognitive self, including public self-consciousness. It occurs only in older children and is absent in infants. (p. 242).

The ability to experience embarrassment thus necessitates the ability to view oneself as a social object while impression management involves using this knowledge about oneself to monitor or alter social behaviour. The question then arises, 'At what age do children develop public self-consciousness?', i.e. develop a role-taking ability or the ability to see oneself as others do.

2. Role-taking and self-consciousness

The ability to see things from another's perspective seems to first develop between the ages of 3 and 6 years, although there is some evidence from later studies that it may occur at an even younger age (Donaldson, 1978). In one early study, Flavell et al. (1968) showed children a set of objects (silk stockings, necktie, toy truck, doll, adult book) and asked them to select a gift for their father, mother, teacher, brother, sister and themselves. Three-year-olds tended to select the same gifts for others as for themselves. Some 4-year-olds, half the 5-year-olds, but all the 6-year-olds chose the appropriate gifts. Thus, at some stage between these ages children learn to distinguish the preferences of others from their own preferences, perhaps indicating a shift from viewing everything from one's own perspective to being able to view events from someone else's perspective.

This gradual change in the assumption from the view that others share their perspective, information, and preferences, to an ability to see things clearly from another's perspective, and in particular take the role of another, has been documented by Selman (1976). He describes four stages of role-taking development.

During the first stage (ages 4–6), the child is able to judge others' emotions, such as sad and happy, in those situations where the child knows his/her own responses. During the second stage (ages 6–8), the child gradually realizes that people feel or think differently as a result of the situations they are in. In spite of this the child still puts himself/herself in the place of others in attempting to make a judgment; the child is also unable to see his/her own actions from someone else's viewpoint. The shift between Stage 1 and Stage 2 involves a change from perceiving others as information collectors to perceiving others as information processors. In the third stage (ages 8–10 years), the child is able to recognize that others can put themselves in his/her position. He/she is unable though to look beyond the two-person perspective or to view it from a third-person point of view. It is only during the fourth stage (ages 10–12) that mutual role-taking occurs. He/she can both put himself/herself in the other's place and consider each party's point of view, realizing that certain actions may have different meanings for different persons.

Whilst this stage approach offers a number of possibilities in terms of the development of embarrassment, there are obviously numerous criticisms which can be levelled against it. In addition to the lack of subtlety of such approaches, and the fact that development does not take place in such invariant, discrete stages, it is questionable whether taking another's perspective occurs as late as 8 years of age. Donaldson (1978) and her colleagues found in their studies that 90 per cent of 3-year-olds were successful in perspective-taking experiments; thus seeing things from another's perspective is likely to develop before this age.

Bearing in mind the variable age at which role-taking abilities occur, it is possible that embarrassment appears in two phases. The first, a type of 'primitive' embarrassment (Modigliani and Blumenfeld, 1979) appears before role-taking abilities develop (ages 6–8 in Selman's stage model) when the child might learn which actions are right and wrong without realizing the meaning these actions might convey to others. Thus certain actions might provoke laughter, teasing, or ridicule and are thus avoided. Embarrassment may well result if these actions are then performed in error. This again raises the issue of whether the definition of embarrassment is placed upon the situation as defined by the act or upon the experience as encountered by the child. Generally the coy, flustered reactions are referred to as embarrassment.

The more 'mature' embarrassment found in older children and adolescents requires more advanced role-taking abilities (the third and fourth stage of Selman's model). It is at this stage that the child is able to reflect upon the meaning of his/her actions from the point of view of someone else. Thus public self-awareness involves a shift from one's own perspective to that of another. As we become more aware of the way in which we present ourselves to others, and more concerned with the reactions of others to that presentation, then the more aware we become of the public aspect of ourselves or publicly self-conscious. Simmons, Rosenberg, and Rosenberg (1973) and Elkind and Bowen (1979) have proposed a curvilinear relationship between self-consciousness and age. They suggest that there is little evidence of self-consciousness in younger children (less than 10 years), a marked increase during early adolescence, with a peak in self-consciousness at 13 or 14 years of age, followed by a gradual decline.

In a direct test of this hypothesis, Tice, Buder, and Baumeister (1985) examined the effect of observation upon skilled performance in children, adolescents, and adults. As mentioned in Chapter 2, the presence of an audience has been used in a number of studies as a reliable means of inducing self-consciousness. Tice *et al.* evaluated the performance of skilled players of video games both with and without an audience presence. The subjects included sixteen children under 13, ten adolescents between 14 and 19, and seven adults over 20. Children generally improved under audience pressure, adolescents showed substantial drops in performance, whilst adults showed moderate drops in performance. Assuming that self-consciousness was indeed the variable manipulated in this study, the results support the curvilinear development of self-consciousness referred to above.

One possible explanation for the adolescent peak of self-consciousness and embarrassment is provided by the work of Elkind (1967). He suggests that, while the attainment of formal operational thinking, which occurs during adolescence, frees the individual in many respects from childhood egocentrism, it entangles him/her in a new version of the same thing. The adolescent not only thinks about his/her own thought, but also about the thought of other people. Elkind argues that this capacity to take account of other people's thinking is the basis of adolescent egocentrism. Because of his egocentrism the adolescent is, either in actual or fantasized social situations, anticipating the reactions of others. Thus, he is continually constructing and reacting to what Elkind calls his 'imaginary audience'. While the presence of a real audience can induce self-consciousness the adolescent *starts* with a higher level of self-consciousness as a direct result of his 'imaginary audience'. Further evaluation increases an already raised level of self-consciousness.

Because the adolescent believes he/she is of importance to so many people (his/her imaginary audience), he/she imagines that everyone is highly aware of the awkward physical and emotional changes he/she is going through. As mentioned in Chapter 2, one aspect of the interaction context which gives rise to self-presentation difficulties involves novel situations in which we are unsure of the correct image to present. As Buss (1980) points out, novelty presents itself as a particular difficulty during adolescence.

Adolescence is marked by rapid bodily growth and the development of secondary sex characteristics. The spurt in growth during this period is likely to give rise to fears about being too tall/short, fat/thin, in comparison to one's peer group. It is not only a time when we are aware of what others must think (i.e. taking the perspective of another) but also a time when we are changing at different rates. The slow or fast developer may feel overconspicuous with regard to his/her peers. Thus Buss (1980) comments:

> while their voices are dropping to an adult pitch, many boys become embarrassed by sudden boyish breaks in their new-found bass voices.

Everything is new, so that adolescents become very conscious of their bodily and sexual changes. They no longer have a clearly defined role, no longer being children but not yet being adults. They have yet to acquire the necessary repertoire of behaviours to play their new roles and are unsure how to present themselves to avoid negative and embarrassing consequences. Lack of knowledge can lead to indecisive and tentative attempts with a lack of confidence in one's ability to perform the desired behaviour appropriately. This is perhaps particularly true in relationships with members of the opposite sex and that daunting 'first date'. As Buss (1980) comments: 'The adolescent is unsure how a "real man" would act with a lady, he has neither the experience or the skill to cope with a first date.' While many adolescents may gradually overcome their nervousness as they adapt to their role, hetero-sexual social anxiety may endure well past adolescence and into adulthood. Arkowitz *et al.* (1978) found that 37 per cent of men and 25 per cent of women in a group of nearly 4000 randomly sampled undergraduates indicated that they were 'somewhat' or 'very' anxious about dating. It may well be the case that adolescent embarrassment inhibits dating to such an extent that, for some, skills may only be acquired at a much later age. Hence confidence in one's ability to cope in such a situation is greatly impaired.

Social perspective-taking, role-taking, and self-consciousness thus clearly play an important part in the development of both embarrassment and impression-management, a process which is perhaps highlighted by the experience of embarrassment during adolescence. This suggestion does, however, involve two further suppositions: first, that the individual is aware of the appropriate way to behave, i.e. possesses appropriate knowledge of the rules of conduct.

3. Knowledge of social rules

Buss's (1980) approach to the development of embarrassment emphasizes socialization practices. All children are taught the ways of their group through various kinds of learning. Children are taught what is right and wrong through the process of being rewarded by goods or affection for prosocial behaviour, and punished physically or verbally for behaviour which ignores the goals of socialization. Buss suggests that one of the most potent forms of verbal punishment is laughter, teasing, and ridicule. While this may occasion 'primi-tive' embarrassment in the younger child (i.e. an ability to anticipate which actions will provoke ridicule while not quite understanding what meaning his/her actions have for others), it may nevertheless form a distinct way in which 'right' and 'wrong' acts can be singled out. For the older child and adolescent, ridicule and laughter may signify that his/her behaviour is erroneous but he/she also realizes why actions appear to be 'wrong'.

Buss (1980) suggests that children are socialized in a sequence which involves self-control, modesty, and manners by means of teasing, laughter, and in short, embarrassing the child for his/her actions. Self-control in the first 3 years of life may be learnt through teasing for 'accidents' involving bladder or bowels. As mentioned above, the child will realize that he/she has behaved inappropriately without perhaps realizing what his/her actions mean. Modesty in later childhood, when children are taught to conceal certain body parts in public and to reserve nakedness for certain occasions (bath) and for certain rooms (bathroom, bedroom), may be acquired as a result of laughter or ridicule for violating the taboo. At first the child may only be aware that he/she has done something wrong; the ridicule has, however, served to indicate which behaviours are socially appropriate, and which are socially inappropriate. Should the child subsequently perform the same actions then the experience of embarrassment can replace external teasing or laughter. As emphasized in Chapter 1, the experience of embarrassment can represent the conditioned aversive stimulation generated by bad behaviour as a result of punishment. For embarrassment to occur, however, the child must not only want to present himself/herself in a way which is acceptable, but must also be aware of the image conveyed to others. Hence, while learning is important, so is cognitive development associated with role-taking, self-presentation, and self-consciousness.

During early adolescence, children are introduced to manners and etiquette; again the penalty for mistakes is often teasing and ridicule. With the development of our ability to manage impressions, the awareness of public aspects of ourselves, and an increasing desire to behave appropriately, we are increasingly motivated to avoid being singled out by laughter and ridicule. Embarrassment then becomes a particularly powerful method by which social rules can be acquired. Similarly, older adolescents quickly learn that certain activities, especially viewing, talking about, or reading about sexual behaviour, must be kept private. This may sometimes have unfortunate consequences. The adolescent, having yet to acquire a clearly defined role, may be unsure about how to behave but may be too embarrassed to ask. This situation prevails in the area of sexuality and is no doubt indicated by the incidence of heterosexual–social anxiety noted earlier. The issue of embarrassment and seeking advice about sexual matters by older adolescents (19-year-old women) has in fact been investigated by Herold (1981). He suggests that embarrassment about seeking contraceptive advice may be due to uneasiness and guilt, or fear about revealing to others the personal fact of being sexually active. For the adolescent, peer and parental pressures may make it difficult to separate 'what is right for me' from 'should I do what peers/parents expect me to do?'. Herold administered a measure of contraceptive embarrassment in addition to a number of other measures including religiosity, sex guilt, and parental and peer attitudes to premarital sex, to 265 young single women who were currently engaged in a sexual relationship. The most important factors related to contraceptive embarrassment were parental attitudes to premarital sex and sex guilt. It is possible that guilt about sex results from parental condemnation of sex as a topic for discussion. Thus, sexuality is linked with embarrassment in later adolescence in the same way that concealing body parts and reserving nakedness for certain occasions is linked with embarrassment in later childhood. It may be the case that fear of embarrassment concerning matters relating to sex is overgeneralized, making it difficult to separate appropriate sexual issues from inappropriate ones.

A further example of the powerful influence of embarrassment in the acquisition of social rules is emphasized in a report by English (1975), mentioned in Chapter 1. She gives an illuminating example from the Eskimo culture:

> The very first time a young child's foot slips through thin ice, the family gathers around him, pointing, laughing, teasing . . . in effect, shaming him at this very young age for an innocent mishap. (p. 25).

> (It should be noted that English refers to embarrassment as a euphemism for shame.)

At another point she asserts that:

> In our culture a two-year-old might be ashamed for wanting to play with faeces or wanting to urinate on the living room carpet. (p. 26).

She concludes that:

> The capacity to feel shame is built into human beings, and it has a civilising effect in adapting a child to his family and culture. (p. 28).

It seems that rule-learning and embarrassment are clearly interlinked, at least in our own culture. While it is undoubtedly the case that all societies have rules, and that there are developmental changes in children's under-standings of these rules and conventions, it seems that laughter, ridicule, and teasing provide a powerful method for inhibiting inappropriate behaviour. In societies which emphasize these means of social learning, embarrassment may be generalized to behaviours which are in fact appropriate in certain circumstances.

4. Summary and conclusions

Having reviewed the few studies investigating developmental changes in embarrassment, and having examined developmental changes in self-presen-tation, self-consciousness and knowledge of social rules, it is possible to draw some tentative conclusions. The limited research on developmental aspects of embarrassment seems to suggest that embarrassment is absent in very young children, perhaps only appearing at about 3 years of age. Over the next few years the occurrence of embarrassment gradually increases until at the age of 6/7 its occurrence seems to be as likely as its occurrence in adults. A peak period of embarrassment, at least in terms of the severity of the experience, seems to occur during adolescence. The explanation seems to be bound up in the development of goal-directed impression-management styles, the emergence of a social self and associated self-consciousness, and through processes of social learning.

Thus, until the age of 4 to 7, the child's behaviour is more likely to be directed by his/her view of what appears to be right to him/her than by what appears to be right to the audience. It is also likely that the child at this age is less able to view himself/herself from someone else's perspective. Children are likely to be aware, however, that certain behaviours provoke ridicule and teasing while others do not. This may well see the emergence of a 'primitive' embarrassment which involves being embarrassed by others' reactions without being fully aware of why the reactions occur. From the age of 8 years it is more likely that the child will wish to convey a particular impression of self recognizing the impression he/she creates for others. As the child's motivation to manage impressions and his/her awareness of how these impressions are viewed by others increases then 'mature' embarrassment is a much more likely outcome should an unintentional transgression occur.

Five factors then appear to be crucial in signalling the emergence of embarrassment:

1. An ability to understand that one is a social object with an outward appearance to others.
2. An ability to see from someone else's viewpoint that impression-management styles influence the way in which the individual is perceived.
3. Knowledge of what constitutes acceptable behaviour within a given culture or setting.
4. An ability to understand that changes in appearance can be conveyed by various impression-management strategies.
5. An ability to understand that one can make inferences about others on the basis of appearance.

Whether the suppositions raised here are indeed correct remains an issue for future research. Rather than asking older children to recall memories, or parents to report on their children's embarrassment, it is important to investigate children's knowledge of, comprehension of, and ability to recognize embarrassment, and to see whether this parallels the development of impression-management ability and self-consciousness.

B. INDIVIDUAL DIFFERENCES IN EMBARRASSMENT

We use the term embarrassibility to refer to a person's susceptibility to embarrassment. Clearly there are substantial individual differences in embarrassibility. Some persons appear to be quite embarrassible, experiencing great discomfort in seemingly innocuous situations, while others appear to be relatively unembarrassible and capable of passing through the most awkward incidents with little discomfort. (Modigliani, 1968, p. 316).

It is frequently noted that some people are more prone to experience embarrassment than others. Some people blush at the slightest provocation while others seemingly do not blush at all. While the issue of blushing is undoubtedly linked to skin colour and skin thickness, it is also likely to be linked to each individual's susceptibility to the experience of embarrassment. As suggested above, some people feel discomfort in seemingly innocuous situations.

The issue of which personality traits are likely to predispose a person to experience embarrassment is closely linked to the issue of which factors are implicated in the development of embarrassment, as discussed in the first part of this chapter. That is, (1) individual differences in our ability and desire to present oneself in a favourable light, and (2) individual differences in our concern with the evaluation of our performance by others. Before discussing these issues in detail, the embarrassibility scale as a measure of an individual's general susceptibility of embarrassment will be evaluated.

1. Embarrassibility scale

The embarrassibility scale was first developed by Modigliani (1966, 1968) and consists of 26 items, each describing a potentially embarrassing situation rated on a scale of 0 (not the least embarrassing) to 9 (acutely embarrassing to the respondent). The respondent's embarrassibility score is the average embarrassment rating taken over all the items.

Little data has been published on the validity and reliability of the scale, with the exception of data published by Modigliani (1968). He reports that the reliability of the scale as assessed by Coefficient Alpha is 0.88, and that the correlations of each item with the total scale score range from 0.64 to 0.85 with a mean value of 0.78. He also found that a meausre of experienced embarrassment (assessed by four bipolar scales; at ease–self conscious; poised–awkward; free–constrained; embarrassed-not embarrassed) for subjects who failed in public, correlated 0.35 ($p < 0.05$) with their scores on the embarrassibility scale. This correlation suggests that the scale has a moderate predictive ability in indicating how severely embarrassed a person will become when he/she is actually placed in a potentially embarrassing situation.

In addition to the above data, there are three studies which report the factor structure of the embarrassibility scale (Modigliani, 1968; Edelmann, 1985d; Edelmann and McCusker, 1986). In the latter two studies the scale used consisted of 22 items derived from the 23 described in detail by Modigliani (1966). An item referring to 'talking in front of an audience' and hence pertaining to audience anxiety was omitted. Details of the factors obtained are discussed below and the full 22-item version of the embarrassibility scale is presented in Table 6.1.

Modigliani's (1966, 1968) factor analysis of the 26-item version of the scale suggested that there were essentially five factors each contributing between 14 and 19 per cent of the common variance. These five factors, which are described as being 'easily interpretable', account for 48 per cent of the total variance. The five factors are as follows:

Table 6.1 Items of the Embarrassibility Scale

---

1. You slip and fall on a patch of ice in a public place, dropping a package of groceries.
2. You are a dinner guest, and the guest seated next to you spills his plate in his lap whilst trying to cut some meat.
3. A group of friends are singing 'Happy Birthday' to you.
4. You discover you are the only person at a social occasion without formal dress.
5. You are watching an amateur show and one of the performers who is trying to do a comedy act is unable to make people laugh.
6. You are calling someone you have just met for the first time in order to arrange a date.
7. You are muttering aloud to yourself in an apparently empty room when you discover someone else is there.
8. You walk into a bathroom at someone else's house and discover that it is occupied by a member of the opposite sex.
9. You are in the audience watching a play when it suddenly becomes clear that one of the actors has forgotten his/her lines, causing the play to come to a standstill.
10. You are being lavishly complimented on your pleasant personality by your partner on your first date.
11. You notice that your tutor has forgotten to do up his fly.
12. You enter an apparently empty room, turn on the light and surprise a couple necking.
13. You are talking to a stranger who stutters badly due to a speech impediment.
14. Your mother/father has come to visit you and was accompanying you to work/ college.
15. You are a dinner guest and cannot eat the main course because you are allergic to it.
16. You are alone in the lift with your professor/boss who has just given you a bad grade/reference.
17. You walk into a room full of people you do not know, and are introduced to the whole group.
18. You trip and fall while entering a bus full of people.
19. You are opening some presents while the people who have given them to you are watching.
20. You ask someone on crutches if they have had a skiing accident and they tell you they were cripped by polio as a child.
21. You have forgotten an appointment with your professor/boss, and remember it as you meet him/her in the entrance the next day.
22. You are talking in a small group which includes a blind person, when someone next to that person unthinkingly makes a remark about everyone being as blind as a bat.

---

1. Situations in which a person discredits his own self-presention through some inadvertent foolishness or impropriety (this consists of items 1, 4, 7, 14, 15, 18).
2. Situations in which a person finds himself unable to respond adequately to an unexpected event which threatens to impede the smooth flow of the interaction (consisting of items 14, 16, 20, 21, 22).
3. Situations in which a person loses control over his self-presentation

through being the centre of attention without having any well-defined role (consisting of items 3, 6, 10, 17, 19).
4. Situations involving empathic embarrassment wherein a person observes another individual who is in a seemingly embarrassing predicament (consisting of items 2, 5, 9, 11, 13, 22).
5. Situations in which an individual is involved in an incident having inappropriate sexual connotations (consisting of items 8, 10, 11, 12).

In the study by Edelman (1985d), three factors emerged which together accounted for over 50 per cent of the variance:

1. The first factor accounting for 34.4 per cent of the variance contained statements which emphasized the central character being made the unexpected centre of attention, and was referred to as 'Centre of Attention' (this consists of items 1, 3, 16, 17, 18, 19).
2. The second factor accounting for 8.8 per cent of the variance included items emphasizing the fact that the central characters' behaviour has caused embarrassment to others, and was referred to as 'Embarrassment to Others' (consisting of items, 6, 7, 8, 10, 15, 20).
3. The third factor accounting for 7.2 per cent of the variance included items emphasizing the fact that someone else's behaviour has caused embarrassment to the central character, and was referred to as 'Other's Behaviour' (consisting of items 2, 8, 10, 11, 12, 13).

These factors do in fact show very little correspondence with the factors obtained by Modigliani (1966, 1968). This is particularly true of the first two factors in Edelmann (1985d) and the first four factors in Modigliani's study, although there is almost complete correspondence between the third factor in Edelmann (1985d) (labelled 'Other's Embarrassment') and Modigliani's fifth factor (labelled Witness to, or Involved in, an Event Having Potential Sexual Overtones').

In our subsequent study (Edelman and McCusker, 1986) we obtained four factors which together accounted for over 50 per cent of the variance:

1. The first factor was very similar to our 'Embarrassment to others' factor described above, and contained items 6, 7, 8, 10, 12
2. The second factor corresponded closely to Modigliani's fourth factor labelled 'Ego is a witness to the embarrassment or potential embarrassment of others', and contained items 2, 5, 9. We have referred to this factor as 'Vicarious Embarrassment'.
3. The third factor corresponded to the third factor in our earlier study labelled 'Others' Behaviour'. In the present study this contained items 11, 12, 13, 16, 21.
4. The fourth factor was similar to Modigliani's first factor labelled 'Ego behaves in a manner which places him/her in danger of appearing foolish

or improper'. This consisted of items 4, 12, 14, 15, 20 and was referred to by us as 'Appearing Foolish'.

The factor structure of our second study thus reflects, to some extent, the factors obtained in the previous two studies (Edelmann, 1985d; Modigliani, 1968). The first and third factors in the Edelmann and McCusker study correspond closely to the second and third factors in the Edelmann (1985d) study, although there were no such factors in the study of Modigliani (1966). Conversely, the second and fourth factors in the study by Edelmann and McCusker correspond closely to factors 1 and 4 in the study by Modigliani, although there were no such factors in Edelmann's (1985d).

Two questions are raised by the studies discussed above: first, 'Is the embarrassibility scale multi- or uni-dimensional?'; and second, 'Why does there appear to be a variable factor structure?'.

Certainly the fact that the first factor accounted for at least a third of the variance in each study, as well as the existence of high inter-item and inter-factor correlations in each study, would suggest that the embarrassability scale is in effect uni-dimensional. It is in effect measuring one construct, i.e. embarrassment.

Why then do studies suggest that the scale is multi-factorial and why does the factor structure obtained vary across studies? The answer seems to lie in the fact that the scale is in effect assessing causes of embarrassment. As discussed in some detail in Chapter 3 there are a number of different situations which can give rise to embarrassment. There are also a number of studies which have attempted to categorize these different causes. As discussed in Chapter 3 these studies do not agree on the categories of cause selected. It is not surprising then that the embarrassibility scale, reflecting different causes of embarrassment, should emerge with different categories across different subject groups. Thus the salience of particular items may differ between the UK samples tested in our own studies and the American sample tested by Modigliani. Also, different population groups were tested in our two studies; the average age of the subjects in our 1985 study was 32, while in our second study the average age was 19. It is likely that incidents found to be embarrassing to 18-year-olds may differ in importance to those regarded as embarrassing to 32-year-olds, even if this is only in terms of severity. Clearly the embarrassibility scale assesses the likelihood that a specific event will occasion embarrassment in any given sample. While some events will be more salient to some individuals than to others it seems plausible to assume that some individuals may be inclined to experience embarrassment more than others.

Having described and discussed the embarrassibility scale we can now turn our attention to factors which might explain the existence of individual differences in the process and experience of embarrassment. As noted in Chapter 2 there are a number of personality variables which affect the likelihood that an individual will adopt a protective rather than an acquisitive self-presentation style. It is likely that individual characteristics which increase the actor's desire to avoid objective signs of failure, are also related to an individual's susceptibility to experience embarrassment. Any personality variables which relate to self-doubts or a lack of confidence in one's ability to present oneself adequately are likely to be implicated. These are discussed in the following sections.

2. Self-monitoring

As has been mentioned, actors are generally concerned to project an image which engenders social approval, or at least avoids engendering social disapproval. Failure to monitor and control one's responses is likely to result in the projection of an image that others deem undesirable and potentially embarrassing. Self-monitoring ability is closely related to impression management skills.

Snyder (1974) has developed a 25-item self-monitoring scale to measure people's tendency to self-monitor. He has argued that some people are particularly sensitive to the social contingencies that surround behaviour, and are primarily responsive to these contingencies. Other people are less sensitive to such matters, and are responsive instead to their own view of themselves. The former are referred to as high self-monitors, the latter as low self-monitors (Snyder, 1974, 1979).

High self-monitors attend more to social cues, are more likely to read these cues adequately, are better at acting out roles, are seen by others as having better control of emotional expression, seem to be more aware of themselves and others as social objects, try to present themselves in ways they deem appropriate and assume that others are likely to do the same (Snyder, 1981, 1979).

In this context, however, it is important to note that recent research suggests that the self-monitoring scale is multi-dimensional with only a relatively stable factor structure. In five separate studies (Briggs, Cheek, and Buss, 1980; Edelmann, 1985d; Gabrenya and Arkin, 1980; Tobey and Tunnell, 1981; Furnham and Capon, 1983) three seemingly consistent factors have emerged, although the item content of these factors has not been entirely consistent across studies.

The first factor to emerge seems to reflect acting elements, such as: 'I would probably make a good actor', or 'I have considered being an entertainer'. These were presumably selected for the original scale on the assumption that self-monitoring involves the ability to manage impressions in a variety of situations, although acting and impression management are not necessarily the same thing.

The second factor, 'other-directedness', seems to be a combination of two tendencies. First, a tendency to seek social cues from others ('When I am uncertain how to act in social situations, I look to the behaviour of others for cues') and second, a tendency to present oneself in a way that is expected or will be liked ('I guess I put on a show to impress or entertain people'). This seems to be applicable to Snyder's (1979, p. 91) definition of high self-monitors as being 'particularly vigilant and attentive to social comparison information that could guide their expressive self-presentation'.

The third factor, 'extraversion', contains items such as 'In a group of people I am rarely the centre of attention', and 'I am not particularly good at making other people like me' (items reversed for scoring).

Most studies suggest that these three factors are relatively independent (we obtained correlations of 0.21 between extraversion and other-directedness; 0.46 between extraversion and acting, and 0.29 between other-directedness and acting) (Edelmann, 1985d).

What then is the relationship between these factors and embarrassibility? In our own study we obtained a correlation of 0.05 between the full self-monitoring scale and embarrassibility; -0.15 between the acting factor and embarrassibility; -0.07 between the extraversion factor and embarrassibility; and 0.17 between the other-directedness factor and embarrassibility. Other-directed people—that is those who seek social cues, try to please others, and wish to be liked—are particularly susceptible to embarrassment. The finding that this particular factor is also positively related to measures of social anxiety and shyness (Briggs *et al.*, 1980; Gabrenya and Arkin, 1980) is in keeping with the present result. Other-directedness seems to typify those actors who are generally concerned with projecting an image which engenders social approval, or at least avoids engendering social disapproval. As embarrassment results from our failure to project a desired image, it is not surprising that actors who most wish to avoid such failure are most prone to experiencing embarrassment.

3. Self-consciousness

While self-monitoring differences may predict where an actor will look to determine behavioural standards, self-consciousness differences may predict the degree to which these standards are used. As mentioned in Chapter 2, Fenigstein (1979) has referred to increased concern with the presentation of self and increased concern about the reactions of others to that presentation as major consequences of self-consciousness. It is likely that self-consciousness plays a major role in the experience of embarrassment. Fenigstein, Scheier, and Buss (1975) have developed a 25-item scale to measure people's tendency to be self-conscious. Factor analysis of this scale has consistently revealed three factors (e.g. Fenigstein *et al.*, 1975; Edelmann, 1985d). The first factor, containing ten items, reflects private self-consciousness and includes statements such as 'I reflect about myself a lot' and 'I'm generally attentive to my inner feelings'. The second factor, containing seven items, reflects public self-consciousness and contains statements such as 'I'm concerned about what other people think of me' and 'I usually worry about making a good impression'. The third factor, containing six items, reflects social anxiety and includes statements such as 'I get easily embarrassed' and 'Large groups of people make me nervous'.

People who obtain high scores on the dimension of public self-consciousness report that they feel as though they are being observed in the company of others, have a high regard for how others regard them, view others' behaviour as having high personal relevance, and demonstrate increased responsiveness to negative interpersonal evaluation (Fenigstein, 1979). In terms of the process of embarrassment outlined previously, individuals who are concerned with the impression they create are more likely to be susceptible to embarrassment; i.e. there should be a positive correlation between embarrassibility and public self-consciousness.

This is indeed what we found in our own study; self-consciousness was significantly positively correlated with embarrassibility ($r = 0.39$). With reference to the subscales both public self-consciousness ($r = 0.36$) and social anxiety ($r = 0.52$) were also significantly correlated with embarrassibility while the private self-consciousness subscale ($r = 0.06$) was not (Edelmann, 1985d). It seems that actors with a particular concern for their observable behaviour (i.e. publicly self-conscious) are particularly susceptible to embarrassment. They are more concerned with managing the impressions they create than people who obtain low scores on the scale (Buss, 1980; Fenigstein, 1979; Fenigstein et al., 1975). Of the remaining subscales listed above, social anxiety was also positively related to embarrassibility, a finding discussed in the following section.

4. Social anxiety

In discussing the social anxiety subscale of the self-consciousness scale, Buss (1980) comments:

> The picture here is of a person who is shy, easily embarrassed and anxious in the presence of others. There is one common denominator underlying this anxiety: the presence of others – in other words social anxiety. (p. 45).

The subscale is in fact rather non-specific with regard to the type of situation or construct to which it is referring. Thus, one statement refers to 'I get easily embarrassed' while anther refers to audience anxiety ('Large groups make me nervous') and another to shyness ('I find it hard to talk to strangers'). In other words it covers several dimensions of social anxiety, all of which seem to involve a concern with the way in which we appear towards others. It is thus perhaps not surprising that embarrassibility and social anxiety, as assessed by the above subscale, are closely related. As mentioned in Chapter 1, socially anxious subjects fear that they will behave in a manner which is embarrassing.

In this context it is relevant to note that we also found that clinically socially anxious subjects reported that they would feel much more embarrassed in specified situations than non-socially anxious subjects (Edelmann, 1985e).

Why the socially anxious should be particularly prone to experience embarrassment is open to debate. It may well be that they fear embarrassment simply because they do not know what to do in social situations, and have learnt from past experience that their behaviur tends to be inadequate and embarrassing. Alternatively they may well know what to do but may fear embarrassment because they fear that they will behave inappropriately or inadequately even though this is unlikely to be the case. The issue of lack of knowledge or lack of confidence as precursors to the experience of embarrassment in clinicaly socially anxious subjects is dealt with in some detail in Chapter 8. Suffice it to say at this point that there is a predicted and expected relationship between social anxiety and embarrassibility.

The picture is emerging, then, of the specific characteristics likely to be associated with embarrassment. Individuals who are particularly concerned with their observable behaviour, and with the expectations of others, and who fear that their behaviour may well fall below some expected and acceptable standard, seem to be especially vulnerable to embarrassment. These individuals are socially anxious, publicly self-conscious and other-directed. Publicly self-conscious subjects tend to describe themselves as emotional, worrying, and nervous, and are particularly quick at making judgments about good and bad aspects of their appearance (Turner, 1978); those who are socially anxious tend to be inhibited and retiring (Zimbardo, 1977). This creates the image of those susceptible to embarrassment as being sensitive to others (especially to others' views), inhibited, and over-concerned with their public image. The tendency to be sensitive to others or to apprehend another person's condition or state of mind is a definition of an empathic individual (Johnson, Cheek, and Smither, 1983). Those who are inhibited (perhaps quiet, retiring, or introspective) during social contacts are often referred to as introverts and the overconcerned (perhaps anxious or worried) are often referred to as neurotic. This gives the impression of those susceptible to embarrassment as being empathic, but neurotic introverts. This is a question we addressed in one of our studies (Edelmann and McCusker, 1986) and which is discussed below.

5. Extraversion

The typical extrovert who likes parties and meeting people may either be less susceptible to embarrassment or less concerned with the experience of embarrassment than the typical introvert, who prefers solitary rather than gregarious activities. The link between introversion and embarrassibility is unlikely, however, to be clear-cut. Some introverts may enjoy quiet and solitude whilst having no difficulty interacting should the occasion demand it—they are neither susceptible to, nor perhaps concerned about, embarrassment. Others who are quiet may be so because they dread social encounters, and in particular embarrassing events or experiences. They are reluctant to be the centre of attention and would be placed in that position should they behave in a way which is discrepant from the way in which they would have wished to behave. The same is true of social anxiety in general; thus, although there is a correlation between introversion and social anxiety (Cheek and Buss, 1981; Pilkonis, 1977; Watson and Friend, 1969), introverted individuals may not be socially anxious.

In our investigation mentioned previously (Edelmann, 1985d), the extraversion factor of the self-monitoring scale was only slightly negatively related to embarrassibility. It is unlikely however that that extraversion factor is as reliable and valid as the measure of extraversion obtained with the EPQ (Eysenck and Eysenck, 1975). We used the latter scale in a further study investigating the relationship between extraversion and embarrassibility (Edelmann and McCusker, 1986). Extraversion was significantly negatively related to the full embarrassibility scale ($r = -0.18$) and the Embarrassment-to Others subscale ($r = -0.22$), the Vicarious Embarrassment subscale ($r = -0.24$), but not the Others' Behaviour ($r = 0.06$) or the Appearing Foolish subscales ($r = -0.15$) of the embarrassibility scale. It seems that introverts have an empathic regard for other people's embarrassment and are most concerned that their behaviour will cause others to feel embarrassed. The links between this finding and neuroticism are discussed below.

6. Neuroticism

Many items on the neuroticism factor of the EPQ have psychological meanings relevant to the construct of embarrassibility. For example, 'Do you often worry about things you should not have said or done?' and 'Do you tend to worry too long after an embarrassing experience?' suggest a link between neuroticism and embarrassibility. Individuals who worry, or are particularly concerned with the image that they create before others felt to be there at the time, are likely to be particularly susceptible to embarrassment. In our own study (Edelmann and McCusker, 1986) we in fact found a significant positive correlation between neuroticism and embarrassibility ($r = 0.32$) and the embarrassment to others ($r = 0.21$) and appearing foolish ($r = 0.17$ subscales. Thus while both neurotics and introverts are concerned that their own behaviour might appear to be foolish to others, introverts feel embarrassed when others behave badly, while neurotics are more concerned that their own behaviour might appear to be foolish to others. Introverts seem to be more susceptible to empathic embarrassment or embarrassment felt for others.

7. Empathy

Empathy, in the broadest sense, refers to the reactions of one individual to the observed experiences of another (Davis, 1983). Johnson, Cheek, and Smither (1983) have referred to an emphatic individual as one who is sensitive to others, or one who is able to apprehend another person's state of mind or condition. While embarrassment generally involves self-concern, as has been mentioned, it is also recognized that an empathic reaction or vicarious embarrassment can occur (Fink, 1975).

The question of what happens when a highly empathic person takes the perspective of an anxious person was investigated in a study by Kendall, Finch, and Montgomery (1978). A group of 30 undergraduates were administered the Hogan Empathy Scale (Hogan, 1969) and a measure of state anxiety. Later in the course, a confederate of the experimenter, posing as an eminent guest speaker, came to the class to give a speech. In the first few minutes of the speech the speaker lost his notes, spilled coffee, and repeated himself several times (i.e. was embarrassing to watch). After the speech, students were asked to retake the state anxiety measure. As predicted, highly empathic individuals' levels of state anxiety had increased above their previous levels, whereas persons low in empathy showed no such increase. This finding was replicated with another group of 40 undergraduates, and in a control study in which the guest speaker performed well, anxiety scores did not vary as a function of empathy. Empathy then is likely to be related to at least one aspect of embarrassment, i.e. vicarious embarrassment.

In a study by Modigliani (1968), empathy, as assessed by a shortened version of the Literature Empathy Test, was found to be significantly positively correlated with embarrassibility ($r = 0.18$). He suggests that the more sensitive a person is to others' evaluations, the more they are made embarrassible by a trait which increases their readiness to assume that others are evaluating them negatively.

In our own study (Edelmann and McCusker, 1986) we administered Hogan's Empathy Scale and the Embarrassibility Scale to over 100 subjects. Hogan's (1966) scale is an easily administered measure of empathy derived from relevant items of the Minnesota Multiphasic Personality Inventory (MMPI) and the California Psychological Inventory (CPI: Gough, 1969). Factor analysis of the Hogan Empathy Scale has revealed a relatively consistent factor structure. Thus, Greif and Hogan (1973) obtained three factors which they labelled 'Even-Tempered Disposition', 'Social Ascendency', and Humanistic–Sociopolitical Attitudes'. Johnson et al. (1983) obtained four factors which they labelled 'Self-Confidence', 'Even-Temperedness, Sensitivity' and 'Nonconformity', the first two and last of which corresponded to Greif and Hogan's (1973) factors. In our study (Edelmann and McCusker, 1986) we also obtained four factors which corresponded closely to those of Johnson et al.

Previous research has suggested that the full empathy scale is significantly positively correlated with extraversion and significantly negatively correlated with neuroticism (Hogan, 1969) and shyness (Johnson et al., 1983), suggesting a close link between empathy and embarrassibility.

In our own study (Edelmann and McCusker, 1986) we actually found an unexpected negative relationship between empathy and embarrassibility ($r =$

−0.25). This was largely accounted for by the 'Social Self-Confidence' and 'Nonconformity' subscales of the Hogan Empathy Scale. The items comprising the former are closely related to elements of extraversion so that the negative relationship is not wholly unexpected. The latter factor suggests someone who 'prefers unstructured, ambiguous and novel situations' (Johnson et al., 1983, p. 1306), situations which tend to give rise to social anxiety (Pilkonis, 1977; Zimbardo, 1977; Lary, 1983a). So again, the negative relationship between nonconformity and embarrassibility is not unexpected.

It is interesting to note that the 'Sensitivity' subscale of the Hogan Empathy Scale is positively correlated (though not quite significantly) with the 'Vicarious Embarrassment' subscale of the Embarrassibility Scale. 'Sensitivity', i.e. motive for acting empathically (Johnson et al., 1983) is perhaps closest of the four factors of the Hogan Empathy Scale to the definition of empathy referred to previously, i.e. the tendency to be sensitive to others or to apprehend another person's state of mind or condition. It seems then that empathy is related to embarrassibility, particularly vicarious embarrassment, although this issue requires further investigation.

8. Other personality factors

It seems then that individual difference factors which reflect concern with the way in which we are evaluated by others are likely to be related to embarrassibility. This may include factors such as our feelings of self-adequacy and self-esteem, as suggested by Modigliani (1966, 1968).

In Modigliani's theorizing, embarrassment was seen to result from a failure to fulfil certain social expectations leading to a diminution of the individual's perceived public esteem, which in turn would lead to a diminution of the individual's esteem. In order to assess this predicted relationship between self-esteem and embarrassment, Modigliani (1968) administered a measure of general self-esteem, a measure of instability of general self-esteem, and a measure of feelings of inadequacy and the embarrassibility scale. He obtained a significant positive correlation between feelings of inadequacy and embarrassibility ($r = 0.50$) and general self-esteem and embarrassibility ($r = 0.25$) but not between instability of general self-esteem and embarrassibility. He suggests that embarrassibility is partly the result of an individual's general readiness to believe that evaluations of others are more negative than they really are. This seems to concur with the suggestion that individuals who are particularly susceptible to embarrassment are concerned with their observable behaviour and with a desire to conform and please others.

A final trait which has been investigated is the relationship between test anxiety and embarrassibility. Modigliani (1968) found a significant positive correlation ($r = 0.33$) between test anxiety and embarrassibility. He suggests that individuals high in test anxiety are by definition more prone to anxiety in situations where they are being evaluated by others. Test anxiety is in fact also positively associated with audience anxiety (Pavio and Lambert, 1959).

As Modigliani points out, it seems reasonable to postulate that high test anxiety reflects a greater concern with, and greater vulnerability to, possible negative evaluations by others.

C. SUMMARY

In this chapter it has been suggested that a distinct set of characteristics identify those who are more likely to be susceptible to the experience of embarrassment. This set involves an over-concern with one's public image, sensitivity to, and over-awareness of, the evaluations of others, with at the same time a tendency to believe that any evaluations of one's behaviour are likely to be negative. This, coupled with slight social inhibition, gives the image of who is likely to be susceptible to the experience of embarrassment.

Those personality factors outlined in Chapter 2 as being associated with the tendency to more or less chronically adopt a protective self-presentation style are thus closely implicated in susceptibility to embarrassment, i.e. variables which relate to self-doubt or lack of confidence in one's ability to present oneself adequately.

Whether embarrassment results from a lack of knowledge about how to behave in particular social encounters, or whether over-concern, sensitivity to, and expectations of, negative evaluations result from *beliefs* about one's social adequacy forms a central part of Chapter 8. This issue obviously has important implications for interventions designed to help those who are socially anxious or who fear embarrassment, as will be discussed in Chapter 9.

Before discussing these issues, however, one further question remains to be answered. The fact that individuals differ in their susceptibility to embarrassment suggests that we may also differ in the extent to which fear of embarrassment functions to constrain our behaviour. Research suggests that we do, in fact, tend to avoid social situations which might engender embarrassment. How fear of potential embarrassment can influence the amount of help we give to others and cause apparently negative responses to the physically disabled or those with a physical stigma is examined in the following chapter.

CHAPTER 7

Social Implications of Embarrassment

A central component of the model of embarrassment proposed in Chapter 5 was the relationship between embarrassment and social rule transgression. As mentioned previously, the structure of rule-governed behaviour is so closely linked with embarrassment that embarrassing events are often classified on the basis of the type of rule violation which gives rise to them. As such, embarrassment is systematically built into our social system, a point emphasized in Chapter 3.

All societies have rules which regulate the everyday behaviour of their inhabitants, including that between participants in social encounters. Where there are rules, these can be unintentionally broken, resulting in the presentation of an image which is discrepant from our desired self-presentation. As pointed out by Goffman (1955) we generally attempt to behave in a manner which is socially appropriate, in order to ensure that a desired image of ourselves is presented to others. It seems feasible to assume therefore that fear of embarrassment can constrain our social behaviour, acting as a social control mechanism. As Armstrong (1974) points out, 'embarrassment is a fusing mechanism for maintaining a single definition of reality' (p. 2), and 'Embarrassment is sociologically important becase it acts as a brake on what can only be described as cultural inflation' (p. 11), i.e. we seek to behave in a way which accords with the behaviour expected within our social group. Social situations which present particular difficulties are thus those in which we are unsure of the appropriate behaviours or self-presentation style, i.e. the novel and ambiguous situations described in Chapter 2.

In these specific situations the actor is often faced with a number of choices: 'Is my action or inaction more likely to result in embarrassment'? 'Is there something inherent in the situation which might affect the likelihood of experiencing embarrassment?' 'How damaging will it be to my desired image should I make the wrong choice?' 'If I make the wrong choice will I be able to remedy the situation?' In novel or ambiguous situations, because we are unsure how to behave, there is an increased risk that we will present ourselves in a way which is inconsistent with the way in which we would wish to present ourselves. There is thus an increased risk that we will receive a negative evaluation for our behaviour and suffer the embarrassing consequences of failure. As pointed out in Chapter 2, it is fear of presenting ourselves inappropriately in such situations, and the negative and embarrassing consequences which can result, which often inhibit our interactions with others.

One specific set of situations which often involve ambiguity and uncertainty are those involving the provision of help or the seeking of help from others. Most situations in which we consider offering help to others are, or at least begin as, ambiguous events (Latané and Darley, 1970). In assessing the helping situation, a factor of importance concerns the costs involved if we make an error of judgment and rush to help when no help is actually required. One possible outcome of such an error is the negative and embarrassing impact on the individual concerned.

Seeking help can also involve presenting oneself in a way which is discrepant from the way in which we would have wished to present ourselves. Seeking help emphasizes one's failure, inferiorities, and incompetencies, and may lead to embarrassment if the help-seekers believe that others are looking down upon them because they need help (Shapiro, 1984).

The part played by fear of embarrassment in inhibiting our help-giving or help-seekng behaviour illustrates the way in which embarrassment can act as a social control mechanism. The numerous factors which affect the likelihood that embarrassment will occur in helping encounters are evaluated in this chapter.

A. EMBARRASSMENT AND HELPING

Providing or seeking help does not always result in embarrassment. There are, however, many aspects of the helping situation and characteristics of both the help-seeker and help-giver which makes its occurrence more likely.

Within the literature examining the extent to which bystanders will provide help to others, much research has focused on facets of the precipitating situation. Factors of importance include: (1) the nature of the act or behaviour which requires assistance; (2) the number of other people present and the actions they take to help the victim; and (3) the ambiguity of the situation. As Latané and Nida (1981) point out:

> The bystander who decides to intervene runs the risk of embarrassment if, say, the situation is misinterpreted and is not actually an emergency—the more people present the greater the risk. The presence of others can inhibit helping when individuals are fearful that their behaviour can be seen by others and evaluated negatively. (p. 309).

In addition to aspects of the target audience, specific aspects of the victim such as status or appearance may also affect the degree of embarrassment inherent in the situation, should we provide the victim with help. It is generally recognized that the presence of a physical disablement, handicap, or stigma can elicit unfavourable reactions from the able-bodied or unstigmatized. One possible explanation for these negative reactions is feelings of repulsion or embarrassment that many able-bodied have towards the disabled.

Finally, whether help is provided may be dependent upon the characteristics of the help-giver or the specific emotional state which he/she is experiencing at the time of the request. It seems that we will provide help if by so doing we are able to avoid embarrassment, or redeem a previously embarrassing situation.

The extent to which we seek help from others is also determined by a similar multiplicity of factors, and has been the subject of a recent review by Shapiro (1983). This review has provided much of the information contained within the latter pages of the present chapter. As Shapiro points out:

> if people believe they will experience embarrassment by seeking help they will be deterred from seeking help. The strength of this avoidance response is a function of two factors: the beliefs about whether their seeking help will lead to unfavourable evaluations from others and the degree to which the person is concerned about these unfavourable evaluations. Both situational and personality variables may affect these two factors. (p. 146)

Any helping situation in which we risk presenting ourselves in a way which is inconsistent with the way in which we would have wished to present ourselves is likely to inhibit help-giving or help-seeking. That is, those situations in which the negative consequences of failure and hence embarrassment are most likely. Each of these factors is reviewed during the course of this chapter.

B. HELP-GIVING

1. Situational and audience factors

Research on the social inhibition of helping has examined the influence of a wide variety of situational factors. These include the extent to which the victim is perceived as being in danger, the extent to which the situation is perceived as likely to place the bystander in danger, whether the situation is perceived as an emergency, and whether the situation is likely to be perceived as ambiguous (Latané and Nida, 1981). Numerous studies have been conducted to investigate these variables. Most of these studies have, however, been primarily concerned with comparing the number of subjects who provide help when alone with the number of subjects who provide help when in the presence of others. Also, few of these studies have directly ascertained the extent to which fear of embarrassment is the crucial variable which inhibits helping. Nevertheless, the studies investigating the inhibiting effects of group size on helping provide results of relevance to the present discussion.

(a) Audience effects

Perhaps the most commonly studied type of emergency is one in which a 'victim' is in danger. In the initial study of this type (Darley and Latané, 1968) participants in a group discussion heard (via an intercom) a fellow participant suffer a seizure. In another group of conceptually similar studies (Smith, Smythe, and Lien, 1972) the experimenter 'fainted' in the next room. In a further study of Latané and Rodin (1969) participants heard a crash in the next room as the experimenter fell while trying to reach a book; whilst in a study by Ross and Braband (1973) the bystanders heard a workman in the next room injure himself with a power saw. In these and other studies the question was whether the participants would help the victim, and whether the number who offered help would decrease as a function of the number of other participants present.

A general finding of these and other studies is that social inhibition is produced by the presence of an audience (i.e. the larger the audience the less people help). In a review of the literature on group size and helping, Latané and Nida (1981) cite 56 published and unpublished comparisons of helping by people who were alone with helping by those who were tested in the presence of confederates or believed other people to be present. In 48 of these 56 comparisons, involving a total of more than 2000 people, there was less helping in the group condition. Overall, three-quarters of individuals tested alone helped, compared with only half of those who were tested with others present.

Three possible explanations have been offered for this phenomenon (Latané and Darley, 1970). First, social influence theory, which suggests that we look towards other people to help us define the situation. The presence of others can thus inhibit helping when an individual sees the inaction of others. Second, diffusion of responsibility, which suggests that we share the costs of nonintervention with others who are present, and hence nonintervention increases with audience size. Third, audiences can inhibit helping when individuals are fearful that their behaviour can be seen by others and hence evaluated negatively (i.e. individuals fear the embarrassing consequences of making an erroneous judgment about the situation).

This latter suggestion has been expanded by Latané (1981), who has discussed these findings in terms of social impact. This he defines as:

> any of the great variety of changes in physiological states and subjective feelings, motives and emotions, cognitions and beliefs, values and behaviour, that occur in an individual, human or animal, as a result of the real, implied, or imagined presence or actions of other individuals. (p. 243).

He further suggests that this social impact or influence of other individuals is a multiplicative function of their strength, immediacy, and numbers. Latané defines strength as the salience, power, importance, or intensity of a given source to the target. This may be determined by the source's status, age, and past or future interaction with the target. Immediacy refers to the perceived closeness of the interactants in space and time with the absence of intervening barriers. Number is simply an assessment of the size of the group of people present. Each of these factors increases the extent of audience influence.

These factors were also discussed in Chapter 2 as those factors likely to influence the adopting of a protective self-presentation style. The threat to our identity and the embarrassing consequences of failure are much greater in front of certain types of audience. Studies investigating the relationship between increased embarrassment in front of larger audiences and audiences of high status, expert others whose opinions we value, were discussed in Chapter 2 (Brown, 1970; Brown and Garland, 1971; Garland and Brown, 1972; Latané and Harkins, 1976; Jackson and Latané, 1981).

As pointed out previously, it seems that we value the impressions, opinions, and reactions of others to our behaviour. The value we attach seems to increase as a result of the audience's size, status, and so on. Should we fail to present ourselves appropriately (which in the present context means providing help when none is actually required), the embarrassment experienced also increases as a result of the size, status, etc. of the audience. As a result, fear of embarrassment in such encounters may inhibit the extent to which we are prepared to offer help. While there are no studies directly assessing the link between audience variables, embarrassment, and helping the explanation matches Latané's (1981) explanation for social impact and inhibition of helping.

One factor which further increases these risks is the degree of ambiguity inherent in the situation. Ambiguity increases the degree of uncertainty (help may be offered when none is required) and hence, possibly via an increase in the embarrassment potential of the situation, the provision of help may be inhibited. This possibility is discussed below.

(b) Ambiguity of the situation

One point to note about the four studies referred to at the beginning of the preceding section is that a sizeable percentage of subjects failed to intervene when they were alone. Thus, 25 per cent failed to intervene in Latané and Darley's (1968) seizure study, 35 per cent in Smith, Smythe, and Lien's (1972) fainting experimenter study, 30 per cent in Latané and Rodin's (1969) falling experimenter study, and 36 per cent in Ross and Braband's (1973) injured workman study. Neither social influence nor diffusion of responsibility theories could be used as explanations for these findings.

The above results can be contrasted, however, with findings from two studies by Clark and Word (1972, 1974). In their earlier study they found 100 per cent helping among subjects who were alone when they were exposed to an emergency, as well as in two-person or five-person groups. (They heard a maintenance man fall, but also call out in agony.) Similar subjects who were confronted with an ambiguous emergency (overhearing an identical fall without the presence of verbal cues to indicate that the victim was injured), helped approximately 30 per cent of the time. In the latter case, subjects who were alone were more likely to help, and responded faster than either the two- or five-person group helpers. Thus the inhibiting influence of groups only occurred when subjects were exposed to an ambiguous emergency. Bystanders who were exposed to a nonambiguous emergency had little, if any, chance of misinterpreting the event, and consequently intervened whether on their own or in the presence of others.

In a further study by Clark and Word (1974), subjects were exposed to one of three emergencies: nonambiguous, moderate ambiguity, and high ambiguity. In the nonambiguous situation the subjects heard and observed the victim sustain what appeared to be a serious shock, simulated by a flash of light and a dull buzzing sound that emanated from the equipment. In the moderate ambiguity condition the victim was located in one corner of the laboratory out of the subject's field of vision. The subject thus only heard the victim and equipment falling, and the victim's cry of pain. In the high ambiguity condition the verbal cue from the victim was eliminated. Thus the sound of the victim and the equipment falling was the only direct indication that the laboratory was occupied. When the subjects clearly heard and observed the accident the victim received help 96 per cent of the time with little variation in this figure according to whether the observers were alone or in groups. The probability of a victim receiving help is therefore high when an individual is exposed to a situation which can be clearly interpreted as an emergency. In weighing up the situation, help-givers are likely to make judgments concering the victim's actual need for help. The higher the degree of ambiguity the greater the risk of making an inappropriate decision, and hence the greater the risk of embarrassment.

One point of importance, however, is that subjects providing help are, in reality, never alone. They are in the presence of at least one other person, the person to whom they are providing help. In an ambiguous situation they may provide help to an individual who does not require it. Providing help to someone who might not need it is potentially embarrassing, simply because the help-giver is likely to be negatively evaluated by the recipient. Hence, the effects of audience inhibition could be used as an explanation for decreased helping in ambiguous situations even when the only audience present is the recipient of the assistance. The potential for embarrassment then increases as a function of the number of observers present.

(c) Embarrassing situations

A further factor inhibiting help-giving is the embarrassment potential of the situation itself. In many instances, performing an embarrassing act can actually lead to the victim receiving assistance. It is not unusual for someone slipping or dropping belongings in front of others to be helped to their feet or given help in collecting their possessions. It also seems that those who have performed an embarrassing act are more likely to offer help if it is requested by observers to that event. This latter finding may be due to attempts by the embarrassing person to redeem him/herself in the eyes of the observer. This is discussed in detail later in this chapter. There are situations, however, which by their very nature inhibit help-giving. In the same way that ambiguous situations inhibit helping due to the increased risk of embarrassment, so can situations which are defined as embarrassing. The issue of whether the embarrassment potential of the situation would affect help-giving was investigated in one of our own studies (Edelmann *et al.*, 1984a).

In this study a casually dressed female confederate overloaded with books, bag, and coat 'accidentally' dropped a small package in front of 40 people selected at random in a south coast resort. The subjects, 20 men and 20 women, were aged from approximately 19 to 60 years old. For half the subjects the package was potentially embarrassing (a box of Tampax tampons), and for the remaining subjects the package dropped was innocuous (a packet of tea). Two observers, following approximately ten paces behind the confederate, coded the subjects' responses according to whether they avoided, signalled to, or picked up the package, and timed the length of any interaction that took place. An avoidance response was recorded as zero seconds of interaction time, but a signalled or pick-up response was recorded from the time the package touched the ground until it was retrieved by the confederate or returned by the subject. Significantly fewer subjects picked up and returned the potentially embarrassing package and, as a result, there was significantly less interaction between subject and confederate when the package returned was potentially embarrassing.

One possible explanation for these findings is that returning the potentially embarrassing package was viewed by the subjects as likely to cause discomfort both to themselves and to the 'victim'. That is, the very act of help-giving could lead to embarrassment, in much the same way as intervening in an ambiguous situation. While this seems a plausible explanation, the conclusion must be treated with a certain amount of caution. Even though the package used in our study was selected as being potentially embarrassing, it is possible that subjects experienced alternative reactions that inhibited their degree of helping. It is obviously difficult from the methodology used to ascertain directly the emotion experienced by the subjects. It does seem reasonable to assume, however, that if the precipitating event is perceived as being potentially embarrassing then this will lead to inhibition in the degree of help offered.

In evaluating situations in which help might be required, one judgment subjects make is the likelihood that providing help will result in embarrassment. The higher the degree of uncertainty the greater the risk of making an inappropriate decision, and hence the greater the risk of embarrassment. Fear of embarrassment is thus likely to inhibit help-giving both in ambiguous situations and those which are potentially embarrassing in their own right, with this fear of embarrassment increasing if our actions are likely to be evaluated not only by the victim to the emergency, but also by other bystanders. A further set of factors which appear to affect the embarrassment potential of the situation and the extent to which help is offered is the characteristics of the victim.

2. Characteristics of the target

The literature on helping has generally suggested that the greater the need on the part of the person being helped (e.g. Harris and Meyer, 1973) and the greater the sympathy for him/her (e.g. Konecni, 1972), the greater the amount of help given. Although one might expect a handicapped person to be viewed with more sympathy than a nonhandicapped, a number of studies suggest that the physically handicapped are often the recipients of unfavourable reactions from the nonhandicapped (Thompson, 1982). The nonhandicapped may even offer less help to a person with a knee brace and arm sling than one who appears completely normal (Pomazal and Clore, 1973).

One explanation for these findings is the suggestion that a physical handicap may serve as a mark of stigma, with the able-bodied reacting unfavourably towards the disabled as a result of negative attitudes, feelings of repulsion, or embarrassment (Goffman, 1963). An alternative explanation is that the presence of a disablement decreases the attractiveness of the individual; facially attractive people generally receive more help (e.g. Sroufe *et al.* 1977; West and Brown, 1975). In both cases one would predict that the degree of the handicap would lead to a decrease in the amount of help given. A study by Samerotte and Harris (1976) tested this supposition.

A confederate, either wearing an eye patch and with a 3¼ inch theatrical scar running from his cheekbone to just above his jaw (disfigured condition), with a bandage wrapped around his forearm (neutral handicap condition), or in a neutral control condition, 'accidentally' dropped envelopes in front of 120 subjects. In all conditions the confederate picked up the envelopes at a slow and steady pace, keeping count of the number he picked up. Whether or not subjects picked up at least one envelope, and the number of envelopes actually picked up by the subject, served as the dependent variable.

Their findings suggested that in the mild handicap condition the confederate received more help than in the disfigured condition. In the mild handicap condition the confederate also received more help than in the control condition. The authors suggest that there might be two components involved in reactions to helping a handicapped person; (1) sympathy, which would tend to increase helping, and (2) a desire to avoid the individual because of repulsion, or embarrassment, or as a result of decreased attractiveness. An alternative explanation is that when a disablement clearly affects the individual's ability to help himself/herself (as with a bandaged arm), this may be sufficient impetus for the help-giver to overcome his/her repulsion or embarrassment with sympathy predominating (although this may not always be the case, as in Pomazal and Clore's study referred to above). The presence of a nondisabling stigma, whether facial or otherwise would not have this effect, and repulsion, embarrassment, etc. may predominate rather than sympathy.

Thus in one of our own studies (Edelmann *et al.*, 1984b) we found that a disabling but not disfiguring handicap did not decrease the amount of help offered. In this study a casually dressed unaccompanied confederate, travelling either in a wheelchair or on foot, dropped a newspaper in front of randomly selected individuals in a shopping precinct. Two men and two women of similar ages acted as confederates. The subjects, 12 men and 12 women, were aged from approximately 20 to 60 years. The design was balanced for sex differences of confederate and subject. Two observers following approximately 18 paces behind the confederate recorded the duration of any interaction which took place when the newspaper was returned. The disabled confederate actually received slightly more (though not significantly more) help than the able-bodied confederates. One possible explanation is that the presence of a wheelchair may cause the able-bodied less discomfort and embarrassment than more disfiguring handicaps. If the disabled person is physically disfigured, then the person approached may feel too embarrassed to help; where the only sign of disablement is a wheelchair then assumed helplessness or sympathy for the target may override these feelings.

The fact that non-disabling but disfiguring stigmas lead to a decrease in helping has been documented in a number of studies. In a study conducted by Piliavin, Piliavin, and Rodin (1975), the confederate appeared either with or without a 'port-wine' stain (a large red birthmark). The confederate, pretending to be blind, fell to the floor of a New York subway train whilst it was in motion. He received help from the public on 61 per cent of occasions when the port-wine stain was present, and on significantly more occasions when the port-wine stain was absent (86 per cent). Those people who helped waited for a shorter period of time before helping (an average latency of 16 seconds) than those who helped in the disfigured condition (an average latency of 27 seconds). In a further study, Bull and Stevens (1981) examined the effect of a facial port-wine stain (a large red birthmark below one eye) upon the amount of money donated to a charity. Although less money was given in the disfigured than in the normal condition, the difference was not significant. It nevertheless supports the notion that facial disfigurement may lead to less helping behaviour. As mentioned, one explanation for this lies in the fact that while facial attractiveness elicits helping, facially disfigured people appear less attractive and so elicit less helping. One problem with this supposition is that it is not only facial stigmas which decrease helping.

In one of our own studies (Edelman *et al.*, 1983) we assessed the affect of a non-facial physical stigma upon helping behaviour (assessed by timing the duration of an interaction) and eye contact in a natural setting. Sixteen male and sixteen female subjects, aged 20 to 60 years and selected nonsystematically, were approached in a coastal town and asked the time of day by a female confederate. For half the subject a natural red birthmark on the confederate's arm was clearly visible, while for the remaining subjects it was concealed. The visibility of the birthmark significantly reduced both the length of interaction and the amount of eye contact. An important feature of this study was the fact that facial attractiveness was constant in both conditions. Also, while six of the subjects glanced briefly at the confederate's birthmark, this on its own was insufficient to account for the decrease in eye contact. As mentioned in Chapter 4, reduced eye contact is one nonverbal sign of embarrassment. It has also been documented that the presence of physical stigma leads to a decrease in eye contact (Kleck, Ono and Hasdorf, 1966). One possibility therefore is that disfigurement elicits embarrassment in the person approached, who is then too flustered to help.

It seems then that in certain cases disablement can elicit sympathy, and hence an increase (or at least no decease) in helping. More disfiguring handicaps seem more likely to elicit negative evaluations and cause certain dilemmas for the nonstigmatized interactant. Should they acknowledge or ignore the presence of the physical stigma? What is the correct way for the interaction to proceed? The introduction of uncertainty into the situation raises the possibility that the nonstigmatized individual will proceed inappropriately. The appropriate way to present oneself (ignoring or acknowledging the stigma either verbally of nonverbally) is unclear. It is possible that fear of behaving inappropriately, and hence causing embarrassment to the help-giver, may constrain our interactions with the physically stigmatized, leading to a reduction in the amount of help we are likely to offer.

3. Characteristics of the help-giver

As well as facets of the situation and aspects of the target person, certain aspects of the help-giver are also likely to influence the extent to which they comply with requests for help. Of importance to the present suggestions, regarding the link between embarrassment and help-giving, is the argument that compliance with a request for help is one way in which people make themselves feel good.

In a study by Cialdini, Darby, and Vincent (1973), a negative state was created for the subjects by setting up a situation where subjects either harmed a confederate or witnessed the harm. Subjects then experienced or did not experience a positive event (the receipt of either money or approval) before receiving a request for help. Both witnesses and harm-doers who experienced the positive event complied with the request for help *less* than did subjects who received neither money nor approval. It seems that those who experienced the positive event (receiving money or approval) were relieved of their negative state and no longer needed the positive experience of helping someone.

Aspler (1975) reports two studies which directly investigated the implications of the above findings for embarrassed help-givers. If compliance with a request for help is a way of making subjects feel good by relieving negative states such as embarrassment, then embarrassed individuals should comply more with requests for help than unembarrassed individuals. Sixty female subjects performed tasks that did or did not make them look foolish to an observer. Two students, one designated the subject and the other a confederate, met the experimenter in a small room with a one-way mirror at one end. The experimenter explained that she was conducting an impression-formation study and that one student would perform some tasks while the other watched through the one-way mirror. Subjects in the high embarrass-ment condition were instructed to (a) turn on a tape recorder and dance to the record; (b) laugh for 30 seconds as if they had just heard a funny joke; (c) sing the 'Star Spangled Banner'; and (d) imitate a 5-year-old having a temper tantrum. Following the completion of the tasks the confederate entered the room and gave the subject the opportunity to comply with a request for help, which involved filling out a questionnaire for up to 20 days. The number of days that the subject was willing to help constituted the measure of compliance. As predicted, embarrassed subjects complied more with the request for help, agreeing to help the confederate for an average of 14.9 days compared with 5.9 days for the non-embarrassed subjects. It seems plausible to assume that the negative affects associated with embarrass-ment can be relieved by the action of compliance with a request for help. As Aspler (1975) comments:

> compliance produces positive feelings that counteract the negative affect created by the embarrassing incident . . . embarrassed subjects' compliance could be interpreted as an attempt to improve the image they presented to an observer of their embarrassing incident. (p. 151).

It seems then that fear of embarrassment may play an important part in determining the likelihood that we will provide help to others. Consistent with this supposition is the finding that people are less likely to provide help in ambiguous situations, in front of larger audiences, and to people with disfigurements, while they are more likely to provide help if they have performed an embarrassed act themselves. In the same way that fear of embarrassment can inhibit help-giving, it has also been suggested that embar-rassment may be a major factor in determining whether people do or do not seek help. This issue is addressed in the second half of this chapter.

C. HELP-SEEKING

A large body of research suggests that, when in need, individuals often refrain from seeking help for their difficulties (e.g. Mechanic, 1976). A number of reasons have been suggested in the social psychological and clinical literature for this reluctance to seek help. Greenberg (1980) has argued, on the basis of equity theory, that feelings of indebtedness toward the helper may be aversive enough in many situations to inhibit help-seeking. A further cost of seeking and receiving help, suggested by Fisher and Nadler (Fisher, Nadler, and Whitcher-Alagna, 1982; Fisher, Depaulo, and Nadler, 1981) is that it presents a threat to the individual's self-esteem. As they point out, while receiving help may provide a number of supportive elements, it may also imply that a person is inadequate or inferior for needing the help. The central element of the loss of self-esteem notion is that help-seeking is inhibited, since needing help is incompatible with the recipient's own self-concept. As mentioned in the preceding chapter, there is a slight relationship between loss of self-esteem and embarrassment. Embarrassment, though, has to do with the *public* exposure of an image which is discrepant from one's desired image, while loss of self-esteem does not necessarily involve public exposure. Shapiro (1983, 1984) has thus discussed embarrassment as a further cost of help-seeking which he regards as being similar to loss of esteem, while emphasizing the public exposure component. As he points out:

> The Fisher and Nadler model emphasizes concern because help is incompatible with the recipient's own self-concept. The Shapiro model of embarrassment emphasizes that people are upset because of other people's supposed reactions. Operationally, the major difference between the two is that embarrassment is possible only if seeking and accepting help are public, while threat to self-esteem may occur even if help seeking is private. (Shapiro, 1984, p. 229).

Self-esteem and embarrassment are often interlinked in the literature on help-seeking. This is emphasized by the fact that a number of authors have suggested that embarrassment is a central process in preventing people from seeking help because seeking help constitutes a threat to self-esteem and emphasizes failures, inferiorities, and incompetencies (De Paulo and Fisher, 1980; Fisher and Nadler, 1976).

As help-seeking inevitably involves a degree of exposure, even if this is to one other person from whom help is sought, it seems likely that fear of embarrassment may play an important part in inhibiting help-seeking behaviour. For example, recipients of social services support are forced to make their personal problems public, a factor which may result in embarrassment and humiliation (Coser, 1965; Williamson, 1974). As a result, many individuals report that they do not seek help because it is too personal and embarrassing (Lieberman and Mullan, 1978). Consistent with previous arguments, if seeking help involves presenting an image which is discrepant from the image which one would wish to present, then the actor may fear the negative evaluations of others and the embarrassing consequences of his/her failure. As with help-giving, a number of factors associated with the situation, the target audience, and help-seeker may affect the embarrassment potential of the situation. In addition, the type of difficulty for which help is sought is likely to have an interactive effect with these factors. Findings that people seek less help for problems which are very intimate (e.g. Greenley and

Mechanic, 1976), stigmatizing (e.g. Perlman, 1975), or imply personal inadequacy (e.g. Gross *et al.*, 1979; Shapiro, 1980) lend support to this notion. As with help-giving, any situation in which we risk presenting ourselves in a way which is inconsistent with the way in which we would have wished to present ourselves is likely to inhibit help-seeking. Each of these factors is reviewed in the remainder of this chapter.

1. Audience effects

As has been mentioned previously, a number of studies have suggested that increased embarrassment occurs in front of larger audiences and audiences of high-status, expert others whose opinions are valued. The link between these factors and inhibition of help-giving was discussed in a previous section of this chapter in relation to social impact theory (Latané, 1981). It seems reasonable to assume that audience presence, and those variables associated with this presence as referred to above, will also inhibit help-seeking via a process of embarrassment.

The effect of an audience on help-seeking has been investigated by Shapiro (1978), who found that subjects were less likely to seek help in public than in private. In this study 60 female undergraduates were randomly assigned to one of four experimental conditions. Subjects performed a task either in public or in private, each of the two groups also being allowed to seek help either in public or in private. When task performance was public, but subjects were allowed to seek help privately, 87.3 per cent of the subjects sought help. Public performance may have provided the subjects with an incentive to improve their performance, while there were few costs involved in seeking help privately. This contrasts with the public performance subjects who were allowed to seek public help; only 33.3 per cent actually did so. In the private performance conditions, 54 per cent of subjects sought help independently of whether this help was public or private. In these two conditions there was likely to be little incentive for the subjects to improve their performances, and thus the demands for seeking help were not as great as in the public performance condition. In this study the relevance of self-presentation concerns is raised at two points: in public exposure during one's performance and in public exposure while seeking help. Concerns with one's public performance may encourage help-seeking at one level (i.e. via incentives), while concerns with publicly seeking help may inhibit help-seeking at another (i.e. the presence of an audience may inhibit help-seeking as a result of the potential embarrassment of revealing one's incompetence).

In relation to the public/private nature of help-seeking, the degree to which one's identity is public or private is also an important factor, i.e. anonymity versus identifiability. Thus, Nadler and Porat (1978) found greater help-seeking when subjects were anonymous than when they were identified by name. Anonymity, like private help-seeking, is likely to reduce the relevance of self-presentational concerns. Performing in a way which results in an image which is discrepant from our desired image is less relevant in private, anonymous circumstances; it is also less likely to result in negative evaluations from others and hence embarrassment. Help-seeking is thus more likely in private, anonymous circumstances.

As well as a public, identifiable performance, certain aspects of the target audience, as mentioned above, are likely to increase self-presentational concerns. In applying social impact theory (Latané, 1981) to help-seeking, one would predict that the frequency of help-seeking would decrease as a function of audience size, lack of immediacy, and status. A study by Williams and Williams (1983) tested this hypothesis. Eighty subjects took part in an examination on a microcomputer that was programmed to break down. The major dependent variable was the time it took to call assistance. The independent variables were number, strength, and immediacy of help-givers. On arrival at the laboratory each participant was asked to report to an office where he/she was greeted by either one (low number), or three (high number), experimenters, who were either neatly dressed experts (high strength), or sloppily dressed non-experts (low strength). In the high immediacy condition the experimenter stated that he or she (or the three experimenters) would be in the room next door; in the low immediacy condition the experimenter stated that he or she (or all three experimenters) would be in the office down the hall. In all conditions the computer was programmed to have a break at the same point for each subject in a sequence of questions that the subjects were answering.

After the participant sought help, one experimenter asked the subject to follow him/her down the hall where the participant filled out a questionnaire concerning the experiment. Questions included manipulation checks, the participants' feelings of stress, embarrassment, and anxiety when the screen froze.

Participants took significantly longer to ask for help if there were three potential help-givers compared to one potential help-giver, in the high strength compared to the low strength condition (although this did not reach significance), and in the low immediacy compared to the high immediacy condition (although this did not reach significance). For reported embarrassment there was a marginally significant effect for number of potential help-givers with the availability of more help-givers resulting in more reported embarrassment. The other two factors produced reports of embarrassment in the predicted direction (i.e. more embarrassment with high strength than low strength others and with high immediacy than low immediacy others) although these were not significant. The general pattern of results thus supports the usefulness of studying help-seeking from a social impact theory perspective and also emphasizes the inhibiting effect of embarrassment upon help-seeking.

Self-presentational concerns and fear of the negative and embarrassing consequences of failure thus seem to play an important part in inhibiting help-seeking. As Nadler, Shapira, and Ben-Itzhak (1982) suggest, three factors may be important in considering help-seeking from a self-presentation perspective:

(a) the degree of *relevance* of self-presentation concerns in a particular help-seeking context. (b) *the intensity of the motivation* for positive self-presentation, and (c) the *meaning* of positive self-presentation in a given helping context. (p. 97; italics in original)

As has been mentioned earlier, self-presentational concerns are increased in front of high-status, expert others, situations which also increase fear of embarrassment. The desire to impress (or at least not to be evaluated unfavourably) increases in front of these specific audiences, the desire to avoid looking foolish increases and hence the embarrassment potential of the situation increases. As a result, help-seeking is likely to decrease in those same situations. As well as general status of the audience, a number of other facets of the helper seem to similarly inhibit help-seeking.

2. Characteristics of the helper

Any characteristics of the helper, which increase our desire to gain social approval (or at least to avoid social disapproval) are likely to increase our fears of embarrassment. The more we value the views and opinions of others (particularly their views of our own performance), the more concerned we will be that our help-seeking will reveal our incompetence or inadequacy.

In this connection, studies suggest that subjects are less likely to seek help from physically attractive than from physically unattractive others (Nadler, 1980; Nadler, Shapira, and Ben-Itzhak, 1982; Stokes and Bickman, 1974). Stokes and Bickman (1974), for example, found that female subjects reported more discomfort in seeking help from an attractive than from an unattractive female. They were also less likely to seek help from the attractive female. When the helper was defined as someone who was there to provide help to the subjects, however, degree of attractiveness did not affect help-seeking. Defining the helper in such specific terms may well have reduced the subject's fear of exposing an inadequacy. Exposure of inadequacy in front of an attractive equal may well engender more embarrassment than similar exposure in front of an unattractive equal or a specifically assigned helper. Also important in the Stokes and Bickman study was the fact that subjects were expected to engage in face-to-face interaction with the helper (the helper sat in the same room as the subject). In view of the links between self-presentational concerns and embarrassment, it seems likely that the extent of interaction with the helper and the expectation of future interaction may also affect the subject's tendency to ask for help.

This has in fact been illustrated in a study by Nadler (1980). Forty female subjects who took a test of knowledge, were provided with a photograph of a female whom they thought was available to them for help on items they could not answer. The photograph depicted one of two persons: a physically attractive, or an unattractive female. (the two photographs were chosen on the basis of a pilot study where twenty independent judges rated sixteen photographs on a five-point scale ranging from 'very attractive' to 'not at all attractive'.) Half the subjects expected a face-to-face meeting in the future with the person from whom they could seek help, the other half of the subjects did not expect a future interaction. The results indicated that subjects were more reluctant to seek help from a physically attractive other than from a physically unattractive other, and they were more reluctant to seek help from another female with whom a face-to-face meeting was expected than from one with whom such a meeting was not expected. As Nadler (1980) suggests:

> it may be that when the subject was to decide whether to seek help, the expectation of a meeting with the other made self-presentation concerns relevant, and the fact that the other was physically attractive increased the ensuing evaluation apprehension (p. 382)

In view of the fact that physically attractive others are valued more than physically unattractive others (Berscheid and Walster, 1974) and one is more motivated to make a favourable self-presentation to valued than less-valued persons (Zanna and Pack, 1975), the negative and embarrassing consequences of admitting failure in front of such others is increased; conversely, seeking help from such others is decreased. It follows, therefore, that in situations in which seeking help is negatively evaluated, doing so will be regarded as a self-presentation failure with embarrassing consequences. There are also, however, occasions where help-seeking will be positively evaluated. Nadler, Shapira, and Ben-Itzhak (1982) investigated help-seeking behaviour as affected by the sex of the needy individual, the sex of the helper, and the physical attractiveness of the helper. Subjects were asked to solve a detective story and were under the impression that correct solutions could be obtained only after a specified number of preliminary questions were answered correctly. Some of these questions were unanswerable, and subjects could ask for help with these items. They found that males sought less help from a physically attractive female than from a less attractive female, but that females sought more help from a physically attractive male than from a less attractive male. They explain these results by pointing out that, for females, displaying dependency on a male is congruent with the feminine sex role; consequently a female's display of relative inferiority by help-seeking actually represents a positive presentation of the self. In this case therefore the helper's physical attractiveness facilitated rather than inhibited help-seeking behaviour. For males, asking females for help violates sex-role definitions of expected behaviour, and hence reflects a negative presentation of self resulting in an increased possibility of embarrassment.

In general, then, a physically attractive helper increases motivation for positive self-presentation which, under certain conditions, inhibits one's willingness to expose inadequacy by help-seeking. To seek help under such circumstances would result in the negative presentation of self with consequent concerns about one's identity and the resultant embarrassment which may well ensue. It seems likely that any other attribute of the helper, or the situation, that increases evaluation apprehension will affect help-seeking.

A situation in which help-seeking would be a clear indication of inferiority, and hence involve a clearly negative presentation of self, involves seeking help from a child. Druian and DePaulo (1977) gave college-age students a spelling test during which approximately half could ask for help from a child, the rest from a same-aged adult. Though both helpers were presented as equally competent spellers, subjects asked for help less frequently from a child than from the adult. The responses of the subjects indicated that they perceived their help requests as an embarrassing acknowledgment of inferiority to the helper. Similar results are reported in a further paper by DePaulo (1978) where she found that adults were less willing to accept free art lessons from competent children than from competent adults. Seeking help from someone of lower status violates the performance expectations derived from the statuses of the participants. Thus, seeking help from a status inferior results in a negative presentation of self in much the same way as seeking help from a status superior. Both may be associated with an increase in embarrassment. The former because we *are* acknowledging our incompetence and inferiority, the latter because we *may* acknowledge our inferiority or incompetence. Thus we are likely to ask for advice and suggestions from high-status others rather than help *per se*.

A further attribute of the helper which is likely to affect the evaluation apprehension inherent in the situation is our relationship with the helper. Brown and Garland (1971) suggest that we are more likely to avoid engaging in embarrassing behaviour in front of friends; it might be expected therefore that we would ask friends for help less than strangers. As Shapiro (1983) points out, however, although we may care more about the evaluations of friends, we may feel that asking a friend for help will involve less embarrassment than asking a stranger. It seems likely that the relevance of self-presentation concerns, our motivation for positive self-presentation, and the meaning of positive self-presentation, will be less in front of friends than in front of strangers. We should therefore be less embarrassed when asking friends for help than when asking strangers.

In a test of this hypothesis, Shapiro (1980) investigated the effect on help-seeking behaviour of the relationship between help-seeker and helper (friend or stranger) and its interaction with costs to the helper of providing help (high or low) and reported task difficulty (hard or easy). Pairs of female undergraduates were presented with a task which neither could solve alone (the task involved attempting to put together the pieces of a puzzle) and each was given the opportunity to seek help from the other. In the friend condition subjects were paired with someone whom they had identified as a friend at an earlier stage in the year, while in the stranger condition subjects were paired with someone from a different class and hall of residence. In the high-cost condition subjects believed that asking for help could interfere with their partner's chance of winning a prize, while high task difficulty was manipulated by informing subjects that few previous subjects had solved the puzzle.

The results suggested that help-seeking was more frequent between friends than strangers; high costs of seeking help deterred help-seeking between strangers but not between friends; the difficulty of the task, however, did not significantly affect help-seeking. As Shapiro (1984) points out, it should be noted that the need for help in the Shapiro (1980) study was due to an inability to solve a puzzle, a reason which should not have resulted in severe embarrassment. In terms of the self-presentation perspective, there may be a curvilinear relationship between help-seeking and friendship. In the case of minor to mild difficulties, it is likely that the relevance of self-presentation concerns will be lower in the presence of friends than with strangers. In the case of severe difficulties, however, self-presentation concerns are likely to be less relevant in the presence of someone who is specifically assigned the role of help-giver than when the person is a peer or friend. Hence, people seeking help are likely to divulge information to the caring professions which might be considered by the client as too personal and embarrassing to reveal even to one's closest friends or relatives. If help-seeking is the expected behaviour in the situation, then such behaviour should produce little embarrassment. As Shapiro (1984) suggests:

> Seeking help may be seen to be the expected behavior when it is sought from a person who occupies a helping role, a role in which providing help to others is a central part of the role definition. . . . People who are able to seek help from someone who occupies such a role should experience less embarrassment and be more willing to seek help that someone who must seek help from a person in a non-helping role. (p. 157).

There are then a range of characteristics of the helper which are likely to affect self-presentation concerns and hence the embarrassment potential of the situation. As mentioned at the beginning of the section, any characteristic of the help-giver which increases our desire to gain social approval (or at least to avoid social disapproval) is likely to be pertinent. If we value someone's view about our behaviour or performance we may, under certain circumstances, be deterred from seeking their assistance. As Nadler, Shapira, and Ben-Itzhak (1982) comment:

> the relevance, intensity and meaning of self-presentation should be considered for a better understanding of the psychological processes that govern help-seeking behaviour, (p. 98).

3. Characteristics of the help-seeker

It seems likely that characteristics of the help-seeker will also affect self-presentation concerns, the potential of the individual for experiencing embarrassment, and hence inhibit help-seeking behaviour. One could predict that the range of personality variables discussed in the previous chapter will be of relevance here. Those individual difference factors related to embarrassibility which reflect a concern with the way in which we are evaluated by others are central to the current argument. Thus one could predict that those who are high scorers on the 'Other-Directedness' factor of the self-monitoring scale, those who are publicly self-conscious, socially anxious, introverted, or neurotic, would be less likely to seek help from others. In line with Nadler, Shapira, and Ben-Itzhak's (1982) suggestion, the relevance, intensity, and meaning of their self-presentations will be particularly pertinent to these individuals. It thus seems reasonable to assume that embarrassibility and associated personality characteristics will be related to a general reluctance to seek help.

Unfortunately, there are few studies investigating personality variables and help-seeking which are of relevance to the present discussion. A number of studies have, however, investigated self-esteem and help-seeking (see Nadler, 1983). This may be of slight relevance, bearing in mind Modigliani's (1968) finding that there was a relationship between general self-esteem and embarrassibility. As mentioned previously, he explained this by suggesting that people who have low self-esteem are more likely to accept and be disturbed by others' evaluations of them. This suggestion is partly in keeping with the personality characteristics referred to above. Modigliani's suggestion does, however, create a dilemma. If low self-esteem people accept others' evaluations of them one would not expect them to be inhibited from seeking help. The fact that they are disturbed by others' evaluations, however, suggests that they may be inhibited from seeking help. If the former case were to apply, self-presentation concerns would be less relevant for a low self-esteem person than for a high self-esteem person who might actually be more disturbed by information that implies an inadequacy. Consistent with this explanation, Nadler, Fisher, and Streufret (1976) found subjects with high self-esteem were more disturbed when receiving help from another that would imply inferiority than were subjects with low self-esteem. In this study, fear of embarrassment might have been a relevant variable as subjects expected future face-to-face interaction with the person who helped them. The issue of embarrassibility, relevant individual difference measures, and their effect upon help-seeking is thus an area which warrants future research.

One final area of research concerning the characteristics of the help-seeker involves the help-seeker's emotional state when the request for help is made. In the same way that an embarrassed person may comply with a request for help in order to relieve their negative state of embarrassment (as in the study by Aspler, 1975, referred to earlier in this chapter), subjects may be more likely to assist an embarrassed help-seeker. This possibility was investigated in a study by Levin and Arluke (1982). They report two studies in which a female confederate, posing as an undergraduate student, was introduced to a class of students as someone who needed assistance with a project. While reading her statements the confederate held a large quantity of papers; in the no-embarrassment condition she had no apparent difficulty in going through the motions of making her request for help. In the embarrassment condition, during her request for help, the confederate 'accidentally' dropped the large quantity of papers on the floor and, in a nervous manner, picked them up before continuing with her statement. The measure of helping consisted of the number of days from 0 to 20 which students were willing to serve as subjects. As expected, embarrassment produced significantly more helping than no-embarrassment, with students volunteering more of their time when the requester experienced a loss of composure than when the requester performed as expected.

Levin and Arluke (1982) also report a second study which replicated and extended the above. In addition to the 'no-embarrassment' and 'embarrassment' conditions, a third condition was introduced in which the confederate, upon dropping the papers, stood as though frozen by anxiety, muttered 'Oh my God! I can't continue', and ran from the room. As with the first study, the confederate received more help in the embarrassed than non-embarrassed condition, yet when the embarrassed individual failed to regain composure, she received significantly less help than when she had not shown embarrassment. It may have been the case that observers of the embarrassed help-seeker were prompted by a desire to help her overcome her embarrassing predicament. In the loss of composure condition, subjects may have perceived the confederate as exhibiting extreme incompetence and hence as incapable of carrying out the study. It may also be the case that a display of mild embarrassment from a help-seeker is regarded as an image-enhancing self-presentation. As mentioned previously, in one of our own studies (Edelmann, 1982), a confederate who displayed embarrassment was seen as being more likeable and causing less discomfort than when he displayed a defiant stare. A display of embarrassment may be seen as an apology for having to ask for help. A person exhibiting such a display may be regarded as likeable, and hence receive more help.

D. SUMMARY

This chapter has argued that any helping situation in which we risk presenting ourselves in a way which is inconsistent with the way in which we would have wished to present ourselves is likely to inhibit help-giving and help-seeking. Specifically it was suggested that embarrassment will be increased and hence help-giving decreased in front of larger, higher-status audiences, in ambiguous situations, in situations with embarrassing overtones, and when the help request is made by someone with a disfiguring handicap. Conversely, help-giving is likely to increase if the request follows an embarrassing act performed by the help-giver. Similarly it was suggested that embarrassment will increase and hence help-seeking decrease in public, in the presence of larger, high-status audiences, if the helper is physically attractive, a child, or a stranger, and if the help-seeker is publicly self-conscious, socially anxious, introverted, or neurotic. On the other hand, a display of embarrassment from a help-seeker is likely to increase the amount of help received.

While embarrassment has been emphasized as an explanatory process, it is also recognized that there are many other reasons why people do not seek or provide help. A discussion of these is beyond the scope of this book. Of central importance to the current argument has been the suggestion that any situational variables or personal characteristics which increase the relevance of self-presentation concerns and our motivation for positive self-presentation are likely to be related to an increase in the embarrassment potential of the situation. It is then this fear of embarrassment which inhibits help-giving and help-seeking due to the potentially aversive nature of experienced embarrassment. For some people the fear that they will behave in a way which is embarrassing may not only constrain help-seeking and help-giving, but may also inhibit all their interactions with others. The part played by embarrassment or fear of embarrassment in cases of social dysfunction forms the central theme of the following chapters.

CHAPTER 8

Clinical Issues

A. EMBARRASSMENT AS A CLINICAL PHENOMENON

It should be stated at the outset that the likelihood of being referred a client who is described as 'suffering from embarrassment' or being able to refer to a clinical text in order to gain an impression of what one might do for such a client are both unlikely occurrences. Although clinicians may occasionally be referred 'chronic blushers', rather more global terms than embarrassment are likely to be used when describing referred clients. As mentioned at the beginning of this book, embarrassment is regarded as a form of social anxiety, and a variety of terms have been used to refer to different types of social anxiety, including stage fright, audience anxiety, shyness, heterosexual–social anxiety, communication apprehension, reticence, and of course embarrassment. Each of these terms refers to variants of a central theme, i.e. concern with the image presented to others who are felt to be evaluating us. Some may be specific to particular social situations. Thus stage fright and audience anxiety are specific to public speaking encounters, heterosexual–social anxiety to dating encounters, and shyness to general social encounters. Embarrassment or fear of embarrassment may be a rather more pervasive phenomenon. Referred clients are thus likely to be called 'socially anxious' or 'shy' without any reference to the part played in their difficulty by fear of embarrassment.

The fact that embarrassment or fear of embarrassment can play an important part in maintaining social anxiety or its subtypes has however been acknowledged both explicitly and implicitly in the literature. Thus, Zimbaro (1977) comments:

> Most shy people . . . learn to avoid any situation which may be potentially embarrassing, thereby further isolating themselves from other people and instead concentrating on their own shortcomings. (p. 29)

In a further study, Greenberg and Stravynski (1985) suggest certain key features that 'patients who complain of social dysfunction' fear would happen to them in a social situation. The commonest feature was the fear that they would be received with ridicule or hostility or would look silly. As the authors point out, unlike agoraphobics who seem to fear 'fear itself', patients with social dysfunction fear ridicule and rejection in social situations. In another paper, Thyer, Himle, and Curtis (1985) state 'The critical feature salient to social phobia involves exposure to the scrutiny of others and consequent fears of embarrassment' (p. 451). It does not take too many inferential leaps to suggest that what is actually feared is the negative consequences of ridicule and rejection, one aspect of which can be the generation of embarrassment. Embarrassment or fear of embarrassment may then be a central and perhaps maintaining factor in some cases of social dysfunction (cf. the DSM-III definition of social anxiety referred to previously).

As has been noted during the course of this book, embarrassment is occasioned by a sequence of events involving a disruption of social routine, an awareness of a discrepancy between present state and a standard for self-presentation with consequent self-directed attention and associated behavioural concomitants. As was noted in Chapter 5, embarrassment can occur as a result both of situationally induced discrepancies and subjectively perceived discrepancies. In the case of social anxiety (i.e. an unpleasant emotional response induced by fear of social situations), it is possible that the fear is occasioned because the actor either (1) fears that his performance (i.e. behaviour) will be below or discrepant from his/her expectations (i.e. inappropriate cognitions), or (2) because he/she simply does not know which behaviour is appropriate in the situation (i.e. a skills deficit)—these two explanations will be discussed in detail in the following section. In either case this fear of failure is really a fear of the negative consequences of failure (i.e. lack of social approval and embarrassment). A similar argument can be advanced for other situation-specific forms of 'social anxiety'. Thus, in heterosexual–social anxiety the fear that one may not behave adequately, or not know the appropriate behaviours, can of itself generate a fear of embarrassment; the risks of disapproval or failure in such situations can be avoided simply by avoiding the situation. As has been noted, one consequence of situations in which one is unsure how to behave (i.e. novel or unfamiliar situations) is the adoption of a protective self-presentation style—this of itself may involve excess modesty or, in extreme cases, social avoidance or withdrawal.

The client referred to as 'socially anxious' or 'shy' may then fear (perhaps as a result of a negative self-view) the embarrassing consequences of failure. In many of these cases it may be appropriate to concentrate upon the reasons for fearing embarrassment. Thus one may focus not only upon whether clients really do know the appropriate behaviours or whether they evaluate themselves appropriately, but also the extent to which they concentrate upon themselves as central characters in the action. Embarrassment then can form a central part of situationally induced social anxiety, and as such one should seek to understand three key issues. Firstly, whether fear of embarrassment is an important maintaining factor within the social anxiety; second, to ascertain whether the fear is based upon lack of knowledge of the appropriate behaviours to perform in the situation or lack of confidence in one's ability to perform the behaviours adequately; and thirdly, the extent to which concern with one's identity is appropriate. The issue of lack of knowledge or lack of confidence is addressed in the second part of this chapter; the issues of concern with one's identity and redirecting attention as a means of alleviating embarrassment are dealt with in the final chapter.

As well as the importance of situationally induced embarrassment, 'subjectively' perceived embarrassment can also be a distressing problem for some clients. In this case the client focuses on one particular aspect of behaviour, namely blushing. It is not the situation as such or general aspects of behaviour which cause concern, the problem centres around the blush, which the client perceives as creating the discrepant image. Thus, 'Competent people do not blush. I blush, therefore others will view me as incompetent and will assume that I am embarrassed even if the situation does not occasion it.' As mentioned in Chapter 5, it is possible to display embarrassment in situations which are not defined by observers as embarrassing. Embarrassment in this case is defined on the basis of the display and not the situation in which it occurs. The issue of chronic blushing is dealt with in the final section of this chapter.

Embarrassment can thus be important clinically both in terms of the part it plays within the general difficulty of social anxiety (i.e. situationally induced) and in terms of the behavioural display (i.e. chronic blushing). Issues central to the former difficulty involve questions posed about social anxiety: 'Is the anxiety a result of previous traumatic experiences with that episode?', 'Is it a result of a lack of knowledge about how to behave in social situations?', 'Does it reflect a lack of confidence in one's ability to perform skills which one actually does possess?'. The role of classical conditioning, behavioural deficits, and cognitive factors in the experience of social anxiety and embarrassment forms the central part of this issue.

As well as being central to the experience of social anxiety, embarrassment can of course occur in individuals who are not so defined. A second issue then involves the strategies by which one might deal with the experience of embarrassment. The various verbal strategies that might be used by the actor to explain away his/her embarrassing behaviour have already been discussed. It is likely that individuals will differ not only in the type of strategy used to deal with embarrassing events but also in their knowledge and/or confidence in their ability to put these strategies into practice. The role of behavioural deficits and cognitive factors in the actor's ability to operationalize coping strategies is thus also an important issue.

In the following sections theoretical explanations of social anxiety will be outlined with specific reference to their relevance to the experience of embarrassment. A study specifically addressing the issue of individual differences in relation to coping with embarrassment and the question of a knowledge/confidence dichotomy will then be evaluated in the light of these explanations.

B. THEORETICAL EXPLANATIONS OF SOCIAL ANXIETY

1. Classical conditioning

According to the classical conditioning model, fears are acquired when a neutral stimulus, which initially does not provoke anxiety, becomes paired or associated with a stimulus which does elicit fear or anxiety. The classical conditioning of fear may result from a single such pairing (single-trial learning) or may be progressively built up over time (Wolpe, 1982). As mentioned in Chapter 1, an influential case in the history of classical conditioning is the conditioned fear elicited in an 11-month-old infant named Albert (Watson and Raynor, 1920). This case was extremely significant as it was regarded as clear evidence that fears could be acquired in this way.

Since the time of Watson, a great deal of research has demonstrated that fears may be conditioned and unconditioned both in humans and animals (Wolpe, 1976, 1982). Social anxiety could also be viewed as a classically conditioned response, resulting from repeated exposure to aversive experiences in social situations. The original classical conditioning theory has been extended and expanded in a number of ways. Mowrer (1950), for example, suggests that anxiety and avoidance are causally linked; the original fear may be acquired as a result of exposure to an aversive experience, fear and anxiety are avoided in future by avoiding the eliciting situation/circumstances. This two-stage theory of fear acquisition could well explain the link between embarrassment and the fear of social encounters referred to as social anxiety. Through ridicule, rejection, or failure in social situations we learn to experience embarrassment; we thus avoid social situations to avoid the embarrassing consequences of failure.

Two assumptions underlie this explanation: first, it is necessary to assume that all people referred to as socially anxious have experienced an aversive social encounter, which has served to condition the person to become anxious in similar settings in the future. The second assumption is that we are able to explain the individual's aversive experiences in social encounters without recourse to his/her own behaviours in the encounter or thoughts about the encounter. In the case of the first assumption it has frequently been note that a traumatic experience relating to the genesis of fears and phobias cannot be found (Eysenck, 1976). While many people are able to trace their concerns over social encounters to specific incidents in which they have had an aversive experience (Zimbardo, 1977) it is likely that many clients referred to as socially anxious have not had the necessary traumatic experiences. Further, most people have had aversive experiences in certain social encounters (particularly during adolescent relationships) and yet the majority of these people do not fear embarrassment associated with social anxiety.

In the case of the second assumption, it is important to understand why the initial aversive encounter has occurred. Perhaps it occurred as a result of the actor's own bad behaviour. This may well result if the actor is unsure how to behave or does not possess the necessary repertoire of behaviours or skills (the links between the skills deficit model and the classical conditioning model are outlined below). An alternative assumption might be that the actor behaved appropriately and possessed the necessary skills but perceived the situation inappropriately or evaluated it in an unnecessarily negative light. Thus the actor may select specific and negative aspects of the inter- action. These inappropriate or faulty cognitions may then be responsible for fear of embarrassment in social encounters rather than an actual aversive experience as such (cognitive factors in the generation of embarrassment and social anxiety are discussed later).

In summary, while learning to fear aversive consequences of a social situation may well explain the generation or maintenance of embarrassment and social anxiety in some cases, this is undoubtedly only one part of the story. The possibility that inappropriate behaviours or faulty cognitions are implicated in the experience of embarrassment and social anxiety also needs to be considered.

2. Skills deficit model

This model presupposes that individuals may not possess the necessary behav- ioural repertoire to meet the demands of the situation. Social anxiety in this case may sometimes arise as a reaction to a problematic situation brought about by one's inability to handle the social demands of a particular encounter. In this sense, social anxiety *results* from a deficit in a person's repertoire of socially skilled responses, the assumption being that the person has either never learned, or has forgotten, appropriate modes of responding to some or all social situations. Consequently, these situations are often associated with undesired outcomes which generate subjective feelings of anxiety and distress.

In the sense that an unskilled actor is likely to receive negative evaluations from others there are links between the skills deficit model and the classical conditioning model. When an individual responds in a way which is perceived as inappropriate to others present, then feedback from others may point out to the actor the embarrassing nature of his/her behaviour. This may lead the actor to fear that his/her behaviour may be inadequate or embarrassing on future occasions.

If the skills model is correct one would expect discernible differences between high and low socially anxious individuals on measures of social skills. Unfortunately the literature presents a rather confusing array of results. This may be a result of (1) the methods used (i.e. observer ratings of general social skill versus measures of specific skill differences); (2) the populations studied (i.e. clinically socially anxious versus analogue studies); or (3) because a deficit in social skills may not be necessary for an individual to view themselves (or be viewed by others) as socially anxious.

Of studies that have used observers' ratings a number have suggested that socially anxious individuals are generally less socially skilled than those who are low in social anxiety (e.g. Arkowitz *et al.*, 1975; Farrell *et al.*, (1979); Twentyman and McFall (1975); and Halford and Foddy (1982).

As a recent example, the latter authors report a study in which judges rated the overt behaviours in a series of simulated social interactions. Judges received 20 hours of training in the scoring of social behaviour from video-tapes. They then judged the subjects during the Social Behaviour Role Playing Test, paying particular attention to the following cues when assessing social anxiety: (1) the presence of non-expressive hand gestures; (2) the presence of lip-biting and swallowing; (3) the presence of rigid, markedly symmetrical body posture; and (4) an absence of eye contact. In assessing social skill, judges were instructed to attend to the following cues; (1) appropriate assertive verbal content (i.e. direct, non-aggressive verbal statements of feelings, needs and wants); (2) short response latency; (3) a strongly audible voice; (4) the presence of smiling; and (5) the appropriate use of hand and body gestures. As predicted, judges rated high-anxious subjects as less skilled and more socially anxious than low-anxious subjects, although the latter difference did not reach significance.

The finding that judges rate socially anxious subjects as less skilled than their non-socially anxious counterparts has been replicated using a number of different judges (trained raters, confederates, and other naive subjects) and in a number of contexts (role-played tasks, videotaped laboratory inter-actions, and real-life interactions). It seems then that socially anxious people are *perceived* as being less skilled than the non-socially anxious.

Although there may be something about the behavioural style of socially anxious people which differentiates them from non-socially anxious, it seems from the studies which have directly assessed the content/amount of specific behaviours that there are not always behavioural differences between these two groups. In a study investigating the behavioural correlates of social anxiety in college students (assigned to high, medium or low social anxiety groups on the basis of their scores on the SAD—Watson and Friend, 1969), Daly (1978) found that high-anxious subjects talked less while listening to instructions and held gaze for less total time and in bouts of shorter duration while they were talking, than low socially anxious subjects, the measures being taken from videotapes of a 3-minute interview.

There were, however, no differences between the subject groups for number of arm movements or self-touching behaviours or eye contact while listening. Further, the variability among high-anxious subjects' average duration of eye contact bouts was significantly greater than among low-anxious subjects. As the author herself points out, within-group variability suggests that nonverbal behaviour should be analysed according to individual, rather than looking for group, differences.

Two recent studies have included both rating measures from judges as well as direct measures of subject behaviour with interesting results. In one study by Newton, Kindness, and McFadyen (1983), groups of clinically socially anxious subjects and non-socially anxious controls were assessed on a number of measures of social performance. Each subject took part in a semi-structured encounter in which they were asked to meet a stranger (a confederate) with whom they were encouraged to engage in a conversation. The confederate used a series of standard prompts to ask about home, work, and interests, using self-disclosure, and when appropriate, following up comments made by the patient. A 5-minute videotape recording of the interaction was then rated by three trained observers. Sixteen aspects of the subject's behaviour were rated on a 0 to 3 scale with 0 representing adequate performance for each item. The three observers also rated their overall impression of the adequacy of social performance on a 0 to 3 scale. In addition to the rating scales three direct measures of subjects' behaviour were included: percentage time of speech, number of questions, and number of smiles.

The results from the ratings showed, as with previous rating studies, significant differences between the two groups. As with the Daly (1978) study of specific behaviours, however, Newton *et al.* report a marked overlap in the range of total performance scores. Some patients' social performance was as adequate as the non-clinical group, with some patients scoring well within the range of the more skilful members of the non-clinical group.

In the case of the direct behavioural measures, the means for the percentage times of speech for the two groups were similar although the patient groups again had a much wider range of scores. As Newton *et al.* comment, this reflects some of the differing social performance difficulties between subjects, from the withdrawn person who speaks little, to the over-talkative person who monopolizes the conversation. There were no differences between the groups on the direct measures of number of smiles and number of questions. Some people presenting with social interaction difficulties seem to have adequate social performance but nevertheless have high social anxiety. In addition, it would seem that even when there are no real differences between socially and non-socially anxious groups in terms of specific behaviours displayed, these individuals are nevertheless judged by others to have behavioural deficits, a point taken up in another recent study in Biedel, Turner, and Dancu (1985).

In this study, 26 socially anxious subjects were compared with 26 non-socially anxious subjects on a series of behavioural tasks: (a) an unstructured interpersonal interaction with an opposite-sex confederate; (b) a similar interaction with a same-sex confederate; and (c) an impromptu talk with a topic selected by the subject. The subject's performance during each of these tasks was videotaped and rated by independent raters blind to group assignment. The behaviours which included intonation, speech loudness, gaze and overall skill were rated on five-point qualitative scales (where 1 was extremely inadequate skill, and 5 a high level of ability). In addition, response duration was timed and speech dysfluencies were counted. Over all these measures the only significant finding was with relation to gaze: during the two unstructured role-plays socially anxious males had lower levels of gaze than either socially anxious females or non-socially anxious males. On the global rating of skill however the non-socially anxious subjects were rated as being more skilful. As the authors themselves conclude:

> Although individual behaviour such as eye contact or voice tone was an insufficient measure by which to discriminate the groups, the synergistic combination of all the molecular variables appeared potent enough to create an impression of unskillfulness in the socially anxious. (Biedel et al., 1985, p. 116)

A number of conclusions can be drawn from the literature: first, it seems clear that some socially anxious people may have a deficit in social performance—it seems equally clear that some do not. Second, in cases where socially anxious people do not have deficits in terms of specific behavioural skills (such as eye contact, gestures, etc.), they may nevertheless have some deficit in the general style of behaviour. Social anxiety is not identified in the same way and with the same deficit in every socially anxious individual.

Assuming that a behavioural deficit can exist in some form in some socially anxious individuals, one is left with the problem of whether this deficit causes social anxiety (i.e. I behave inappropriately which generates anxiety) or is a consequence of social anxiety (i.e. 'I am anxious which generates poor behavioural responses'). In the case of a causal explanation one could argue that inappropriate behaviour receives a negative response, perhaps generating embarrassment, and hence the fear that this response may recur in future interactions (along the lines of classical conditioning). In this case the behaviour creates an image which is perhaps viewed as being discrepant from the image we would wish to convey, i.e. we have self-presentational difficulties which might generate embarrassment.

If, however, inappropriate performance is a consequence of being anxious, i.e. anxiety interferes in some way with performance, it may be the case that anxiety or worry generates self-attention which leads to an overconcern with the evaluations of others, hence embarrassment and performance failure. If one assumes, however, that anxiety rather than behaviour is causal, this necessitates invoking notions such as anxious preoccupations or expectations about performance or irrational beliefs about one's social adequacy. Cognitive factors may thus be important in determining social anxiety and embarrassment.

3. Cognitive factors

> Many people who seek treatment are neither incompetent nor anxiously inhibited, but they experience a great deal of distress stemming from excessively high standards of self-evaluation, often supported by unfavourable comparisons with models noted for their extraordinary achievements. (Bandura, 1969, p. 37).

A number of authors have suggested that faulty patterns of self-perception or faulty cognitions play a major role in the maintenance of social anxiety in socially anxious individuals. Faulty cognitions or cognitive styles which have been implicated include: negative self-evaluations of social performance (Glasgow and Arkowitz, 1975; Clark and Arkowitz, 1975; Curran, Wallander and Fischetti, 1980b), negative self-statements before and during social encounters, (Biedel *et al.*, 1985; Glass *et al.*, 1982; Cacioppo, Glass, and Merluzzi, 1979; Halford and Foddy, 1982), irrational beliefs (Glass *et al.*, 1982; Sutton-Simon and Goldfried, 1979), excessively high performance standards (Bandura, 1969) or selective memory for negative versus positive information about oneself and one's social performance ('O'Banion and Arkowitz, 1977)

These various biases in self and other perception in social interaction may well affect the use of socially skilled or socially appropriate behaviour. Thus at the level of inappropriate cognitions as a consequence of social anxiety, a socially anxious individual may not use his/her available skills simply because he/she doubts his/her ability to put them into practice. At the level of inappropriate cognitions as a cause of social anxiety, an individual may become anxious as a result of his/her negative/irrational or inappropriate thoughts about his/her ability to perform successfully in social encounters. As with the social skills explanation, embarrassment may form a central part of this process of bias in self-belief. For example, a socially anxious person may fear embarrassment as a direct result of negative expectations about his/her own performance, with these very fears leading to further increases in social anxiety. It is worth considering the various types of cognitive bias which have been proposed as giving rise to the experience of social anxiety.

(a) Negative self-evaluations

The underlying theme of this supposition is that people experience social anxiety when they evaluate themselves negatively or believe that they will not be able to present the image that they wish to present; i.e. they presume that their presented image will be discrepant from their desired image and hence embarrassing.

The general method of the studies investigating this supposition is to obtain ratings from socially anxious subjects concerning their views of their own interactions, for comparison with their views of the interactions of others. In this way it is possible to gain an impression of the extent to which socially anxious subjects negatively evaluate their own performances. Thus, in the study by Clark and Arkowitz (1975), subjects participated in two brief conversations with female confederates. Each subject rated his own and others' conversations on social skill, anxiety, and females' response. High socially anxious subjects (as indicated by the Fear of Negative Evaluation Scale—Watson and Friend, 1969) underestimated positive aspects of their performance (i.e. their social skill) and overestimated negative aspects of themselves (i.e. their degree of social anxiety). In a more recent study by Curran *et al.*, (1980b), 96 subjects, half of whom were not socially anxious and half of whom were socially anxious (as indicated by their scores on the

Situation Questionnaire—Rehm and Marston, 1968), took part in a simulated heterosexual–social situation. They were then classified, on the basis of behavioural ratings, for degree of anxiety exhibited and level of social skill displayed. Subjects then viewed a series of videotapes to evaluate their own skill performance and the performance of bogus subjects during the same interaction. All subject groups were accurate in rating the performance of the bogus subjects but the high-anxious/high-skill subjects underestimated (in comparison to judge's ratings) their own skill, while high-anxious/low-skill subjects accurately assessed their poor performance.

This latter study is of particular interest as it points to the need for careful assessment in the case of social anxiety. As pointed out, not all socially anxious subjects are deficient in the necessary skills and not all socially anxious subjects are inappropriately negative about their performance. Fear of embarrassment may in some cases be due to a lack of knowledge about how to perform in certain situations, while in other cases it may be due to doubts that one will be able to perform adequately. In certain of the latter cases one's doubt will in effect be confirmed.

(b) Negative self-statements

While the self-evaluations referred to in the previous section are aimed specifically at aspects of one's behavioural performance, other studies have attempted to examine self-relevant cognitions or self-statements and their role in mediating self-evaluation. Negative self-statements are identified with Meichenbaum (1977) and reflect the notion that thoughts that contain negative feedback and poor self-evaluation, or are task-irrelevant, interfere with adaptive functioning and therefore result in anxiety. Thus Cacioppo *et al.*, (1979) assessed the number of positive, negative, and neutral self-statements generated by groups of high and low socially anxious males (as determined by the Social Avoidance and Distress Scale—Watson and Friend, 1969) prior to an anticipated interaction with a female (no interaction actually took place) in addition to a self-evaluation of their attitude towards themselves and the impending interaction. As predicated, the anticipation of a discussion with an unfamiliar woman led to the spontaneous generation of more negative self-statements and a more negative self-evaluation by high than by low socially anxious men.

In an attempt to gain a clearer picture of the type of self-statements generated by highly socially anxious subjects, Glass *et al.*, (1982) have developed a questionnaire (Social Interaction Self-Statement Test—SISST) designed to assess self-statements prior to, during, or following social interaction. The 30-item questionnaire contains fifteen positive and fifteen negative self-statements that were derived by asking subjects to list thoughts while imagining difficult social situations. Item analysis suggested four factors emphasizing self-depreciation (e.g. 'I wish I could leave and avoid the whole situation'); positive anticipation (e.g. 'We probably have a lot in common');

fear of negative evaluation (e.g. 'I'm really afraid of what she'll think of me'); and coping ('What do I have to lose? It's worth a try'). As predicted, following a 3-minute interaction with a male confederate, high socially anxious female subjects (as assessed by the SADS) scored significantly higher on negative self-statements and significantly lower on positive self-statements than low socially anxious female subjects (the socially anxious sample were all female). Correlations between the SISST scores and behavioural ratings by confederates (immediately after the interaction) and judges (scored from videotape) were significant between negative self-statements and judgments of skill and anxiety. Also the other person in the interaction rated subjects with higher levels of negative internal dialogue as less skilful and more tense.

In further studies using this scale, Biedel *et al.*, (1985), in a study referred to previously, found differences between clinically socially anxious and non-socially anxious subjects for both the positive and negative subscales of the SISST across three different role-play situations.

An additional study, using another self-statement checklist (Halford and Foddy, 1982), found that socially anxious subjects (as defined by their scores on the SADS) made significantly more negative statements but not less positive self-statements than a non-socially anxious control group.

It is of interest to note that both the SISST and the self-statement questionnaire devised by Halford and Foddy contain items which seem to reflect anticipation of the effects of self-presentation failure, e.g. 'I might say the wrong thing'; 'This person thinks I am foolish' (Halford and Foddy); 'I feel awkward and dumb, she's bound to notice'; 'What I say will probably sound stupid' (Glass *et al.*). Thus, a central concern for these people seems to be that they will perform inadequately, say the wrong thing, and receive a negative evaluation. This is perhaps not surprising when one recalls the relationship between public self-consciousness (i.e. a particular concern with one's observable behaviour) and embarrassibility. It would thus be of particular interest to investigate the relationship between negative self-statements, embarrassibility and social difficulty—no study as yet exists.

(c) Irrational beliefs

A further cognitive variable which has been investigated in relation to social anxiety is the existence of irrational beliefs. In an interesting study, Sutton-Simon and Goldfried (1979) compared the incidence of irrational thoughts with negative self-statements in socially anxious subjects. Both types of cognition reflect different patterns of faulty thinking. The first form of faulty cognition is discussed by Ellis (Ellis, 1962; Ellis and Harper, 1975) and reflects the tendency to maintain absolutist beliefs and imperative assumptions about oneself and the world, even in the face of contradictory evidence. The latter form of faulty cognition is, as mentioned, associated with Meichenbaum, and reflects the notion that task-irrelevant or poor self-evaluations interfere with performance.

Subjects were 25 male and 33 female adults requesting therapy at a community clinic. They were assessed on two indices of anxiety—the Social Avoidance and Distress Scale, and the Fear of Heights Survey—and on two measures of faulty thinking—the Irrational Beliefs Test and the Situations Questionnaire. The former consisted of 100 statements of rational and irrational content for which subjects indicated strength of agreement; the latter consisted of an open-ended questionnaire in which subjects had to indicate what they might think in each of five situations. Interestingly, social anxiety was correlated with irrational beliefs, and like the previous studies cited was related to negative self-statements although the latter figure was not significant. It may well be the case that social anxiety is mediated by irrational beliefs about other interactants' adequacy and their own inadequacy, beliefs which are maintained by negative self-statements. This in turn may generate a belief that embarrassing encounters only happen to them, perhaps influenced by selectively recalling such previous events

(d) Selective memory

In view of the fact that cognitive formulations of social anxiety emphasize the importance of self-focused, negative patterns of thought, the extent to which subjects both produce and attend to these patterns of thinking is likely to affect their degree of social anxiety. One way in which overly negative self-evaluations may arise is if individuals selectively remember negative versus positive information about themselves and their performance. In a study by O'Banion and Arkowitz (1977), high and low socially anxious women (as identified by their scores on the SADS) interacted with a male confederate who was trained to respond positively (success) to half the subjects in each group and negatively (failure) to the other half. Following this interaction, subjects were given identical feedback, supposedly consisting of the confederates' impressions of them. This feedback consisted of a set of positive and negative adjectives describing personality traits, and was identical for all subjects. After viewing the ratings, subjects were asked to recall the male's rating of them. Consistent with their predictions, highly socially anxious women remembered a significantly higher number of negative adjectives than low socially anxious women.

It seems that selective memory for information about oneself may be an important factor in the mediation and maintenance of social anxiety. It is also likely that selective memory for such information is closely associated with negative self-evaluations, negative self-statements, and irrational beliefs. Thus socially anxious individuals may be inclined to recall certain negative or embarrassing experiences, or the feelings and thoughts associated with those experiences, and hence develop a distorted image of what to expect from social encounters with an increased concern over the evaluations of others.

This notion is partially reflected in a study by Smith, Ingram, and Brehm

(1983), who investigated recall of self-relevant information by socially anxious subjects. High and low socially anxious subjects (as determined by their scores on the SADS) were assigned at random to a stress or no-stress condition. Subjects in both conditions were told that they were participating in an experiment concerned with the effects of personal information on impression formation and change. The stress condition was intended to arouse anxiety through a social-evaluative threat. Subjects in this condition were told that they would each stand individually in front of a group and provide some brief personal information. Each of them would be rated by the others in the group on three dimensions (i.e. poise, intelligence, and attractiveness). They were also told that they would be asked to stand in front of the group a second time in the experiment to provide some additional, more personal, information about themselves, and that the evaluative ratings would be repeated at that time.

Subjects in the stress condition then completed the first introductions and ratings before taking part in a depth-of-processing task. This task represented the main purpose of the study but was introduced to subjects as being designed to provide a brief time lag between the two impression rating tasks.

In the depth-of-processing task all subjects listened to a tape recording of 48 trait adjectives. After hearing each adjective subjects responded to one of four types of question (counterbalanced across traits) corresponding to four levels of processing: structural (i.e. 'Was the word read by a male or female voice?'); semantic (i.e. 'Does the word mean the same as/opposite of?'); private self-reference (i.e. 'Does the word describe you?'); and public self-referent (i.e. 'Would someone who knows you or who had just met you say that the word desctibes you?'). Following the 48 trials subjects were asked to turn over their task rating sheets and write down in any order as many of the adjectives as they could remember.

The results of the study showed that socially anxious individuals under social-evaluative threat had increased recall of words processed on the public self-referent task but no difference in recall of words processed on the private self-referent, semantic, or structural tasks in relation to non-socially anxious controls. As the authors themselves conclude, maladaptive overt behaviours of socially anxious individuals may be due to the direct effect of increased preoccupation with the evaluations by others and the fact that they may be anticipating negative evaluation from others, i.e. they may be ruminating about what others think of them. This suggestion links directly to the issues raised in previous chapters of this book concerning the public self-consciousness and self-presentational concerns of those most susceptible to the experience of embarrassment. As mentioned previously, it may well be these concerns and fears of embarrassment that are central to social anxiety.

It seems likely, then, that a number of cognitive factors play an important part in the generation and maintenance of social anxiety. Some socially anxious individuals may possess the necessary behavioural repertoire but may for a variety of reasons outlined above anticipate more negative evaluation than non-anxious individuals. While much of the foregoing discussion has centred around social anxiety, the same arguments can be applied to the experience of embarrassment. Socially anxious individuals may well experience more embarrassment, not because they behave inappropriately but because they think their performance is in some way deficient. As there were no studies which specifically tested the performance deficit (lack of knowledge) versus cognitive (lack of confidence) models with relationship to embarrassment, we devised a study directed specifically towards answering this question.

Of particular importance within the process of embarrassment is the use of remedial tactics invoked by the actor to deal with the embarrassing event (as discussed in Chapter 3). One possibility is that socially anxious individuals risk being embarrassed more frequently than their non-socially anxious counterparts because, due to behavioural deficits, they are much less adept at dealing with social predicaments. The alternative possibility suggested by the cognitive model is that socially anxious individuals underestimate parameters of their own performance and thus negatively evaluate their ability to deal with embarrassment should such a predicament occur.

C. DEALING WITH EMBARRASSING EVENTS: COGNITIVE OR BEHAVIOURAL DIFFICULTIES

In our study (Edelmann, 1985a) we tested a patient group of 20 subjects (12 female and 8 male) and a non-clinical group of 22 subjects (14 females and 8 males). On the basis of their scores on the SADS (Watson and Friend, 1969) 19 of the patient group scored within the socially anxious range and 20 of the non-clinical group scored within the non-socially anxious range.

Each subject was provided with six scenarios (see Table 8.1) each describing an embarrassing episode which happens to a central character 'P'. All the scenarios were derived from the Embarrassibility Scale described in Chapter 6. Two of the scenarios were derived from each of the three factors obtained in the study by Edelmann (1985c). Criteria for inclusion were: (1) high loading on the factor concerned; (2) the question was exclusive to one factor; and (3) the questions from each factor were dissimilar in basic content and wording. The six scenarios were stapled together in random order.

A series of five questions followed each scenario. The first four were answered on a seven-point scale (numerical end points 1 and 7). The first question asked how embarrassed the respondent would personally feel in the described situation ('not at all' to 'extremely'). The second question looked at identification with an embarrassed and hence negative target, and asked respondents how closely the person in the description resembled them. The third and fourth questions, looking more explicitly at negative self-evaluations, dealt with, respectively, the extent to which respondents would have been clear about how to react in the situation ('not at all' to 'extremely') and how well they felt they would have dealt with the situation ('not at

Table 8.1 Scenarios of embarrassing incidents and described methods of dealing with each embarrassing event.

1. P is walking through snow and ice in a public place full of people. Suddenly P slips and falls, dropping a bag of groceries which spill onto the ground. P picks himself/herself up whilst some of the onlookers start to pick up the groceries.
   There are many possible ways of dealing with the incident described above. For example P might have apologized for his/her action, but attempted to justify it in some way. Thus P might comment: 'I'm sorry, I always seem to be doing this sort of thing, I shall have to be more careful'.

2. As P enters his/her room at work all his/her colleagues begin to sing 'Happy Birthday to You', P stands in the doorway until the singing has stopped and the noise has died down.
   There are many possible ways of dealing with the incident described above. For example P might have apologized and found an excuse for not knowing what to say. Thus P might comment: 'I'm sorry, I'm totally lost for words.'

3. P enters a room containing high-back chairs and thinking he/she is alone in the room starts muttering loudly to himself/herself. Suddenly P realizes that someone is sitting in one of the chairs.
   There are many possible ways of dealing with the incident described above. For example P might apologize, but attempt to excuse his/her action in some way. Thus P might comment: 'I'm sorry, it was so dark I didn't see you.'

4. P is at a party when a fellow guest enters the room on crutches and stands next to P. P asks the fellow guest if he has had a skiing accident. The fellow guest says: 'No, I had polio as a child.'
   There are many possible ways of dealing with the incident described above. For example, P might have apologized but attempted to justify his/her remark in some way. Thus P might comment: 'I'm sorry, I expect lots of people assume you have had a skiing accident.'

5. P is a dinner guest at a relatively formal lunch. The guest sitting next to P is trying to cut some meat when the plate falls in his/her lap. P is well aware of what has happened and moves his/her chair back to help, not knowing at first whether to laugh, ignore what has happened or look away.
   There are many possible ways of dealing with the incident described above. For example, P might have apologized for his/her reaction to the incident and attempted to excuse it in some way. Thus P might have commented: 'I'm sorry, accidents do happen.'

6. P is at a party at a friend's house and decides to look around upstairs. P enters an apparently empty room, but when he/she puts on the light suprises a couple engaged in an intimate embrace.
   There are many possible ways of dealing with the incident described above. For example, P might apologize for entering the room, but attempt to justify his/her action in some way. Thus P might comment: 'I'm sorry, I always seem to be disturbing people.'

all' to 'extremely'). The fifth question was a free-response item in which respondents had to describe how they would have attempted to deal with the situation, including details of what they might have said and how they would have behaved. This question was aimed specifically at self-reported knowledge of behavioural/verbal skills for dealing with embarrassing events and was subsequently coded into the following eight responses: (1) an apology; (2) an excuse or justification; (3) an apology with an excuse or justification; (4) laughter or joking; (5) thank you for any help received; (6) an empathy response or an offer of help to others; (7) no response; and (8) other.

Following question 5, subjects turned to a second page for each scenario, where a description of a possible way of dealing with the described embarrassing episode was presented (see Table 8.1). For three of the scenarios (one for each factor), an apology/justification combination was described, whilst for the other three scenarios an apology/excuse combination was described. Following each method of dealing with embarrassment, subjects were asked two further questions rated on a seven-point scale which examined specifically the question of how subjects evaluate performance standards. These two questions dealt with respectively how 'appropriate' they thought the central character's reaction had been ('not at all' to 'extremely') and how well they thought the central character had dealt with the situation ('not at all' to 'extremely').

The results of this study were: firstly, socially anxious subjects reported that they would experience more embarrassment than non-socially anxious in the described situations; secondly, they reported being less clear about how to react and reported that they would not have dealt as well with the situation in comparison to their non-socially anxious counterparts. This result generally supports the notion that socially anxious individuals evaluate themselves negatively and overevaluate others as suggested by the literature on social anxiety referred to previously (Clark and Arkowitz, 1977; Cacioppo et al., 1979; Glass et al., 1982; O'Banion and Arkowitz, 1977). One possibility is that the clinically socially anxious experience more embarrassment in potentially embarrassing situations simply because they *believe* that they are not able to deal with the situation adequately. They fear self-presentation failure and associated negative evaluations of self, even if this self-presentation failure does not in fact occur. Because they believe they are going to perform inadequately those who are particularly susceptible to embarrassment may well overemphasize the extent to which they focus on the impression they create with others.

This possibility is emphasized by the third finding from the study, that socially anxious subjects were more likely to rate the central character as having coped well with the situation (i.e. 'Anyone would be much clearer about what to do and would do it much better than I can').

It is of interest to note that analysis of the free-response items dealing with subjects' self-reported accounts of how they might deal with each embarrassing episode showed no differences between socially anxious and non-socially anxious subjects. The average percentage responses of each code category used by both groups of subjects are presented in Table 8.2. The almost complete lack of any difference in self-reported techniques for dealing with embarrassing episodes is perhaps surprising. One possible explanation is that highly socially anxious subjects would attempt the same response as non-socially anxious subjects, but it would differ in style or quality. This possibility could obviously not be explored in the study described. It does seem to be plausible, however, in view of the studies referred to previously in which judges rated socially anxious subjects as being less skilled even if there were not actually behavioural differences between them and non-socially anxious subjects. If socially anxious subjects evaluate themselves negatively and overevaluate others, then this may lead to a rather cautious or overly self-protective performance while the behaviours themselves are not affected in overall content.

Table 8.2 Average percentage response of each category used by socially anxious and non-socially anxious subjects as a means of dealing with embarrassment.

	Socially anxious	Control
An apology	19.5	15.5
An excuse or justification	10.5	14.0
An apology with an excuse or justification	13.0	10.0
Laughter or joking	5.0	8.5
'Thank you' for any help received	22.0	21.0
An empathy response or an offer of help to others	10.5	10.0
No response	11.5	12.5
Other	8.0	8.5

A second possibility is that the skills available may be dependent upon the nature of the performance under investigation. Thus, skills for dealing with embarrassing events may be more readily available than those for dealing with, for example, heterosexual–social encounters. As mentioned, however, embarrassment or fear of embarrassment may well play an important part in many social encounters for the socially anxious individual. The skills for dealing with many or most social encounters may well be available, both to socially anxious and non-socially anxious alike. The former group, however, may well fear the negative consequences of self-presentation failure to such an extent that their negative view of themselves and their positive view of others causes them to focus on their observable behaviour. This very self-focus may then result in negative evaluations about otherwise satisfactory performances. Trower (1982) has suggested that adequate social functioning involves both attention to one's own internal state and a focus on the situational demands of the external interaction. Both social anxiety and embarrassing events appear to increase attention to one's own internal state, and in particular how this state affects the image conveyed to others.

Intervening with socially anxious subjects and/or those most susceptible to embarrassment should depend upon the deficit displayed by the individual, i.e. whether it is a behavioural/performance deficit or a cognitive/confidence deficit. It is clear that not all socially anxious subjects have behavioural deficits, and a number of studies now suggest that a variety of inappropriate cognitions may be central to social difficulties. In our own study it would seem that those subjects who believe their performance to be inadequate are more likely to focus on the impression they create on others. This involves those actors with a particular concern for their observable behaviour, with a particular desire to conform and please others (Edelmann, 1985d) and who are inhibited and overconcerned with their public image (Edelman and McCusker, 1986). These individuals have a strong concern with approval and disapproval, and are more concerned with adopting a protective self-presentational style in an attempt to avoid significant losses in social approval. This suggests that while social skills training may be effective for some socially anxious or excessively embarrassible individuals, and cognitive interventions may be effective for others, particular attention should be paid to strategies aimed at directing attention towards others and decreasing concern with one's own behaviour and its appropriateness. These issues of intervention are discussed in the final chapter. Before discussing these issues, however, another important factor needs to be evaluated. While behaviours and thoughts no doubt play an important role in the cause and/or maintenance of social anxiety and susceptibility to embarrassment, physiological responsivity is also likely to be an important factor, particularly in relation to the issue of chronic blushing.

D. BLUSHING AND PHYSIOLOGICAL ASPECTS

The few studies on physiological responses to embarrassment have been reviewed in Chapter 4, and the problems involved in these findings discussed. The information with regard to physiological arousal in social anxiety is also somewhat meagre. In one study of relevance, Borkovev et al., (1974) found that heart rate was significantly higher in heterosocially anxious males than non-heterosocially anxious males during a 3-minute social interaction. Similar elevated arousal was noted by Lang et al., (1983), who reported increased heart rate in phobic subjects when delivering a speech. This study, however, did not include a non-fearful control group. Particularly in a public-speaking situation, individuals who do not report fear when in a performance situation might still demonstrate increased cardiac response. The discriminating factor might be that they do not experience concomitant cognitive distress or label this arousal as 'anxiety', as do the socially anxious. This latter point is of particular importance in the experience of embarrassment (cognitive distress versus physiological reactions) and will be taken up later in this section.

A final study which has investigated physiological aspects of social anxiety is that by Biedel et al. (1985), outlined earlier in this chapter. During participation in three behavioural tasks, physiological reactivity was monitored continuously. Three channels were assessed: heart rate as indicated by interbeat interval, systolic and diastolic blood pressure. The results indicated that the socially anxious group demonstrated significant increases in physiological reactivity, when compared to the non-socially anxious group, during opposite-sex interaction and during an impromptu speech, but not when interacting with a person of the same sex. For the opposite-sex interactions there were significant differences between the group both for systolic blood pressure and heart rate measures. While giving an impromptu speech, the socially anxious group demonstrated significantly higher elevations on systolic blood pressure but there were no differences in diastolic blood pressure or heart rate. The authors of this article conclude that:

> The fact that interaction in the same-sex task did not elicit significant differences between the groups in arousal is an indication that social anxiety is to some extent situationally specific. Therefore, in future studies, individualized tasks will be necessary. (p. 115).

The issue of both situational and individual differences is indeed a very important one for assessment and intervention purposes, as well as for theoretical ones. It would seem, on the basis of the evidence, that socially anxious individuals are more physiologically responsive in certain situations than non-socially anxious. Although there are no studies of which the author is aware, one could speculate on a possible link between physiological reactivity and blushing (remembering that the only studies on physiological reactivity and embarrassment suggest a heart rate deceleration—see Chapter 4). The question could be 'Do socially anxious subjects blush more readily than non-socially anxious subjects?'. If this were indeed the case then blushing could well be the starting point for embarrassment or fear of embarrassment in certain subjects, i.e. 'I know that I blush in certain situations. Observers to my blushing will then assume that I am embarrassed, this causes me to focus on myself and have negative thoughts about myself causing me to be flustered and apparently lacking in social competence.' There are likely then to be certain client groups for whom intervening at the blushing stage becomes central, i.e. when blushing or fear of blushing is causal in the link between social situations and cognitive or social skills deficits. Which intervention is appropriate for which clients is discussed in the final section of this chapter, while the interventions themselves are discussed in the final chapter.

E. INTERVENTION ISSUES

The first part of this book addressed itself to the issue of self-presentational concerns and embarrassment. A key point was the fact that we have our own standards for presentation based upon assumptions of the identity image that we feel is most appropriate for us to present. They key point of the present chapter has been the fact that these self-presentational concerns may be based upon our lack of behavioural skills to convey the desired image, physiological reactivity leading us to believe that the image conveyed is inappropriate, or inappropriate thoughts leading us to believe that we will not or cannot convey the appropriate image. Fear of embarrassment, or concern with the impression that one creates for others, may thus be the result of a behavioural deficit, inappropriate cognitions or physiological reactivity (particularly in the form of blushing). The question of intervention then becomes one of whether to intervene in all systems (behavioural, cognitive, physiological) or with only one. As will be described in the next chapter, intervention has in fact taken place within each framework.

The crucial question, 'Which intervention is appropriate?', is obviously dependent upon a thorough assessment of the client's presenting difficulty. As mentioned at the beginning of this chapter, it is unlikely that a referred client will be described as suffering from 'chronic embarrassment' or even chronic blushing or self-presentational concerns. A more likely referral would describe general anxiety or perhaps social anxiety or interaction difficulties. It thus becomes crucial to ascertain the behavioural, physiological, or cognitive difficulties that the client is experiencing. A clear picture can be obtained from a thorough functional analysis (see Emmelkamp, 1982, for an excellent summary) with a number of scales and assessment measures available to back up one's judgment.

Within the past decade, the field of behavioural assessment has grown dramatically. This growth is reflected by the numerous books on this topic (e.g. Barlow, 1980; Ciminero, Adams, and Calhoun, 1977; Hersen and Bellack, 1981; Kendall and Hollon, 1981) and the interested reader is referred to these for thorough and comprehensive accounts. It is not intended to review the issues here, but to provide a summary comment.

Any comprehensive assessments should include self-report, physiological, and behavioural measures, considering that different anxiety assessment channels do not correlate highly (Martinez-Diaz and Edelstein, 1980). The importance of situational specificity in behavioural assessment has also been noted (e.g. Kazdin, 1979) and as mentioned is likely to be particularly pertinent in the case of fear of embarrassment. Moreover, within each assessment channel it seems important to include a broad range of measures. Dow, Biglen, and Glaser (1985), for example, suggest self-report measures, peer rating, laboratory social interactions, and self-monitoring of *in vivo* social behaviour.

The following are examples of assessments which have been used in a few recent studies to provide measures by which to monitor interventions.

As a starting point it is useful to gain an impression of the social activities, contacts, and situations in which the client experiences difficulty. Butler *et al.*, (1984), for example, measured the frequency of social activities and social contacts by asking clients to complete (a) a diary recording all phobic situations encountered during the 2-week period preceding each assessment, and (b) a form detailing all social contacts other than forced or casual interactions during the 7 days immediately before the assessment.

Newton, Kindness, and the McFadyen (1983) used the Social Situations Questionnaire (Trower, Bryant, and Argyle, 1978) in an attempt to measure the degree of difficulty experienced in various social situations as well as the frequency of social contacts. Many studies have also used standard questionnaires, such as the SADS (Watson and Friend, 1969), as mentioned previously.

In terms of behavioural deficits a variety of methods are available (see Curran and Monti, 1982) including assessment of role-plays, peer judgements, and observer ratings for evaluation of both verbal and nonverbal skills during interactions.

The cognitive component can be assessed via a range of questionnaires aimed at tapping the various aspects of inappropriate cognitions. The Irrational Beliefs Test and the Social Interaction Self-Statement Test are examples of assessment procedures referred to earlier in the chapter.

Finally, there is the question of assessing physiological reactivity, or the behavioural manifestation of this in the form of blushing. Physiological reactivity can obviously be measured continuously throughout participation in behavioural tasks (e.g. Biedel et al., 1985; Öst, Jerremalm and Johansson, 1981) providing a more accurate and reliable measure than patient's self-reports of arousal or blushing. As fear of blushing may form a central problem in the experience of embarrassment, however, self-reports of frequency, in addition to the antecedent events and consequences, can provide useful clinical information. In a study by Timms (1980), for example, two measures were taken in relation to blushing. Firstly, feelings in relation to situations in which the client might expect to blush; second, extent of blushing when in situations in which the client might expect to blush.

Assessment and intervention then can be directed towards the cognitive, behavioural, or physiological manifestations of embarrassment or fear of embarrassment in social encounters. Particular attention, however, needs to be directed towards a central aspect of embarrassment, i.e. a tendency to focus upon the evaluations of oneself made by others. Whether behavioural training or physiological control can provide the means for achieving this goal would seem to be doubtful. It is clear from issues discussed in this chapter that not all those with interaction difficulties are deficient in socially skilled behaviour, nor is it necessary that they are all physiologically responsive to the same degree. There does seem to be good evidence, however, for assuming a degree of self-presentational concern and a tendency towards distorted cognitions which tend not to reflect a true impression of reality. Any adequate intervention, then, must certainly take account of the cognitive component. This issue and other issues of intervention are discussed in the following chapter.

CHAPTER 9

Therapeutic Intervention

In this chapter the issue of therapeutic intervention will be discussed. The first and major part of the chapter evaluates treatment strategies based on the theoretical explanations of social anxiety discussed previously. Each explanation has given rise to a treatment strategy for the remediation of social anxiety: (1) systematic desensitization and other interventions emphasizing exposure to the anxiety-arousing situation: (2) social skills training; and (3) cognitively oriented treatments. Each method of intervention will be discussed with an evaluation of the implications for methods of dealing with embarrassment.

The second issue is centred on the social implications of embarrassment, as discussed in Chapters 3 and 7, i.e. certain situations provoke embarrassment, and due to the potentially aversive nature of experienced embarrassment, fear of embarrassment may inhibit our behaviour in certain situations. Pairing thoughts of embarrassment with undesirable behaviours can thus be used as a means of eliminating those behaviours. This issue will be discussed briefly at the end of this chapter.

A. TREATMENT OF SOCIAL ANXIETY

Barlow and Wolfe (1981), summarizing the findings of the National Institute of Mental Health–State University of New York Conference on treatment of anxiety disorders, stated:

> Exposure treatments produce the most consistent improvement particularly when applied to agoraphobia and obsessive–compulsive disorders [but] the effectiveness of psychosocial treatments with other anxiety disorders is either unknown or undemonstrated. These include a broad range of problems referred to as social anxieties or social phobias. (pp. 448–9).

While there are numerous studies evaluating various approaches to anxiety in social situations the majority of what is now a sizeable literature is directed to studies evaluating the remediation of subclinical levels of social anxiety among college students or community volunteers. As the above quote indicates, clinically significant social anxiety has received less attention. The part played by embarrassment as a major factor or possible mediator variable in this process has received no attention.

A further factor which has undoubtedly led to a dearth of clinical studies in this area is the fact that *social phobia* became an official subcategory of the anxiety disorders only with the publication of DSM-III. As mentioned in Chapter 1, according to DSM-III *social phobia* is:

> A persistent, irrational fear of, and compelling desire to avoid, situations in which the individual may be exposed to the scrutiny of others. There is also fear that the individual will behave in a manner that will be *humiliating or embarrassing*. Marked anticipatory anxiety occurs if the individual is confronted with the necessity of entering such a situation, and he or she therefore attempts to avoid it. (DSM–III, 1980, p. 227; present author's italics).

Several facets of this definition deserve some comment: first, all the components referred to previously (i.e. cognitive, behavioural and physiological) are encapsulated by this definition. Thus the irrational component presupposed a cognitive element, although obviously the extent to which a fear is irrational will be judged by the therapist in conjunction with the client. The fear that *behaviour* may be humiliating or embarrassing presupposes a behavioural deficit; and anticipatory 'anxiety' could be taken to refer to the physiological component. Obviously not all these elements are present for all clients referred to as 'socially anxious'. As discussed previously, some components may be more salient for some individuals than for others. Thus the individual with a clear skills deficit may be entirely rational in his/her fears of social encounters, as may 'physiological reactors'. In contrast the socially competent non-physiologically reactive client who fears social encounters may do so due to his/her irrational judgment concerning his/her performance in such encounters.

Second, the central part played by fear of embarrassment requires careful scrutiny. As mentioned previously, fear of embarrassment may play a central part in mediating social anxiety as a result of either a behavioural and/or cognitive deficit. One aspect of central importance is the possibility that intervention can be directed solely towards alleviating fears of embarrassment; something which all studies have singularly failed to do. This issue is raised in the latter part of this chapter.

A third factor concerns the use of the term 'phobic' in the above definition. All phobias tend to be irrational and to produce avoidance behaviour in the client (usually total avoidance). If one considers social phobia, however, there may well be clients whose fears are far from irrational (i.e. based upon a real behavioural deficit) or who do not avoid all social situations in spite of their anxiety. It may be most appropriate to consider social anxiety as a continuum from 'not anxious in social situations' through 'anxious in and *sometimes* avoids social situations' (socially anxious) to 'fearful of and *usually* avoids social situations' (social phobic). The cut-off point for seeking help for social anxiety may well be different from other phobias, i.e. well below the mid-point on the above continuum.

While social phobia/extreme social anxiety is a new category for DSM-III, its existence outside the USA has been recognized for some time. Early investigations such as those by Gelder *et al.* (1973) and Gillan and Rachman (1974) treated social phobics as part of a sample of mixed phobics (using systematic desensitization as an intervention), but did not report the results by type of phobia. Within the past 10 years, however, an increasing, but still surprisingly small, number of studies (cf. Barlow and Wolfe, 1981), have investigated treatments involving rather more homogeneous groups of social phobic/socially anxious clients. The following sections look at these studies under two broad headings—behavioural and cognitive interventions. The former encompasses the various exposure and skills training interventions based upon the classical conditioning and skills deficit paradigms including less frequently used methods such as paradoxical intention. The cognitive interventions encompass such strategies as cognitive restructuring and rational emotive therapy, based upon various facets of the cognitive paradigm outlined in the preceding chapter. As some of the most recent studies have compared the two broad approaches there is of necessity a certain amount of overlap.

1. Behavioural approaches

(a) Exposure-based methods

It follows from the classical conditioning approach that any response that was classically conditioned is potentially unconditionable through the same general process operating in reverse. Thus, if social anxiety was conditioned initially when aversive stimuli were associated with certain social settings or kinds of people it may be deconditioned by pairing the aversive stimuli with factors that elicit more positive responses. If a response that inhibits anxiety, such as relaxation, can be evoked in the presence of the stimulus that causes the person to feel anxious, the conditioned bond will be weakened (Wolpe, 1982).

There is in fact consistent evidence from research with agoraphobics that for successful treatment it is essential to encourage clients to return repeatedly to situations that they have avoided (e.g. Mathews, Gelder, and Johnston, 1981). This exposure is then supplemented by a range of factors, from training in muscle relaxation to advice about ways of coping with the symptoms of anxiety. Exposure may be graded, as in systematic desensitization, or at extreme levels as in flooding. Exposure may also be *in vivo* or in imagination.

Two descriptions of exposure methods from recent studies will serve by way of illustration. Emelkamp *et al.* (1985) describe the use of six 2½-hour group sessions of exposure *in vivo* for the treatment of twelve-socially phobic patients. During the first ½ hour of the session the patients exchanged information about the onset and development of the social phobia. In the remainder of the session, and during the other sessions, patients had to confront their feared situations in the group and in real social situations. Structured exercises included giving a speech in front of the group, keeping eye contact while standing in front of the group, and walking through the main street while looking at the pedestrians. Patients had to perform a number of difficult assignments, such as making enquiries in shops and offices, speaking to strangers, visiting bars, etc. This *in vivo* treatment was compared with the findings from 22 subjects treated by two cognitively based interventions. These results are discussed in a later section of this chapter.

In a further recent study, Heimberg *et al.* (1985) describe both imaginal and performance-based exposure in the treatment of seven socially phobic clients. In the imaginal exposure sessions subjects were asked to sit comfortably, close their eyes, and actively imagine the anxiety-provoking stimuli provided by the therapist. This consisted of a scene which involved public speaking. Each session of imaginal exposure was followed by performance-based exposure in which the imaginal session was simulated in the group setting. Cognitive restructuring was also used at a later stage of the intervention. Comparative results are discussed in a later section of this chapter.

Both the structured *in vivo* exposure of Emmelkamp *et al.* and the flooding *in vivo* and in imagination of Heimberg *et al.* differ from the graded exposure with relaxation commonly used in the earlier studies with socially anxious subjects (Shaw, 1979; Trower *et al.*, 1978b; Hall and Goldberg, 1977; Marzillier, Lambert, and Kellet, 1976) dating anxiety (Curran, 1977; Curran and Gilbert, 1975) and speech anxiety (Paul, 1968; Meichenbaum, Gilmore, and Fedoravicius, 1971).

One of the first studies to demonstrate the efficacy of systematic desensitization for reducing socially based anxieties was that by Paul (1968). He assigned highly speech-anxious subjects to one of four treatment groups, one of whom received graded exposure with relaxation, i.e. standard systematic desensitization. Compared with the other three groups who received either insight-oriented therapy, a placebo pill, or a no-treatment control, subjects receiving systematic desensitization showed the greatest improvement on all measures of anxiety (self-reports, physiological, and behavioural indices). Follow-up data also showed that the group who received systematic desensitization scored lower on measures of speech anxiety than the other two treatment groups after 2 years.

Other studies have also tended to show that for socially based anxieties exposure tends to be more effective than no-treatment controls for reducing measures of social anxiety. Perhaps of more interest are those studies comparing the relative efficacy of other established behavioural methods, and in particular social skills training for dealing with social anxiety. These will be evaluated following a brief summary of the basic skills training approach.

(b) Social skills training

The basic assumption of the skills deficit approach is that the source of anxiety in social situations is due to an inadequate or inappropriate behavioural repertoire. Thus an individual may never have learned the appropriate behaviour, or may have learned inappropriate behaviour. Given this inadequate repertoire the individual does not behave appropriately in a given situation and hence experiences aversive consequences that elicit anxiety. (As mentioned in the preceding chapter it is likely that embarrassment is one of the major aversive consequences and that fear of embarrassment may constrain social interaction.) There is generally a 'strong' or a 'weak' version of the skills deficit model. The 'strong' version tends to assume that deficiencies in appropriate social skills lead to aversive consequences that produce social anxiety. Treatment then follows a *response acquisition approach* (Bandura, 1969) and assumes that the acquisition of the appropriate behavioural repertoire leads to successful performance in social situations and hence reduces levels of anxiety. The 'weak' version assumes that individuals do in fact possess the necessary skills and only need practice in how and when to employ these skills. This *response practice approach* (Curran, 1977) further assumes that mere exposure to the feared social encounters can lead to appropriate use of social skills with the subsequent reduction of social anxiety. As will be discussed later, this latter model has led a number of writers to suggest that one reason for the effectiveness of social skills training is that it operates via a process of exposure as outlined in the preceding section (see Emmelkamp, 1982).

Social skills training has tended to follow a method described by Trower, Bryant, and Argyle (1970a). Initially a list is drawn up of the particular social difficulties experienced in particular social situations, and appropriate techniques for dealing with these situations are identified. Then the specific skills themselves are taught through demonstrations, use of role-play and feedback from videotaped recordings. The various skills identified by Trower *et al.* include observation, listening, speaking, meshing, and finally a category referred to by them as nonverbal deficits. Observational skills involve, for example, recognizing emotions from nonverbal cues. People may be both trained to recognize emotions from pictures of others, and asked to role-play the emotions themselves. Videotaped feedback may then be given to the client, giving them some idea of their success. An example of listener skills involve the use of appropriate listener responses such as head nods to indicate continued interest and attention to the other's conversation. Meshing skills refer to the way in which the participants regulate the conversation through, for example, turn-taking. The fact that a failure of meshing is one category of cause of embarrassment has been discussed in a previous chapter where the term encompassed failure, not only of turn-taking, but failure to agree on the broader roles of the participants present. Being interrupted at inappropriate junctures of the interaction can, of itself, be embarrassing. Finally, skills training procedures are used to modify what can best be described as nonverbal deficits. That is, characteristic actions or mannerisms which are inappropriate during the interaction and which can be modified via video-taped feedback.

A number of studies have evaluated the effectiveness of variants of the skills training approach in relation to socially anxious clients. As mentioned, many of these studies compared the effectiveness of social skills training with the effectiveness of systematic desensitization as referred to in the previous section.

Trower *et al.* (1978b) compared 20 patients judged to be socially unskilled with 20 patients diagnosed as socially phobic. Half the patients in each group were randomly assigned to one of two treatment conditions: social skills training or systematic desensitization. It was predicted that the socially unskilled group, in view of the fact that their skills deficit could be regarded as the cause of their problem, would respond better to the skills training treatment. The social phobics, on the other hand, in view of the fact that their skills problem was a direct result of anxiety, would respond better to the desensitization treatment. Results from a self-report questionnaire did in fact show that the socially unskilled group reported significantly less social difficulty after skills training than after desensitization; for the phobic group, however, improvement was the same whether they received skills training or desensitization. As mentioned previously, skills training may work simply through exposing clients to feared situations (i.e. in role-played and practice sessions) and hence desensitization may be implicit within the skills training approach.

In a further study, Hall and Goldberg (1977) compared the relative effectiveness of systematic desensitization and a training programme involving role-playing with feedback. Thirty socially anxious patients were assigned at random to one of the two conditions each receiving an introductory session followed by eight training sessions. In the training programme subjects viewed, role-played, and discussed a videotape demonstrating different strategies and behaviour that might be used in problem social situations. In the desensitization group, subjects were taught self-relaxation and were exposed to imaginal desensitization. Both groups showed a significant reduction in self-reported anxiety after treatment, suggesting that the possible implication of exposure in skills training as an important variable may be correct. The social skills training group also showed a significant improvement with their particular social behaviour difficulties, while the systematic desensitization group showed a significant improvement in self-reported frequency of social participation. Social skills training may thus alleviate behavioural difficulties in social situations, as well as anxiety occasioned by those situations, through exposure to the problem situation as in desensitization.

This possibility also receives some support from a study by Shaw (1979), who randomly assigned 30 social phobics to one of three treatment conditions: desensitization, flooding, or social skills training. Each patient was seen for one assessment session followed by ten weekly treatment sessions. In these sessions, treatment was geared around a hierarchy developed by the assessor. As the author states:

> Naturally in the desensitization this hierarchy was ascended, whereas in the flooding most therapeutic effort was concentrated at the top of the hierarchy. Social skills training . . . was not so closely geared to the hierarchy, instead early sessions were devoted to listening and expressive skills, followed later by role-playing situations relevant for each patient. (Shaw, 1979, p. 621).

All three forms of therapy thus involve some form of exposure to the feared situation, in addition to some form of practice within that situation. The emphasis may then differ between therapies while the content may be very similar. In fact in the study referred to above all groups of patients improved over the treatments and improvement remained constant over the follow-up period 6-months later.

Behavioural interventions for social anxiety/social phobia thus meet with some degree of success, although the mechanism by which they operate is open to some debate. A further point of relevance, referred to earlier in this chapter, is the notion of individual differences in the salience of the components of social anxiety, i.e. the physiological, behavioural, and cognitive aspects. Very often subjects are randomly assigned to treatment conditions with very little regard for the role of individual differences in anxiety–response components. In the case of a complex phobia such as social phobia, this would seem to be of particular importance in light of the part played by blushing and 'flustered' embarrassed behaviour. One study highlights the importance of noting the subjects' response patterns. Öst, Jerremalm, and Johansson (1981) classified social phobics as 'behavioural reactors' or 'physiological reactors' based on standardized scores derived from two sets of measures. The behavioural measures consisted of 17 items concerned with voice, posture, gesture, proximity, orientation, speaking, and turn-taking taken from videotape recordings of a brief interaction between the subject and one male and one female confederate. The physiological measures consisted of a continuous record of the patient's heart rate taken during the interactions with the confederates.

The 'physiological reactors' were sixteen patients with high heart rate reactions but small overt behaviour reactions, while the sixteen 'behavioural reactors' had large behavioural reactions but little or no heart-rate reactions. Eight of the initial 40 subjects assessed in the interview task had either low or high reactions in both systems, and so were excluded from the treatment study.

The two groups of sixteen subjects were then randomly assigned to two treatment groups—applied relaxation and social skills training. One treatment corresponded to the patient's response pattern (i.e. relaxation to the physiological response and social skills training to the behavioural response). This creative study highlights the need and importance of assessing social anxiety in subjective, behavioural, and physiological response systems. This can be illustrated by reference to the role of embarrassment in social anxiety. As mentioned, DSM–III refers to socially phobic individuals as those who fear that they will behave in a manner that will be humiliating or embarrassing. The question which arises is: 'What do these subjects actually fear?' Is it the fact that they react physiologically, perhaps blushing visibly? In this case the patients' fear may centre on a concern that observers will label their facial display as one of embarrassment and, as a result, evaluate them negatively. Is it the fact that they react behaviourally, perhaps not possessing the necessary behavioural repertoire? In this case the patients' fear may centre on a concern that observers will evaluate their behaviour negatively, perhaps regarding the behaviour itself as embarrassing. Finally, is it the fact that they think negatively about themsleves (in Öst et al.'s terms this might be referred to as cognitively reactive)? In this case the patients' fear may centre on the belief that everyone else is much more adequate than they are, and that their own behaviour is embarrassingly inadequate, even if this is not in fact the case. Intervention should then be tailored to meet the client's needs, highlighting the need for careful assessment. As Emmelkamp and Foa (1983) point out, the time seems ripe for investigators to stop subscribing to the myth of patient uniformity, and to systematically match treatment to a particular client's characteristics. Desensitization or applied relaxation may then be appropriate for the physiologically responsive, social skills training for the behaviourally responsive, and cognitive interventions for the cognitively responsive. The cognitive question will be dealt with in a later section. Before turning to this issue, however, one final behavioural intervention requires some comment. This involves the few studies which have attempted to tackle by behavioural means the question of blushing.

2. Treatment of chronic blushing

Three reports in the literature refer to attempts to reduce directly the occurrence of blushing 'behaviour'. Salter (1952) reports very briefly the case of a 45-year-old man complaining of chronic blushing, who was treated by using techniques designed to increase the patient's self-assertiveness. As an adjunct to this therapy, Salter instructed his patient in the deliberate expression of emotion and spontaneity as opposed to its inhibition. As Salter explained to his client:

> I want you to *deliberately* practice blushing. Tell yourself to blush at all times: when you're alone, and when you're with people. Get practice in sending logical electricity to your face instead of emotional electricity, and that will put logic in charge of blushing. It will neutralize the involuntary emotional impulses, and condition, or train, a deliberate control over your blushing. When you control it, that will be the end of it. (Salter 1952, p. 106; italics in original).

It seems that this intervention was remarkably successful, as Salter comments:

When I saw him a week later, he was a bit perplexed. 'You know' he said, 'I find that I can't blush whether I want to or not. It's the darnedest thing.' (p. 106).

This technique, by which a patient attempts to deliberately bring on symptoms, has been termed paradoxical intention. It has been developed mostly from the standpoint of existential psychiatry (Frankl, 1975). Its commonest use by behaviour therapists has been in the treatment of insomnia (Ascher and Turner, 1979), although two other studies have attempted to use similar procedures to eliminate blushing.

A more detailed account of an intervention similar to Salter's is given by Gibbs (1965). It is interesting to note that he refers to chronic blushing or symptomatic erythema as a condition that is rarely mentioned in the therapeutic literature; further commenting:

It seems likely that although patients may be embarrassed by these symptoms, they are often reluctant to seek therapeutic attention for fear that their problem will not be taken seriously. (p. 261).

This state of affairs would seem to be particularly unfortunate if the client is sufficiently aware of the blushing so that it interferes with everyday interactions with others. It may also explain why clients are unlikely to be referred due to chronic blushing or chronic embarrassment, but by the more generic and acceptable term of social anxiety.

The patient referred to by Gibbs was a 26-year-old male bank employee, whose complaint was that his blushing embarrassed him in his employment and social life. The patient's symptomatology is described by Gibbs (1969) as follows:

The symptom was first noticed by the patient as embarrassing during his employment as a chemist's assistant. Thereafter it worried him in social situations when attention was focussed on him and in informal work relationships at the bank. He did not feel particularly shy, he participated freely in social activities and felt no special embarrassment in the company of men or women. However, he was conscious of blushing when he spoke amongst a group, to customers of the bank, and to other bank officers. (p. 262).

This patient then meets the criteria stressed in the previous section. Physiological responsiveness, manifested as blushing, is of particular salience, in the absence of behavioural difficulties as indicated by the patient's self-reports. The blushing itself gives rise to cognitions relating to the way in which the client feels he is being evaluated in social situations. Whilst one could argue that the client's cognitions should be the starting point for intervention (i.e. that they are unduly negative, faulty, etc.) it could also be argued that the client's cognitions are indeed accurate (i.e. his blushing is noticed and reflected upon by those present) and thus the blushing itself becomes a central focus of intervention. The issue of whether the client's perceptions or symptoms should be the centre of intervention is, however, addressed by Gibbs (1965):

> The perceptions . . . [of social relationships] arouse autonomic activity leading to dilation of the blood vessels. The blushing exacerbates the anxiety in a secondary way since the symptom itself embarrasses the patient. (p. 263).

As suggested in Chapter 5, it would perhaps be wrong to assume that the generation of embarrassment is an either/or of situation versus reaction. Our attention is likely to alternate between the two sources of information so that cue salience becomes of paramount importance. In the case described by Gibbs, blushing seems to be the cause of concern in specific social situations; the emphasis is thus on the former rather than the latter aspect.

The therapeutic intervention used by Gibbs involved an application of Wolpe's (1958) reciprocal inhibitory techniques for altering acquired habits of unadaptive behaviour. The objective of the treatment was to extinguish the anxiety responses together with the 'secondary' symptoms of blushing. The patient was first taught to respond assertively to everyday life situations followed by instruction in Salter's 'techniques for increasing excitation', referred to above. Intervention was terminated 3 weeks after instruction in the two aspects of intervention.

Six months later the patient was sent a letter in which he was requested, amongst other details, to 'estimate his improvement or deterioration in regard to: (i) his feelings in relation to other people, and (ii) his blushing when in contact with other people'. This follow-up evaluation showed an 80 per cent improvement in feelings, and a 70 per cent improvement in blushing.

In an extention of the methodology used by Gibbs, Timms (1980) presents a case of chronic blushing using only the second part of Gibbs's intervention strategy (i.e. paradoxical intention, without the first phase of self-assertiveness training). The client reported was a 25-year-old female who estimated that she would suffer between five and ten blushing attacks a week, in which she would flush up quickly, taking up to 2 hours for the sensation to pass.

Intervention, as mentioned, concentrated on the use of paradoxical intention using instructions suggested by Salter: 'I want you to deliberately practice blushing. Tell yourself to blush at all times: when you're alone, and when you're with people' (Salter, 1952, p. 106).

The assessment procedures replicated those used by Gibbs (1965). At 6-month follow-up the client reported a 37 per cent improvement in feelings and 67 per cent improvement in blushing. As Timms (1980) concludes, 'The technique reported here provides effective treatment for the presenting problem and client satisfaction in return for a relatively low investment of clinic time.' In other words, careful assessment of the presenting problem is essential. As has been pointed out, likely referrals will be under general headings such as social anxiety or social phobia—if the salient difficulty for the client involves physiological responsivity rather than a behavioural or cognitive difficulty then clearly intervention can be effectively directed towards this area. It is worth bearing in mind, however, a warning note sounded by Salter (1952, p. 108): 'Successful results with it [i.e. paradoxical intention] may sometimes preclude deeper treatment'. Deeper treatment, in Salter's writing, refers to attempts to alter a wider behavioural repertoire. In current terms this deeper treatment might be taken to refer to cognitions. In both the Salter and Gibbs papers the client's perception of his blushing was regarded as secondary to his perception of the situation i.e. the situation was evaluated as one likely to produce a particular response (i.e. blushing), the occurrence of that response then enhanced the reaction of blushing itself. This perhaps contrasts with Timms's client, who was happy at work and enjoyed putting her ideas across to others unless the hot environment would lead to blushing. In the latter case, cognitions about blushing (i.e. 'Observers will label me as being embarrassed and perhaps think negatively about me') seem to be particularly salient; in the former two cases cognitions about both the situation (i.e. 'This is the type of situation in which I am likely to blush') and the subsequent blush (i.e. embarrassed and negatively evaluated) seem to be salient. In either case it could be argued that cognitive interventions aimed at re-evaluating perceptions of the situation and/or the response which occurs in that situation are of particular relevance.

3. Cognitive approaches

The implication of a number of cognitive factors in the experience of social anxiety has been outlined in the preceding chapter. These mirror the growth in cognitive therapies which have appeared within the past decade. Two developments in particular have been important in creating contemporary cognitive therapy. One stems from Ellis's (1962) Rational-Emotive Therapy (RET), emphasizing the need to alter the client's irrational cognitive responses; the other from Meichenbaum's emphasis on self-verbalization or Self-Instructional Training (SIT) (Meichenbaum, Gilmore, and Fedoravicius, 1971). Central concepts of both these approaches are:

> (1) Humans emit a covert, verbal 'running commentary' upon most of the behaviours in which they engage, particularly in a social context; (2) some commentaries may unhelpfully focus upon unpleasant or threatening aspects of the situation, and thus serve to disrupt behaviour, while other commentaries productively quell anxiety and facilitate the desired performance; and (3) anxious subjects, in particular, may be *trained* to abandon their anxiety-inducing reflections and emit more productive self-statements, resulting in a reduction of anxiety in other response classes (e.g. autonomic, behavioral). (Thorpe) *et al.*, 1976, p. 505).

Cognitive therapies for social anxiety, performance anxiety, or public speaking have varied, with some emphasizing an RET approach (e.g. Kanter and Goldfried, 1979; Lent, Russel, and Zamostny, 1981; Shahar and Merbaum, 1981; Heimberg *et al.*, 1985) whereas others (e.g. Hayes and Marshall, 1984) have emphasized an SIT approach.

As an example of the former RET intervention, Kanter and Goldfried (1979) state that their treatment taught the client (1) to recognize the unrealistic and self-defeating nature of thoughts that led to anxiety (e.g. 'I'm going to say something foolish to these people and they're going to think I'm really dumb'), and (2) to substitute more reasonable thoughts for the unrealistic ones (e.g. Chances are I won't say anything foolish. Even if I do, it really doesn't mean that I'm a dumb person').

As an example of the latter SIT intervention, Hayes and Marshall (1984) describe three phases of treatment. The first involved encouraging subjects to identify inappropriate thoughts (i.e. to become aware of the thoughts and verbalizations the subject emitted); the second phase involved monitoring these negative cognitions; the third phase involved the subject in changing their perceptions of how they behaved in social situations (i.e. training in self-statements that would facilitate task performance).

RET is generally assumed to give the client 'general insight' into his/her difficulties, while SIT is assumed to concentrate on instructional rehearsal. Studies comparing the effectiveness of these two components (i.e. insight versus self-instructional training) in reducing performance anxiety have produced conflicting results. Thorpe *et al.*, (1976) found that insight into irrational beliefs contributed more to cognitive restructuring than self-instructional training. The reverse result was found by Glogower, Fremouw, and McCroskey (1978).

In spite of the difficulties involved in identifying the precise mediator of change, cognitive interventions have nevertheless been successful in treating social anxiety. There are, however, few studies evaluating the relative effectiveness of cognitive versus behavioural interventions for social anxiety (Kanter and Goldfried, 1979; Butler *et al.*, 1984; Heimberg, *et al.*, 1985; Emmelkamp *et al.*, 1985).

Kanter and Goldfried (1979) compared the efficacy of rational restructuring and self-control desensitization as interventions for 68 socially anxious community residents. Each participant was assigned to one of two anxiety levels (high or moderate on the basis of scores on the SAD–Watson and Friend, 1969). The groups were then randomly assigned to one of three treatment conditions or a waiting list control. Three categories of measures were taken at three stages: before intervention, post-intervention, and at follow-up 9 weeks after the completion of therapy. The three measures were an observational measure of behavioural manifestations of interpersonal anxiety; self-report measures of interpersonal, non-social, and general anxiety; and a physiological index of anxiety.

The three interventions involved systematic rational restructuring (described earlier in this chapter), self-control desensitization, and a combination of systematic rational restructuring and self-control desensitization. Self-control desensitization involved relaxation training, imagery training, and desensitization (i.e. imaginal exposure). The findings indicated that each of the three therapeutic procedures resulted in significant decrements in anxiety at post-testing which were either maintained or improved upon at follow-up. Between-group comparisons revealed that rational restructuring was more effective than desensitization in reducing state anxiety, trait anxiety, and irrational beliefs. Rational restructuring also produced significant within-group improvement on many more variables than did desensitization. Finally, when compared to the waiting list controls, rational restructuring was also significantly more effective on a greater number of variables than was desensitization. The authors conclude that: 'The results of the present study support the relative superiority of rational restructuring in the treatment of social anxiety' (Kanter and Goldfried, 1979, p. 489).

In a further study Emmelkamp *et al.* (1985) compared the relative effectiveness of exposure *in vivo*, self-instructional training (SIT), and rational emotive therapy (RET) for 34 socially phobic patients assigned at random to the three treatment groups. Assessments involved a battery of self-reports (including the SAD and the Irrational Beliefs Test) as well as pulse rate taken pre-treatment, post-treatment, and at follow-up 1 month after the termination of treatment. Treatment in each case involved six sessions lasting 2½ hours each.

The findings indicated that, as with the Kanter and Goldfried (1976) study, each of the three therapeutic procedures resulted in a significant reduction in anxiety at post-testing that was either maintained or improved at follow-up. Only the cognitive treatments, however, resulted in significant changes in cognitions as measured by the Irrational Beliefs Test. Only exposure led to a decrease in pulse rate with the cognitive interventions leading to an increase (although these results did not reach significance). The differential effects of the therapies, with changes in dependent measures being consonant with the treatment approach, emphasize the importance of careful assessment of individual patient's needs, as outlined previously. If social skills training alters a client's behaviour, desensitization alters arousal patterns, and cognitive therapy alters patterns of thinking, then the itervention should be tailored to the particular client's characteristics. Using Öst *et al.*'s (1981) terms, 'physiological' reactors will benefit from desensitization, 'behavioural' reactors from skills training, and 'cognitive' reactors from cognitive therapy. As mentioned, Öst *et al.* suggest that this is indeed the case for the former two groups. In a further study of relevance, Shahar and Merbaum (1981) categorized 54 volunteer subjects who were high in interpersonal anxiety into strong or weak physiological reactors and autonomic perceivers. Physiological reactivity was determined by the difference in a 15-second pulse rate measure before and after hearing a tape recording of a stressful social situation. Autonomic perception was assessed by a modified version of the Mandler, Mandler, and Uviller (1958) autonomic perception questionnaire.

Subjects classified as strong reactors and strong perceivers (SS) or weak reactors and strong perceivers (WS) were randomly allocated to one of two experimental groups (Systematic Rational Restructuring or Self-Control Desensitization) or a waiting list control. Generally the SS subjects improved more with desensitization while the WS subjects improved more with rational restructuring. In terms of the part played by embarrassment in social anxiety, physiological responsiveness in the form of blushing will require a different intervention strategy to behavioural deficits in the form of flustered or inadequate behaviour, which in turn will require a different intervention to faulty cognitions in the form of over concentration on the negative aspects of oneself and the impression conveyed to others. Whether to concentrate on one intervention aimed at a particular response system or a multimodal approach is also worth considering.

Such an approach to the treatment of social phobia was used by Heimberg *et al.* (1985). Subjects were seven patients who experienced clinically significant anxiety in situations involving public speaking or heterosexual performance and who received a DSM–III diagnosis of social phobia. A range of measures were taken pre-test, post-test, and at 3- and 6-month follow-ups. Each patient (1) completed a range of self-report measures, including the SAD and the Irrational Beliefs Test; (2) was assessed on a range of behaviours scored from a 4-minute videotape recording of a simulated interview; (3) was assessed for physiological arousal by the measurement of heart rate during the behavioural simulations, and (4) completed a self-report of subjective distress taken in anticipation of the interaction.

Treatment consisted of fourteen 90-minute sessions in a number of phases. Session 1 was devoted to an introduction and explanation of treatment; the second, fifth, eighth, and eleventh sessions were spent in imaginal exposure; each session of imaginal exposure was followed by two sessions of combined performance-based exposure and cognitive restructuring.

The rationale for cognitive restructuring is of particular relevance to the current argument about the role of embarrassment in social interaction difficulties. Following the exposure simulation, each subject was asked to recall his/her thoughts. Reported cognitions fell into a relatively few homogeneous categories: (a) concern that others would detect the anxiety and evaluate him/her negatively; (b) fears of embarrassment and humiliation; and (c) negative evaluation of his/her own social performance. The issue of fear of embarrassment and evaluation of one's performance has been discussed in the previous chapter, and will be discussed in terms of our own intervention package at a later stage in this chapter.

In the Heimberg *et al.* study, subjects showed a significant reduction on all the anxiety measures (the change on the irrational beliefs scale did not reach significance), as well as demonstrating significant improvement in behavioural performance and quality of performance during the behavioural simulations. Several patients also showed a decrease in heart rate during the behavioural simulation. In spite of the fact, then, that no attempts were made to teach the patients behavioural skills, they nevertheless showed significant improvement in this aspect of their difficulty as well as in cognitive and physiological measures. As mentioned previously, social skills training may have been effective because it involved exposing the client to the feared situation; it may also have been effective because the client was allowed to develop confidence in his/her ability and hence was mediated by cognitive factors.

One final study of interest compared exposure-based treatment with cognitive and relaxation techniques for controlling anxiety responses in socially phobic outpatients (Butler *et al.*, 1984). Forty-five patients were randomly assigned to one of two treatment conditions or a waiting list control group. One treatment group received exposure and anxiety management training, the other treatment group received exposure with a nonspecific 'filler' treatment instead of anxiety management. The anxiety management consisted of helping patients to identify the early symptoms of anxiety and then to control them. The control techniques involved relaxation, distraction, and rational self-talk. While all patients learned all three techniques they were allowed to focus on the technique they found most helpful (i.e. allowing the patients to concentrate on relaxation or physiological control versus distraction, and self-talk, or cognitive control).

Patients were treated individually for seven weekly sessions, each lasting 1 hour. Two additional booster sessions were given 2 weeks and 6 weeks after the end of treatment. Assessments were conducted 2 weeks before the start of treatment, at post-treatment (after the seven weekly sessions) and at 3- and 6-month follow-up. Measures taken included the Social Avoidance and Distress Scale (SAD) and the Fear of Negative Evaluation Scale (FNE) (Watson and Friend, 1969), the frequency of social activities, and contacts assessed from diary recordings.

At the end of treatment, and at 6-month follow-up, the exposure plus anxiety management group had lower scores than the exposure group on both the SAD and FNE. The waiting list group did not change during the same interval. No patient in the exposure and anxiety management group requested further treatment within a year, whereas 40 per cent of the exposure group did so. While exposure is effective in the treatment of social phobia, it seems that anxiety management helps the client to develop skilled use of techniques for controlling anxiety symptoms. As the authors themselves conclude:

> Attention to cognitive factors may be particularly important in the treatment of social phobia because negative evaluation of social behaviour is an important part of this disorder. (p. 649).

> It seems that the natural first stage in managing anxiety is to direct attention away from anxiety provoking stimuli. (p. 659)

Social anxiety, or the fear that one will behave in a manner which is embarrassing, can then be treated from a number of perspectives:

1. exposure, relaxation, and paradoxical interventions directed specifically at reducing the physiological aspects of social anxiety (heart rate or blushing);

2. social skills training directed specifically towards providing necessary skills in order to ensure an adequate and non-embarrassing performance;
3. cognitive interventions aimed specifically at alleviating irrational or overly negative fears about the adequacy of one's performance or an overconcentration upon aspects of one's own behaviour.

As has been emphasized, the salience of physiological, behavioural, or cognitive aspects may differ from individual to individual, so that intervention obviously needs to be tailored to the needs of the client. A client who clearly lacks behavioural skills, or who blushes chronically in the absence of behavioural difficulties, may well benefit from skills training or paradoxical interventions. Anxiety in the absence of a skills deficit may also be ameliorated by exposure to the anxiety-provoking situation. It seems clear, however, that for many clients an overconcern with their own behaviour and its appropriateness plays a central part in the experience of social anxiety. It is perhaps here that fear of embarrassment becomes a crucial factor. This fear may be generated as a result of anticipated skills failure or anticipated blushing, which may or may not be based upon a realistic appraisal of behaviour or context. Ultimately, however, the fear that one may behave in a way which is humiliating or embarrassing is exacerbated by (if not caused by) an overconcentration on aspects of one's own performance. It is this tendency to chronically attend to one's own behaviour, arousal, and thoughts which seems to play a crucial part in embarrassibility, concern with blushing, and social anxiety. It is for this reason that our own intervention package concentrates on the reduction of self-attention.

B. REDUCING SELF-ATTENTION

A consistent theme in recent literature is the notice that reducing self-attention may be an effective strategy for warding off embarrassment (Fenigstein, 1979; Edelmann, 1985a,b,c). Thus strategies aimed at directing attention towards others and decreasing concern with one's own behaviour and its appropriateness should form a central component of any intervention programme.

That changing self-focus has important consequences has been demonstrated in both the experimental and clinical literature. Brockner and Hulton (1978), for example, evaluated the effect on the performance of low self-esteem subjects of directing attention away from themselves and onto the task. In this study subjects performed a task under three conditions: (1) in the presence of an audience where self-focused attention was presumably high; (2) in a control group in which attention was not manipulated; (3) with instructions to concentrate on the task diligently. In the latter condition subjects were told:

This task is not *extremely* difficult although it can be somewhat tricky. Therefore, I can't emphasize strongly enough just how important it is that you maintain your complete undivided attention on the task at all times. People who have done this experiment in the past frequently mention the importance of concentrating on the task at hand. So, just remember to keep focusing on the task as much as possible. Again, I can't emphasize this strongly enough. (Brockner and Hulton, 1978, p. 568).

When instructed in this way, subjects low in self-esteem performed better than high self-esteem subjects. As the authors point out, this finding is generally consistent with the test anxiety literature. Here, to improve the performance of the high test-anxiety subjects, a number of techniques have been introduced to direct the attention of high test-anxious subjects away from themselves and onto the task. For instance, Sarason (1958) told subjects not to worry about what they were doing, but rather to concentrate on the task so that they would find the task easier to learn. The assumption behind this instruction was that anxious self-preoccupation or self-focusing are the cognitive processes that interfere in test anxiety (Sarason, 1975, 1978). In our own study (Edelman and Hardwick, 1986) the use of relaxation and distraction as methods of coping were related to lower levels of anxiety. The former may reduce anxiety levels; the latter may reduce cognitive interference and hence enhance performance levels.

Within the test anxiety and speech anxiety literature a number of studies have followed Meichenbaum's (1972) suggestions for reducing test anxiety. Meichenbaum emphasized the need for insight into unadaptive self-verbalizations and self-instructions that the subject emitted while thinking about the speech situation. Meichenbaum (1972) offered his test-anxious subjects several subprocedures for dealing with their anxiety. This included the use of any personally generated self-statements which would facilitate their attending to the task and inhibit task-irrelevant thoughts. As mentioned in an earlier section of this chapter, applications of Meichenbaum's self-instructional training have generally produced successful results with socially anxious subjects (Emmelkamp *et al.*, 1985) and with speech-anxious subjects (Hayes and Marshall, 1984) using the techniques developed by Meichenbaum (1975) and the procedure recommended by Meichenbaum and Genest (1980).

In an extension and adaptation of these procedures we have added a specific dimension focusing particularly upon instructing subjects to focus outward on aspects of the environment rather than upon aspects of their own behaviour. As the views and reactions of others are of particular relevance to the socially anxious, we felt that redirecting attention outward towards the behaviour of others present, rather than focusing upon dimensions of their own behaviour, was particularly important. One component of the exposure-based treatment used by Emmelkamp *et al.* (1985) did in fact ask patients to complete a structured exercise which involved walking through the main street while looking at the pedestrians.

As recommended by Meichenbaum and Genest (1980) the initial therapy session is devoted to conceptualizing the problem by preparing the subjects to accept the rationale and treatment intervention. The goal of this conceptualization phase is to define the client's problems in terms of 'irrational, self-defeating and self-fulfilling thinking styles' (Meichenbaum and Genest, 1980, p. 409). An additional concept is added, however, in our own treatment which involves discussing with the client the way in which their thinking pattern is likely to specifically focus on aspects of their own behaviour. Subjects are then encouraged to consider how this particular pattern of thinking might influence behaviour and feelings. Thus, within the context of social anxiety, fear of embarrassment or chronic blushing, a client may not only believe that his/her performance is inadequate and that of others more adequate, but may also disrupt the interaction by focusing on his/her own behaviour. Subjects are asked to monitor their thoughts and feelings prior to the next session.

The second treatment session involves a continued discussion of the therapeutic rationale to consolidate points raised in the first session in the light of the clients' monitoring of their cognitions. Subjects are asked to continue monitoring their negative cognitions, but in addition are asked to pay particular attention to the behaviour of others during the course of any interactions. They are asked to pay particular attention to various elements of nonverbal behaviour, either during their own interactions with others or by observing people around them. Should a client express doubts about specific behaviours such as his/her ability to maintain eye contact, clumsiness or tendency to gesture or blush, he/she is asked to pay particular attention to these behaviours in others.

At the third session two main elements are discussed: the nature of the client's own behaviour in relation to others and strategies for dealing with anxiety which may occur. Emphasis is placed upon evaluating the extent to which clients' perceptions of their own behaviour differs from, or is similar to, their perceptions of the behaviour of others, based upon the task assignment from the second session. Clients are also encouraged to offer examples of cognitive strategies of self-statements that they could use to cope with or control their anxiety. As clients begin to pay more attention to the behaviour of others, their anxiety, which may be generated by self-attention, is likely to decrease.

The remaining sessions (generally between five and seven) consist of brief discussions of any problems or difficulties encountered by the client. In addition the client continues to monitor negative self-statements, attempts to replace them with positive coping self-statements, and continues and extends his/her monitoring of the behaviour of others. Emphasis upon negative self-statements is reduced over the sessions with increased emphasis upon attending to the reactions, behaviours of others, and ways in which these may be influenced by the client's own behaviour.

The programme is currently being evaluated in a series of single case studies; initial results are promising, but no follow-up data are yet available.

Each subject is assessed at the beginning and end of treatment on four separate self-report measures:

The Social Avoidance and Distress Scale (SAD)
The Self-Consciousness Scale (SCS)
The Self-Monitoring Scale (SMS)
The Embarrassibility Scale (ES)

The average pre-treatment scores on these scales for the first three patients in the series were:

SAD   18,
SCS   65,
SMS   13,
ES   125,

while the average post-treatment scores were:

SAD   15,
SCS   48,
SMS   13,
ES   95.

A further follow-up assessment will also be undertaken 6 months after the termination of treatment.

C. EMBARRASSMENT AS AN AVERSIVE STIMULUS

Having examined ways of helping patients overcome chronic embarrassment and/or chronic blushing we can turn our attention to the way in which the very experience of embarrassment can be used as an aversive stimulus to eliminate unwanted or undesired behaviours. As mentioned in Chapter 3, embarrassment can be viewed as a method of constraining behaviour within the bounds of social convention. The role of self-presentation concerns in influencing our behaviour and the way our behaviour is constrained by social rules and conventions has been discussed in previous chapters. The way in which we attempt to avoid behaviours or actions which could be potentially embarrassing has also been discussed. In view of the fact that anything that is unpleasant is a potential source of aversive conditioning (Wolpe, 1982, p. 267), it seems reasonable to assume that induced embarrassment should act as an aversive agent. The essence of aversion therapy is to administer an aversive (unpleasant) stimulus simultaneously with an unwanted emotional response, with the objective of inhibiting the latter and consequently diminishing its likelihood of occurrence. Most early studies employed electrical aversion or nausea-producing drugs (Rachman and Teasdale, 1968) although a number of other aversive agents including verbally suggested aversion–covert sensitization (Cautela, 1967) and rapid inhalation for smoking (Orleans *et al.*, 1981) have been used. The negative consequences of embarrassment have also been used in a number of studies to eliminate undesired behaviours and in particular deviant sexual acts.

One of the first examples of the use of embarrassment in this way is a reference by Serber (1970) to shame aversion therapy. He describes how the technique developed as an incidental result of photographing a transvestite patient cross-dressing.

> I had planned to use classical aversion therapy—to project photographed scenes of the patient cross-dressing and then administer painful electric shocks to one of his extremities. . . . He appeared to be too reluctant to begin. He said he was too embarrassed and ashamed to be observed while cross-dressing. . . . He became markedly anxious. He flushed, felt weak and had to sit down several times. He was unable to get sexually excited in the least.

The patient was subsequently asked to repeat his cross-dressing on two subsequent occasions in front of the therapist and two other mental health workers. No judgmental remarks were made and the patient was only encouraged to go on. At 1-year follow-up the patient had not cross-dressed, and denied any urge to do so. Serber (1970) reports eight other patients treated by shame aversion therapy. They included cases of transvestism, voyeruism, exhibitionism, pedophilia and frotteurism, all of at least 10 years duration. At 6-month follow-up five of the patients had remained free of their asocial behaviour. As Serber points out, a prerequisite for successful shame aversion therapy is that the patient must be ashamed of the act, and must desire not to be observed in its execution. Exhibitionists typically feel shame or guilt after acts but rarely before or during an exhibition (Schaefer, 1976). It is thus possible that embarrassment rather than shame is the essential ingredient. As the aversive content is dependant upon the observation of the event it could be surmised that the patient is embarrassed by the observation and potential evaluation of himself by the observer.

Further reports of the use of similar aversion techniques to those referred to above are given by Reitz and Keil (1971), Schaefer (1976), and Wardlaw and Miller (1978). Reitz and Keil report the treatment of an exhibitionist who was instructed to exhibit himself to nurses under controlled conditions in the therapist's office. The client experienced strong feelings of guilt, shame, and embarrassment under these conditions and requested a termination of the exhibiting requirement. Treatment was terminated, and in a follow-up 14 months later the client reported complete absence of exhibitionistic behaviour. A similar treatment was reported by Schaefer (1976). As mentioned, he noted that exhibitionists typically experience feelings of guilt and shame after, but rarely before or during, an exhibition. Wardlaw and Miller (1978) report the application of a technique based upon this assumption to three cases of exhibitionism. Treatment involved having subjects exhibit themselves at regular intervals under controlled conditions.

> Emphasis was placed upon causing the subjects to experience the feelings of shame, guilt, and embarrassment that they typically felt after an exhibition, before an attempted exhibition. (p. 27).

Subjects were instructed to make 'practice' exhibitions under controlled conditions starting immediately upon waking in the morning and occurring once every hour until retiring at night. Subjects were instructed not to perform the practice exhibitions in situations which usually set the occasion for exhibiting behaviour in the natural environment. The majority of such exhibitions thus occurred in their own home or in secluded parts of their place of work. During the exhibition the subjects were asked to imagine how stupid they felt, and in general to try and experience all the negative feelings they normally experienced after an exhibition in public. Follow-ups 4 years after treatment for two subjects and 3 years for a third, showed that none had experienced any uges to exhibit nor any actual exhibitions since termination of treatment.

As the authors themselves conclude:

> The important aspect of this procedure appears to involve causing the client to experience the feelings of shame, embarrassment etc before an instance of exhibition, rather than subsequently, as is usually the case. (Wardlaw and Miller, 1978, p. 32).

The important aspect in all the studies described, however, involves controlling the observer's reaction to the patient. In the case of Serber (1970) this involved using health workers as observers to the act, while Reitz and Keil (1971) used nurses as observers; Wardlaw and Miller asked subjects to imagine negative feelings in the presence of an imagined observer. The manipulation in each case was thus the use of an inappropriate observer (for the client's act) or an inappropriate setting. Remove the sexual connotations as perceived by the client and the act becomes socially inappropriate; the client is presenting himself in a way which is likely to be evaluated negatively by others and thus experiences acute embarrassment. The technique, as Wardlaw and Miller (1978) comment, provides a relatively quick (2–3 months) and simple method for dealing with exhibitionism.

D. SUMMARY

In this chapter the various therapeutic approaches to social anxiety and implications of this research for treating chronic blushing or fear of embarrassment have been evaluated. The need to take into account individual patient differences in determining the choice of a particular treatment strategy in clinical practice was pinpointed. Patients with high levels of

dysfunctional cognitions are most likely to benefit from cognitive interventions, while 'physiological' reactors and 'behavioural' reactors are most
likely to benefit from exposure-based or skills training programmes respectively. The possibility that social anxiety or fear of embarrassment results
from patients attending to specific aspects of their own behaviours, arousal
or thoughts suggest that the therapeutic intervention should vary to match
particular clients' concerns. Our own intervention package aims to reduce
self-attention by focusing specifically on the reactive domain of relevance to
the client. The fact that embarrassment and chronic blushing are aversive
experiences which cause distress to the clients concerned, needs to be given
greater consideration in the clinical literature. The aversive nature of embarrassment is illustrated by the fact that undesirable behaviours can be eliminated by encouraging subjects to imagine the feelings of embarrassment while
performing the behaviour.

CHAPTER 10

Concluding Comments

The main aim of this review was to draw together the various strands of research dealing with embarrassment in order to build up a comprehensive picture of a common and often dramatic experience with which nearly everyone is familiar. The review has focused upon both the multiplicity of issues which give rise to the experience of embarrassment and the impact that this experience can have upon our everyday lives. While it is clear that a number of research issues have been adequately resolved, it is also clear that there are still gaps in our knowledge, and many questions remain unanswered. The aim of this brief final chapter is to summarize the main conclusions to be drawn from this review and to highlight those areas where further research is required.

The central theme of this review is that embarrassment is a complex emotion which is made up of several components and aspects, the salience of which can vary between individuals. The experience of embarrassment necessitates the individual making appraisals of the social event and the physiological and behavioural consequences of that event. In appraising the social event, self-presentational difficulties and a concern with social rules are central issues. Embarrassment has to do with a failure to present a desired image to others whom we regard as evaluating our performance. Given that we have our own standards of presentation based upon assumptions of the identity image we feel is most appropriate in a given situation, any disrupting or discrediting event can have negative consequences. A public violation of a social rule, when we are aware of the rule and wish to behave in a manner that is prescribed by that rule, threatens our identity image and hence increases the risk of embarrassment.

The involvement of self-presentational difficulties in the experience of embarrassment seems to be well established in the literature. The implication of particular self-presentation strategies (protective and self-handicapping), discussed in Chapter 2, derives in part from research in the related areas of shyness and social anxiety, and merits further research dealing specifically with embarrassment. The involvement of social rule violation and embarrassment is also well established in the literature, although future research examining categories of rule-breaking episodes would benefit from a clearly defined classification system. As mentioned in Chapter 3, orthogonal dimensions of rules known–rules not known; intentional action–accidental action; actor responsible–observer responsible; could provide a useful starting point.

The fact that embarrassment is characterized by a fairly well defined behavioural display is also well established in the literature. Eye contact is reduced, while there is an increase in body motion, speech disturbances, and smiling. Reduced eye contact could be viewed as a behaviour that decreases contact with others and hence is disaffiliative; increased body motion and speech disturbances could be regarded as nervous responses; whilst smiling may, in some cases, be an attempt to protect one's image following a disruption of social routine. These behaviours also act as cues for recognizing embarrassment in others. While the nonverbal reaction associated with embarrassment is well established, carefully conducted studies are still required in order to evaluate the physiological response to embarrassing events. The relationship between skin temperature, heart rate, and blushing still remains to be adequately investigated. Future research in this area is of particular importance given the line of reasoning developed in Chapter 5, i.e. that feedback from facial and bodily signs of emotion plays a central part in the experience of embarrassment. The possibility that the facial flush leads directly to the experience of embarrassment seems to be supported by the evidence from clinical cases. If, as Tomkins (1981) suggests, the skin of the face is particularly important in producing feelings of affect, then blushing and embarrassment may provide a good empirical test for the facial feedback hypothesis. One would predict that the more intense the expression of embarrassment, particularly skin temperature changes associated with blushing, the more intense the subjective experience of embarrassment.

While the first part of this review investigated factors giving rise to the experience of embarrassment, the second half reviewed the way the experience of embarrassment affects our everyday lives. Chapter 6 was concerned with two central questions: 'At what ages do the components of embarrassment become salient and why?', and 'What personality characteristics are salient to the experience of embarrassment?' The set of characteristics identifying those who are more likely to be susceptible to the experience of embarrassment is well researched. This set involves an overconcern with one's public image, sensitivity to, and awareness of, the evaluations of others; with at the same time a tendency to believe that any evaluations of one's behaviour are likely to be negative. The issues with regard to developmental changes in embarrassment are not so clearly defined. While the development of goal-directed impression management, social perspective-taking and self-consciousness are clearly linked to the development of embarrassment, the nature of the age changes involved clearly remains an issue for further research. The available studies based upon parental reports or memories of past embarrassing experiences do not adequately address the complex questions involved in developmental aspects of embarrassment.

The final three chapters of this review examined the influence that fear of embarrassment can exert upon our everyday behaviour. It was argued that fear of embarrassment is a major reason why people may not give help or seek help. The studies reviewed provide ample evidence that fear of embarrassment can account for variation in help-giving and help-seeking. Of central importance to the current argument was the suggestion that any situational variables or personal characteristics which increase the relevance of self-presentational concerns and our motivation for positive self-presentation are likely to be related to an increase in the embarrassment potential of the situation. It is then this fear of embarrassment which inhibits our behaviour due to the aversive nature of experienced embarrassment. For some socially anxious people, the fear that they will behave in a way which is embarrassing may inhibit their interactions with others. While the mechanisms underlying social anxiety and the remediation of clinically significant social anxiety has received increased attention in recent years, further research is clearly required. The evaluation of treatments for social anxiety has received insufficient attention and the part played by embarrassment as a major or possible mediator variable in social anxiety, while suggested both by the DSM–III classification of social phobia and discussed in the final two chapters of this book, has received no attention from researchers. Given the present overview, perhaps this situation will be redressed in the not too distant future.

As a final comment it should perhaps be emphasized that embarrassment is not entirely negative. While fear of embarrassment may excessively inhibit our behaviour in certain circumstances, and may cause particular distress to some people, embarrassment is systematically built into our social system. What would society be like without embarrassment? Many writers have taken up Goffman's (1956) theme that embarrassment serves a social function. As he comments, 'embarrassment is not an irrational impulse breaking through socially prescribed behaviour but part of this orderly behaviour itself' (p. 273). Embarrassment can be subtle and pervasive in its constraints and pressures, perhaps acting as a homeostatic mechanism within society. Further, what would an individual be like who could not be embarrassed? Would he/she be socially uninhibited to such an extent that his/her behaviour would be seen as brash and insensitive? In Goffman's terms, 'Too little perceptiveness, too little *savoir-faire*, too little pride and considerateness, and the person ceases to be someone who can be trusted to take a hint about himself or give a hint that will save others embarrassment' (1955, p. 229).

References

Ables, B. (1972). The three wishes of latency age children, *Developmental Psychology*, **6**, 186.

Altman, L. L. (1969). *The Dream in Psychoanalysis*, International Universty Press, New York.

American Psychiatric Association (1980). *Diagnostic and Statistical Manual of Mental Disorders*, 3rd ed, American Psychiatric Association, Washington, DC.

Amies, P. L., Gelder, M. G., and Shaw, P. M. (1983). Social phobia: a comparative clinical study, *British Journal of Psychiatry*, **142**, 174–179.

Argyle, M. (1969). *Social Interaction*, Methuen, London.

Argyle, M. (1981). Social competence and mental health. In *Social Skills and Health* (eds. M. Argyle), pp. 158–187, Methuen, London.

Argyle, M., and Cook, M. (1976). *Gaze and Mutual Gaze*, Cambridge University Press, Cambridge.

Argyle, M., Furnham, A., and Graham, J. A. (1981). *Social Situations*, Cambridge Universty Press, Cambridge.

Arkin, R. M. (1981). Self-presentation styles. In *Impression Management Theory and Social Psychological Research* (ed. J. T. Tedeschi), pp. 311–333, Academic Press, New York.

Arkowitz, H., Hinton, R., Perl, J., and Himadi, W. (1978). Treatment strategies for dating anxiety in college men based on real-life practice, *The Counseling Psychologist*, **7**, 41–46.

Arkowitz, H., Lichtenstein, E., McGovern, K., and Hines, P. (1975). The behavioral assessment of social competence in males, *Behavior Therapy*, **6**, 3–13.

Armstrong, W. D. (1974). The social functions of embarrassment. Unpublished doctoral dissertation, University of Michigan.

Asch, S. E. (1956). Studies of Independence and conformity. 1: A minority of one against a unanimous majority, *Psychological Monographs*, **70** (9, Whole No. 416).

Ascher, L. M., and Turner, R. M. (1979). Controlled comparison of progressive relaxation, stimulus control and paradoxical intention therapies for insomnia, *Journal of Consulting and Clinical Psychology*, **47**, 500–508.

Asendorpf, J. (1984). Shyness, embarrassment, and self-presentation: A control theory approach. In *The Self in Anxiety, Stress, and Depression* (ed. R. Schwarzer), pp. 109–114, North Holland, Amsterdam.

Asendorpf, J. (1985). Embarrassed smiles: from lay judgment to expert coding. Paper presented at the Annual Conference of the British Psychological Society, Swansea, 1985.

Aspler, R. (1975). Effects of embarrassment on behaviour toward others, *Journal of Personality and Social Psychology*, **32**, 145–153.

Austin, J. L. (1970). *Philosophical Papers* (2nd edn.), Oxford University Press, New York.

Ausubel, D. P. (1955). Relationship between shame and guilt in the socializing process, *Psychological Review*, **62**, 378–390.

Baldwin, A. (1955). *Behavior and Development in Childhood*, Dryden, New York.

200

Baldwin, A. L., and Lervin, H. (1958). Effects of public and private success or failure, *Child Development*, **29**, 363–372.

Bandura, A. (1969). *Principles of Behavior Modification*, Holt, Rinehart and Winston, New York.

Barlow, D. H. (1980). *Behavioural Assessment of Adult Dysfunctions*, Guildford Press, New York.

Barlow, D. H., and Wolfe, B. E. (1981). Behavioral approaches to anxiety disorders: A report on the NIMH-SUNY, Albany, research conference, *Journal of Consulting and Clinical Psychology*, 3 448–454.

Baumeister, R. F., and Cooper, J. (1981). Can the public expectation of emotion cause that emotion? *Journal of Personality*, **49**, 49–59.

Bem, D. J. (1967). Self-perception: an alternative interpretation of cognitive dissonance phenomena, *Psychological Review*, **74**, 183–200.

Bem, D. J. (1972). Self-perception theory. In *Advances in Experimental Social Psychology*, vol. 6 (ed. L. Berkowitz), pp. 1–63, Academic Press, New York.

Benedek, T. (1925). Notes from the analysis of a case of erythrophobia, *International Journal of Psycho-Analysis*, **6**, 430–439.

Berglas, S., and Jones, E. E. (1978). Drug choice as a self-handicapping strategy in response to non-contingent success, *Journal of Personality and Social Psychology*, **36**, 405–417.

Bergler, E. (1944). A new approach to the therapy of erythrophobia, *Psychoanalytic Quarterly*, **13**, 43–59.

Berlyne, D. (1969). Laughter, humour and play. In *Handbook of Social Psychology*, vol. 3 (eds G. Lindzedy and E. Aronson), pp. 795–852 Addison, Wesley, New York.

Berlyne, D. E. (1972). Humor and its kin. In *The Psychology of Humor* (eds J. H. Goldstein and P. E. McGhee), pp. 43–60, Academic Press, New York.

Berscheid, E., and Walster, E. (1974). Physical attractiveness. In *Advances in Experimental Social Psychology*, vol. 7 (ed. L. Berkowitz), pp. 104–148, Academic Press, New York.

Biedel, D. C. Turner, S. M., and Dancu, C. V. (1985). Physiological, cognitive and behavioural aspects of social anxiety, *Behaviour Research and Therapy*, **23**, 109–117.

Birdwhistell, R. L. (1952). *Introduction to Kinesics: An Annotation System for Analysis of Body Motion and Gesture*, University of Louisville, Louisville, Kentucky.

Birdwhistell, R. L. (1970). *Kinesics and Context*, University of Pennsylvania Press, Philadelphia.

Blumer, D., and Benson, D. F. (1975). Personality changes with frontal and temporal lobe lesions. In *Psychiatric Aspects of Neurologic Disease* (eds D. F. Benson and D. Blumer), pp. 151–170, Grune and Stratton, New York.

Borkovec, T. D., Stone, N., O'Brien, G., and Kaloupek, D. (1974). Identification and measurement of a clinically relevant target behavior for analogue outcome research, *Behavior Therapy*, **5**, 503–513.

Briggs, S. R., Cheek, J. M., and Buss, A. H. (1980). An analysis of the self-monitoring scale, *Journal of Personality and Social Psychology*, **38**, 679–686.

Brockner, J., and Hulton, A. J. B. (1978). How to reverse the vicious cycle of low self-esteem: the importance of attentional focus, *Journal of Experimental Social Psychology*, **14**, 564–578.

Brown, B. R. (1970). Face-saving following experimentally induced embarrassment, *Journal of Experimental Social Psychology*, **6**, 255–271.

Brown, B. R., and Garland, H. (1971), The effect of incompetency, audience acquaintanceship, and anticipated evaluative feedback on face-saving behaviour, *Journal of Experimental Social Psychology*, **7**, 490–502.

Bryant, B., and Trower, P. (1974), Social difficulty in a student population, *British Journal of Educational Psychology*, **44**, 13–21.

Buck, R. W. (1980), Nonverbal behaviour and the theory of emotion: the facial feedback hypothesis, *Journal of Personality and Social Psychology*, **38**, 811–824.

Buck, R. W., and Parke, R. D. (1972). Behavioural and physiological response to the presence of a friendly or neutral person in two types of stressful situations, *Journal of Personality and Social Psychology*, **24**, 143–153.

Buck, R. W., Parke, R. D., and Buck, M. (1970), Skin conductance, heart rate, and attention to the environment in two stressful situations, *Psychonomic Science*, **18**, 95–96.

Bull, R., and Stevens, J. (1981). The effects of facial disfigurement on helping behaviour, *Italian Journal of Psychology*, **8**, 25–33.

Buss, A. H. (1980). *Self-Consciousness and Social Anxiety*, W. H. Freeman, San Francisco.

Buss, A. H., Iscoe, I., and Buss, E. H. (1979). The development of embarrassment, *Journal of Psychology*, **103**, 227–230.

Butler, G. Cullinton, A., Munby, M., Amies, P., and Gelder, M. (1984). Exposure and anxiety in the treatment of social phobia, *Journal of Consulting and Clinical Psychology*, **52**, 642–650.

Buytendijk, F. (1950). The phenomenological approach to the problem of feelings and emotions. In *Feelings and Emotions* (ed. M. I. Reymert), pp. 127–141, McGraw-Hill, New York.

Cacioppo, J. T., Glass, C. R., and Merluzzi, T. V. (1979). Self-statements and self-evaluations: a cognitive-response analysis of heterosocial anxiety, *Cognitive Therapy and Research*, **3**, 249–262.

Cannon, W. B. (1929). *Bodily Changes in Pain, Hunger, Fear and Rage*, Appleton-Century, New York.

Carver, C. S. (1979). A cybernetic model of self-attention processes, *Journal of Personality and Social Psychology*, **37**, 1251–1281.

Carver, C. S., and Scheier, M. F. (1981). *Attention and Self-Regulation: A Control-Theory Approach to Human Behavior*, Springer-Verlag, New York.

Carver, C. S., Blaney, P. H., and Scheier, M. F. (1979). Focus of attention, chronic expectancy, and responses to a feared stimulus, *Journal of Personality and Social Psychology*, **37**, 1186–1195.

Cautela, J. R. (1967). Covert sensitization, *Psychological Reports*, **20**, 459–467.

Chapman, A. J. (1983). Humor and laughter in social interaction and some implications for humor research. In *Handbook of Humor Research, Volume I: Basic Issues* (eds P. E. McGhee and J. H. Goldstein), pp. 135–157, Springer-Verlag, New York.

Cheek, J. M., and Briggs, S. R. (1982). Self-consciousness and aspects of identity, *Journal of Research in Personality*, **16**, 401–408.

Cheek, J. M., and Buss, A. H. (1981). Shyness and sociability, Journal of Personality and Social Psychology, **41**, 330–339.

Cialdini, R. B., Darby, B. L., and Vincent, J. E. (1973). Transgression and altruism: a case for hedonism, *Journal of Experimenal Social Psychology*, **9**, 502–516.

Ciminero, A. R., Adams, H. E., and Calhoun, K. S. (1977). *Handbook of Behavioral Assessment*, Wiley, New York.

Clark, J. V. and Arkowitz, H. (1975). Social anxiety and self-evaluation of interpersonal performance, *Psychological Reports*, **36**, 211–221.

Clark, R. D., and Word, L. E. (1972). Why don't bystanders help? Because of ambiguity?, *Journal of Personality and Social Psychology*, **24**, 392–400.

Clark, R. D., and Word, L. E. (1974). Where is the apathetic bystander? Situational characteristics of the emergency, *Journal of Personality and Social Psychology*, **3**, 279–287.

Colby, C. Z., Lanzetta, J. T., and Kleck, R. E. (1977). Effects of expression of pain on autonomic and pain tolerance responses to subject-controlled pain, *Psychophysiology*, **14**, 537–540.

Coleman, J. C. (1980). *The Nature of Adolescence*, Methuen, London.

Collett, P. (1977). The rules of conduct. In *Social Rules and Social Behaviour* (ed. P. Collett), Basil Blackwell, Oxford.

Cook, M. (1969). Anxiety, speech disturbances and speech rate, *British Journal of Social and Clinical Psychology*, **8**, 13–21.

Coser, L. A. (1965). The sociology of poverty, *Social Problems*, **13**, 140–148.

Crowne, D. P., and Marlowe, D. (1964). *The Approval Motive: Studies in Evaluative Dependence*, John Wiley, New York.

Curran, J. P. (1977). Skills training as an approach to the treatment of heterosexual-social anxiety: a review, *Psychological Bulletin*, **54**, 140–157.

Curran, J. P., and Gilbert, F. S. (1975). A test of the relative effectivness of a systematic desensitization program and an interpersonal skills training program with date anxious subjects, *Behavior Therapy*, **6**, 510–521.

Curran, J. P., and Monti, P. M. (1982). *Social Skills Training: A Practical Handbook for Assessment and Treatment*, Guildford Press, New York.

Curran, J. P., Miller, T. W., Zwick, W. R., Monti, P. M., and Stout, R. L. (1980a). The social inadequate patient: Incidence rates, demographic and clinical features, and hospital and posthospital functioning, *Journal of Consulting and Clinical Psychology*, **48**, 375–382.

Curran, J. P., Wallander, J. L., and Fischetti, M. (1980b). The importance of behavioural and cognitive factors in heterosexual-social anxiety, *Journal of Personality*, **48**, 285–292.

Daly, S. (1978). Behavioural correlates of social anxiety, *British Journal of Social and Clinical Psychology*, **17**, 117–120.

Dann, O. T. (1977). A case study of embarrassment, *Journal of the American Psychoanalytic Association*, **25**, 453–470.

Darley, J. M., and Latané, B. (1968). Bystander intervention in emergencies: Diffusion of responsibility, *Journal of Personality and Social Psychology*, **8**, 377–383.

Darwin, C. (1873). *The Expression of Emotion in Man and Animals*, Murray, London. Reprinted University of Chicago Press, Chicago, 1965.

Davis, M. H. (1983). Measuring individual differences in empathy: evidence for a multidimensional approach, *Journal of Personality and Social Psychology*, **44**, 113–126.

De Beauvoir, S. (1957). *The Second Sex*, Knopf, New York.

DePaulo, B. M. (1978). Accepting help from teachers—when the teachers are children, *Human Relations*, **31**, 459–474.

DePaulo, B. M., and Fisher, J. D. (1980). The cost of asking for help, *Basic and Applied Social Psychology*, **1**, 23–35.

Devinsky, O., Hafler, D. A., and Victor, J. (1982). Embarrassment as the aura of a complex partial seizure, *Neurology*, **32**, 1284–1285.

Dixon, N. F. (1980). Humor: A cognitive alternative to stress? In *Stress and Anxiety*, vol. 7 (eds I. G. Sarason and D. Spielberg), pp. 281–289, Hemisphere Publishing Corporation, Washington, DC.

Donaldson, M. (1978). *Children's Minds*, Fontana/Collins, Glasgow.

Dow, M. G., Biglan, A., and Glaser, S. R. (1985). Multimethod assessment of socially anxious and socially nonanxious women, *Behavioral Assessment*, **7**, 273–282.

Druian, P. R., and DePaulo, B. M. (1977). Asking a child for help, *Social behaviour and Personality*, **5**, 33–39.

Duval, S., and Wicklund, R. A. (1972). *A Theory of Objective Self-Awareness*, Academic Press, New York.

Edelmann, R. J. (1981a). Embarrassment in social interaction. Unpublished doctoral dissertation, University of London.

Edelmann, R. J. (1981b). Embarrassment: The state of research, *Current Psychological Reviews*, **1**, 125–138.

Edelmann, R. J. (1982). The effect of embarrassed reactions upon others, *Australian Journal of Psychology*, **34**, 359–367.

Edelmann, R. J. (1984). The process of embarrassment: self-awareness and embarrassibility. Paper presented at the 2nd European Conference on Personality, University of Bielefeld, W. Germany.

Edelmann, R. J. (1985a). Social embarrassment: an analysis of the process, *Journal of Social and Personal Relationships*, **2**, 195–213.

Edelmann, R. J. (1985b). Cross-cultural aspects of embarrassment: Preliminary report of the British sample. Paper presented at the Annual Conference of the British Psychological Society, Swansea, 1985.

Edelmann, R. J. (1985c). Embarrassment, laughter and humour. Paper presented at the Fifth International Conference on Humour at University College, Cork, Ireland, 1985.

Edelmann, R. J. (1985d). Individual differences in embarrassment: self-consciousness, self-monitoring and embarrassibility, *Personality and Individual Differences* **6**, 223–230.

Edelmann, R. J. (1985e). Dealing with embarrassing events: socially anxious and non-socially anxious groups compared, *British Journal of Clinical Psychology*, **24**, 281–288.

Edelmann, R. J., and Hampson, S. E. (1979). Changes in non-verbal behaviour during embarrassment, *British Journal of Social and Clinical Psychology*, **18**, 385–390.

Edelmann, R. J., and Hampson, S. E. (1981a). The recognition of embarrassment, *Personality and Social Psychology Bulletin*, **7**, 109–116.

Edelmann, R. J., and Hampson, S. E. (1981b). Embarrassment in dyadic interaction, *Social Behavior and Personality*, **9**, 171–177.

Edelmann, R. J., and Hardwick, S. (1986). Test anxiety, past performance and coping strategies, *Personality and Individual Differences*, **7**, 255-257.

Edelmann, R. J., and McCusker, G. (1986). Introversion, neuroticism, empathy and embarrassibility, *Personality and Individual Differences*, **7**, 133–140.

Edelmann, R. J., Childs, J. Harvey, S., Kellock, I., and Strain-Clark, C. (1984a). The effect of embarrassment on helping, *Journal of Social Psychology*, **124**, 353–354.

Edelmann, R. J., Evans, G., Pegg, I., and Tremain, M. (1983). Responses to physical stigma, *Perceptual and Motor Skills*, **37**, 294.

Edelmann, R. J., Scott, A., Scott, J., Singh, E., Trotter, R., and Wright, M. (1984b). Disablement and helping, *Psychological Reports*, **54**, 453–454.

Ekman, P., and Friesen, W. V. (1969). The repertoire of non-verbal behaviour—categories, origins, usage and coding, *Semiotica*, **1**, 49–98.

Ekman, P., and Friesen, W. V. (1972). Hand movements, *Journal of Communication*, **22**, 353–374.

Ekman, P., and Friesen, W. V. (1975). *Unmasking the Face*, Prentice Hall Inc., Englewood Cliffs, New Jersey.

Ekman, P., and Oster, O. (1982). Review of research, 1970–1980. In *Emotion in the Human Face*, 2nd edn. (ed. P. Ekman), pp. 147–173, Cambridge University Press, Cambridge.

Elkind, D. (1967). Egocentrism in adolescence, *Child Development*, **38**, 1025–1034.

Elkind, D., and Bowen, R. (1979). Imaginary audience behavior in children and adolescents, *Developmental Psychology*, **15**, 38–44.

Ellis, A. (1962). *Reason and Emotion in Psychotherapy*, Lyle-Stuart Press, New York.

Ellis, A., and Harper, R. A. (1975). *A New Guide to Rational Living*, Prentice Hall, Englewood Clifs, New Jersey.

Ellsworth, P. C., and Carlsmith, J. M. (1968). Effects of eye contact and verbal content on affective response to a dyadic interaction, *Journal of Personality and Social Psychology*, **10**, 15–20.

Ellsworth, P. C., and Tourangeau, R. (1981). Our failure to confirm what nobody ever said, *Journal of Personality and Social Psychology*, **40**, 363–367.

Ellsworth, P. C., Friedman, H. S., Perlick, D., and Hoyt, M. E. (1978). Some effects of gaze on subjects motivated to seek or to avoid social comparison, *Journal of Experimental Social Psychology*, **14**, 69–88.

Emerson, J. P. (1970). Behaviour in private places: sustaining definitions of reality in gynecological examinations. In *Recent Sociology*, No. 2: *Patterns of Communication Behavior* (ed. H. P. Dreitzel), pp. 74–97, Macmillan, New York.

Emmelkamp, P. M. G. (1982). *Phobic and Obsessive-Compulsive Disorders: Theory Research and Practice*, Plenum Press, New York.

Emmelkamp, P. M. G., and Foa, E. B. (1983). Failures are a challenge, in *Failures in Behavior Therapy* (eds P. M. G. Emmelkamp and E. B. Foa), Wiley, New York.

Emmelkamp, P. M. G., Mersch, P. P., Vissia, E., and Van der Helm, M. (1985). Social phobia: A comparative evaluation of cognitive and behavioral interventions, *Behaviour Research and Therapy*, **23**, 365–369.

English, F. (1975). Shame and social control, *Transactional Analysis Journal*, **5**, 24–28.

Exline, R. V., Gray, D., and Schuette, D. (1965). Visual behaviour in a dyad as affected by interview content and sex of respondent, *Journal of Personality and Social Psychology*, **1**, 201–209.

Eysenck, H. J. (1976). The learning model of neurosis, *Behaviour Research and Therapy*, **14**, 251–267.

Eysenck, H. J., and Eysenck, S. B. G. (1975). *The Manual of the Eysenck Personality Questionnaire*, Hodder and Stoughton, London.

Farrell, A. D., Mariotto, M. J., Conger, A. J., Curran, J. P., and Wallander, J. L. (1979). Self-ratings and judges' ratings of heterosexual social anxiety and skill: a generalizability study, *Journal of Consulting and Clinical Psychology*, **43**, 522–527.

Feldman, S. (1941). On blushing, *Psychiatric Quarterly*, **15**, 249–261.

Fenichel, O. (1945). *The Psychoanalytic Theory of Neurosis*, Norton, New York.

Fenigstein, A. (1979). Self-consciousness, self-attention, and social interaction, *Journal of Personality and Social Psychology*, **37**, 75–86.

Fenigstein, A., Scheier, M. F., and Buss, A. H. (1975). Public and private self-consciousness: assessment and theory, *Journal of Consulting and Clinical Psychology*, **43**, 522–527.

Fink, E L. (1975). An empirical analysis of vicarious embarrassment: a study of social interaction and emotion. Unpublished doctoral dissertation, University of Wisconsin.

Fink, E. L., and Walker, B.A. (1977). Humorous responses to embarrassment, *Psychological Reports*, **40**, 475–485.

Fish, B., Karabenick, S. A., and Heath, M. (1978). The effects of observation on emotional arousal and affiliation, *Journal of Experimental Social Psychology*, **14**, 256–265.

Fisher, J. D., and Nadler, A. (1976). Effect of donor resources on recipient self-esteem and self-help, *Journal of Experimental Social Psychology*, **12**, 139–150.

Fisher, J. D., DePaulo, B. M., and Nadler, A. (1981). Extending altruism beyond the altruistic act: the mixed effects of aid on the help recipient. In *Altruism and*

Helping Behavior: Social, Personality and Developmental Perspectives (eds J. P. Rushton and R. M. Sorrento), pp. 367–422, Lawrence Erlbaum and Associates, Hillsdale, New Jersey.

Fisher, J. D., Nadler, A., and Witcher-Alagna, S. (1981). Recipient reactions to aid, *Psychological Bulletin*, **91**, 27–54.

Flavell, J. H., Botkin, P., Fry, C., Wright, J., and Jarvis, P. (1968). *The Development of Role-Taking and Communication Skills in Children*, John Wiley, New York.

Frankl, V. E. (1975). Paradoxical intention and dereflection, *Psychotherapy: Theory, Research and Practice*, **14**, 520–530.

Freud, S. (1900). *The Interpretation of Dreams, Standard Ed. 4 & 5*, Hogarth Press, London, 1953.

Furnham, A., and Capon, M. (1983). Social skills and self-monitoring processes, *Personality and Individual Differences*, **4**, 171–178.

Gabrenya, W. K., and Arkin, R. M. (1980). Self-monitoring scale: factor structure and correlates, *Personality and Social Psychology Bulletin*, **6**, 13–22.

Garfinkel, H. (1963). Trust and stable actions. In *Motivation and Social Interaction* (ed. O. J. Harvey), pp. 187–238, Ronald, New York.

Garland, H., and Brown, B. R. (1972). Face-saving as affected by subjects' sex, audiences' sex and audience expertise, *Sociometry*, **35**, 280–289.

Gelder, M. G., Bancroft, J. H. J., Gath, D. J., Johnston, D. W., Mathews, A. M., and Shaw, P. M. (1973). Specific and non-specific factors in behaviour therapy, *British Journal of Psychiatry*, **123**, 445–462.

Gibbs, D. N. (1965). Reciprocal inhibition therapy of a case of symptomatic erythema, *Behaviour Research and Therapy*, **2**, 261–266.

Gillan, P., and Rachman, S. (1974). An experimental investigation of desensitization in phobic patients, *British Journal of Psychiatry*, **124**, 392–401.

Ginsburg, G. P., Argyle, M. Forgas, J. P., and Holtgreaves, T. (1981). Reactions to rule-breaking. In *Social Situations* (eds M. Argyle, A. Furnham, and J. A. Graham), pp. 156–163, Cambridge University Press, Cambridge.

Glasgow, R. E., and Arkowitz, H. (1975). The behavioral assessment of male and female social competence in dyadic heterosexual interactions, *Behavior Therapy*, **6**, 488–498.

Glass, C. R., Merluzzi, T. V., Biever, J. L., and Larsen, K. H. (1982). Cognitive assessment of social anxiety: Development and validation of a self-statement questionnaire, *Cognitive Therapy and Research*, **6**, 37–55.

Glogower, F., Fremouw, W. J., McCroskey, J. C. (1978). A component analysis of cognitive restructuring, *Cognitive Therapy and Research*, **2**, 209–223.

Goffman, E. (1955). On face-work, *Psychiatry*, **18**, 213–231.

Goffman, E. (1956). Embarrassment and social organisation, *American Journal of Sociology*, **62**, 264–271.

Goffman, E. (1959). *Presentation of Self in Everyday Life*, Doubleday, New York.

Goffman, E. (1963). *Stigma*, Free Press, Englewood Cliffs, New Jersey.

Goffman, E. (1971). *Relations in Public*. Basic Books, New York.

Goldstein, A. J., and Chambless, D. J. (1978). A reanalysis of agoraphobia, *Behavior Therapy*, **9**, 47–59.

Gordon, J. E. (1963). *Personality and Behaviour*, Macmillan, New York.

Gough, H. G. (1969). *Manual for the California Psychological Inventory* (Revised edn), Consulting Psychologists Press, Palo Alto, Calif.

Greenberg, D., and Stravynski, A. (1985). Patients who complain of social dysfunction as their main problem: 1. Clinical and demographic features, *Canadian Journal of Psychiatry*, **30**, 206–211.

Greenberg, M. S. (1980). A theory of indebtedness. In *Social Exchange: Advances in Theory and Research* (eds K. J. Gergen, M. S. Greenberg, and R. H. Willis), pp. 3–26, Wiley, New York.

Greenley, J. R., and Mechanic, D. (1976). Patterns of seeking care for psychological problems. In *The Growth of Bureaucratic Medicine* (ed. D. Mechanic), Wiley, New York.

Greif, E. B., and Hogan, R. (1973). The theory and measurement of empathy, *Journal of Counseling Psychology*, **20**, 280–284.

Gross, A. E., Fisher, J. D., Nadler, A., Stiglitz, E., and Craig, C. (1979). Initiating contact with a woman's counselling service: Some correlates of help utilization, *Journal of Community Psychology*, **7**, 42–49.

Gross, E., and Stone, S. P. (1964). Embarrassment and the analysis of role requirements, *American Journal of Sociology*, **70**, 1–15.

Gutheil, E. (1939). *The Language of the Dream*, Macmillan, New York.

Hager, J. C., and Ekman, P. (1981). Methodological problems in Tourangeau and Ellsworth's study of facial expression and experience of emotion, *Journal of Personality and Social Psychology*, **40**, 358–362.

Halford, K., and Foddy, M. (1982). Cognitive and social correlates of social anxiety, *British Journal of Clinical Psychology*, **21**, 17–28.

Hall, R., and Goldberg, D. (1977). The role of social anxiety in social interaction difficulties, *British Journal of Psychiatry*, **131**, 610–615.

Harris, M. B., and Meyer, F. W. (1973). Dependency, threat and helping, *Journal of Social Psychology*, **90**, 239–242.

Hayes, B. J., and Marshall, W. L. (1984). Generalization of treatment effects in training public speakers, *Behaviour Research and Therapy*, **22**, 519–533.

Heider, F. (1958). *The Psychology of Interpersonal Relations*, Wiley, New York.

Heimberg, R. G., Becker, R. E., Goldfinger, K., and Vermilyea, B. A. (1985). Treatment of social phobia by exposure, cognitive restructuring and homework assignments, *The Journal of Nervous and Mental Disease*, **173**, 236–245.

Hellpach, W. (1913). Vom Ausdruck der Verlegenbheit, *Archives of General Psychology*, **27**, 1–62.

Herold, E. S. (1981). Contraceptive embarrassment and contraceptive behaviour among young single women, *Journal of Youth and Adolescence*, **10**, 233–242.

Hersen, M., and Bellack, A. S. (1981). *Behavioral Assessment. A practical handbook*, 2nd edn., Pergamon Press, New York.

Hitschmann, E. (1943). Neurotic bashfulness and erythrophobia, *Psychoanalytic Review*, **30**, 438–446.

Hodges, W. F., and Felling, J. P. (1970). Types of stressful situations and their relation to trait anxiety and sex, *Journal of Consulting and Clinical Psychology*, **34**, 333–337.

Hogan, R. (1969). Development of an empathy scale, *Journal of Consulting and Clinical Psychology*, **33**, 307–316.

Horowitz, E. (1962). Reported embarrassment memories of elementary school, high school, and college students, *Journal of Social Psychology*, **56**, 317–325.

Hull, J. G., and Levy, A. S. (1979). The organizational functions of the self: an altenative to the Duval and Wicklund model of self-awareness, *Journal of Personality and Social Psychology*, **37**, 756–768.

Izard, C. E. (1971). *The Face of Emotion*, Appleton-Century-Crofts, New York.

Izard, C. E. (1977). *Human Emotions*, Plenum, New York.

Izard, C. E. (1981). Differential emotions theory and facial feedback hypothesis of emotion activation: comments on Tourangeau and Ellsworth's 'The role of facial response in the experience of emotion', *Journal of Personality and Social Psychology*, **40**, 350–354.

Jackson, M. J., and Latané, B. (1981). All alone in front of all thoese people: stage fright as a function of number and type of co-performers and audience, *Journal of Personality and Social Psychology*, **40**, 73–85.

James, W. (1884). What is an emotion?', in *The Nature of Emotion* (ed. M. Arnold), pp. 17–36 Penguin, Harmondsworth, 1968.

Johnson, J. A., Cheek, J. M., and Smither, R. (1983). The structure of empathy, *Journal of Personality and Social Psychology*, **45**, 1299–1312.

Jones, E. E., and Berglas, S. (1978). Control of attributions about the self through self-handicapping strategies: the appeal of alcohol and the role of underachievement, *Personality and Social Psychology Bulletin*, **4**, 200–206.

Jones, E. E., and Gerard, H. B. (1967). *Foundations of Social Psychology*, Wiley, New York.

Jones, E. E., and Pittman, T. S. (1982). Toward a general theory of strategic self-presentation. In *Psychological Perspectives on the Self*, vol. 1 (ed. J. Suls), pp. 231–262, Lawrence Erlbaum Associates, Hillsdale, New Jersey.

Jones, W. H., and Russell, W. D. (1982). The social reticence scale: a measure of shyness, *Journal of Personality Assessment*, **46**, 629–631.

Kami, A. G., and McOsker, T. G. (1982). Attention and stuttering: do stutterers think too much about speech?, *Journal of Fluency Disorders*, **7**, 309–321.

Kane, T. R., Suls, J., and Tedeschi, J. T. (1977). Humour as a tool of social interaction. In *It's a Funny Thing Humour* (eds A. J. Chapman and H. Foot), pp. 13–16, Pergamon Press, Oxford.

Kanter, N. J., and Goldfried, M. R. (1979). Relative effectiveness of rational restructuring and self-control desensitization in the reduction of interpersonal anxiety, *Behavior Therapy*, **10**, 472–490.

Karch, F. E. (1971). Blushing, *Psychoanalytic Review*, **58**, 37–50.

Kazdin, A. E., (1979). Situational specificity. The two-edged sword of behavioral assessment, *Behavioral Assessment*, **1**, 57–75.

Kendall, P. C., and Hollon, S. D. (eds) (1981). *Assessment Strategies for Cognitive-Behavioral Assessment*, Academic Press, New York.

Kendall, P. C., Finch, A. J., and Montgomery, L. E. (1978). Vicarious anxiety: a systematic evaluation of vicarious threat to self-esteem, *Journal of Consulting and Clinical Psychology*, **5**, 997–1008.

Kleck, R., Ono, H., and Hasdorf, A. (1966). The effects of physical deviance on face to face interaction, *Human Relatins*, **19**, 425–436.

Kleck, R. E., Vaughan, R. C. Cartwright-Smith, J., Vaughan, K. B., Colby, C. Z., and Lanzetta, J. T. (1976). Effects of being observed on expressive, subjective, and physiological responses to painful stimuli, *Journal of Personality and Social Psychology*, **34**, 1211–1218.

Konecni, V. J. (1972). Some effects of guilt on compliance: a field study, *Journal of Personality and Social Psychology*, **23**, 30–32.

Kraut, R. E. (1982). Social presence, facial feedback, and emotion, *Journal of Personality and Social Psychology*, **42**, 853–863.

Krout, M. H. (1954). An experimental attempt to a produce unconscious manual symbolic movements, *Journal of General Psychology*, **51**, 93–120.

Lacey, J. I. (1959). Psychophysiological approaches to the evaluation of psychotherapeutic process and outcome. In *Research in Psychotherapy*, Vol. 1 (eds E. Rubenstein and Mr. Parloff), pp. 161–196, American Psychological Association, Washington, DC.

Lacey, J. I., Kagan, J., Lacey, B. C., and Moss, H. A. (1963). The visceral level: Situational determinants and behavioural correlates of autonomic response. In *Expressions of Emotions in Man* (ed. P. Knapp), pp. 160–208, International University Press, New York.

Laird, J. D. (1974). Self-attribution of emotion: the effects of expressive behaviour on the quality of emotional experience, *Journal of Personality and Social Psychology*, **29**, 475–486.

Laird, J. D. (1984). The role of facial response in the experience of emotion: a reply to Tourangeau and Ellsworth, and others, *Journal of Personality and Social Psychology*, **47**, 909–917.

Lang, P. J., Levin, D. N., Miller, G. A., and Kozak, M. (1983). Fear behavior, fear imagery, and the psychophysiology of emotion: the problem of affective response intergration, *Journal of Abnormal Psychology*, **92**, 276–306.

Lanzetta, J. T., Biernat, J. J., and Kleck, R. E. (1982). Self-focused attention, facial behaviour, autonomic arousal and the experience of emotion, *Motivation and Emotion*, **6**, 49–63.

Lanzetta, J. T., Cartwright-Smith, J., and Kleck, R. E. (1976). Effects of nonverbal dissimulation on emotional experience and autonomic arousal, *Journal of Personality and Social Psychology*, **33**, 354–370.

Latané, B. (1981). The psychology of social impact, *American Psychologist*, **36**, 343–356.

Latané, B., and Darley, J. (1968). Group inhibition of bystander interventions in emergencies, *Journal of Personality and Social Psychology*, **10**, 215–221.

Latańe, B., and Darley, J. (1970). *The Unresponsive Bystander: Why Doesn't He Help?* Appleton-Century-Crofts, New York.

Latańe, B., and Harkins, S. (1976). Cross-modality matches suggest anticipated stage fright: A multiplicative power function of audience size and status, *Perception and Psychophysics*, **20**, 482–488.

Latańe, B., and Nida, S. (1981). Ten years of research on group size and helping, *Psychological Bulletin*, **89**, 308–324.

Latańe, B., and Rodin, J. (1969). A lady in distress: inhibiting effects of friends and strangers on bystander intervention, *Journal of Experimental Social Psychology*, **5**, 189–202.

Leary, M. R. (1982). Social anxiety. In *Review of Personality and Social Psychology*, vol. 3 (ed. L. Wheeler), pp. 97–120, Sage, Beverley Hills, California.

Leary, M. R. (1983a). *Understanding Social Anxiety*, Sage: Beverley Hills, California.

Leary, M. R. (1983b). Social anxiousness: the construct and its measurement, *Journal of Personality Assessment*, **47**, 66–75.

Leary, M. R., and Schlenker, B. R. (1981). The social psychology of shyness: a self-presentational model. In *Impression Management Theory and Social Psychological Research* (ed. J. T. Tedeschi), pp. 335–358, Academic Press, New York.

Lent, R. W., Russell, R. K., and Zamostny, K. P. (1981). Comparison of cue-controlled desensitization, rational restructuring, and a credible placebo in the treatment of speech anxiety, *Journal of Consulting and Clinical Psychology*, **49**, 608–610.

Leventhal, H. (1979). A perceptual-motor processing model of emotion. In *Advances in the Study of Communication and Effect*, vol. 5: *Perceptions of Emotions in Self and Others* (eds P. Pliner, K. R. Blankstein, and I. M. Spigel), pp. 1–46, Plenum Press, New York.

Leventhal, H. (1980). Toward a comprehensive theory of emotion. In *Advances in Experimental Social Psychology*, vol. 13 (ed. L. Berkowitz), pp. 139–207, Academic Press, New York.

Leventhal, H., and Mosbach, P. A. (1983). The perceptual-motor theory of emotion. In *Social Psychophysiology: A Sourcebook* (eds J. T. Cacioppo and R. E. Petty), pp. 353–387. Guildford Press, New York.

Levin, J., and Arluke, A. (1982). Embarrassment and helping behavior, *Psychological Reports*, **51**, 999–1002.

Lieberman, M. A., and Mullan, J. T. (1978). Does help help? The adaptive consequences of obtaining help from professionals and social networks, *American Journal of Community Psychology*, **6**, 499–517.

Lowy, S. (1942). *Psychological and Biological Foundations of Dream Interpretation*, Stechert, New York.

Lynd, H. (1958). *On Shame and the Search for Identity*, Harcourt Brace, New York.

McCroskey, J. C. (1977). Oral communication apprehension: a summary of recent theory and research, *Human Communication Research*, **4**, 78–96.

McEwan, K. L., and Devins, G. M. (1983). Is increased arousal in social anxiety noticed by others?, *Journal of Abnormal Psychology*, **92**, 417–421.

Magnusson, D., and Ekehammar, B. (1975). Anxiety profiles based on both situational and response factors, *Multivariate Behavior Research*, **10**, 27–43.

Mandler, G. (1975). *Mind and Emotion*, Wiley, New York.

Mandler, G., Mandler, J. M., and Uvillier, E. T. (1958). Autonomic feedback: the perception of autonomic activity, *Journal of Abnormal and Social Psychology*, **86**, 367–373.

Manstead, A. S. R., and Semin, G. R. (1981). Social transgressions, social perspectives, and social emotionality, *Motivation and Emotion*, **5**, 249–261.

Marks, I. B. (1970). The classification of phobic disorders, *British Journal of Psychiatry*, **116**, 377–386.

Martin, R. A., and Lefcourt, H. M. (1983). Sense of humor as a moderator of the relationship between stressors and mood, *Journal of Personality and Social Psychology*, **45**, 1313–1324.

Martinez-Diaz, J. A., and Edelstein, B. A. (1980). Heterosocial competence: Predictive and construct validity, *Behavior Modification*, **4**, 115–129.

Marzillier, J. S., Lambert, C., and Kellet, J. A. (1976). A controlled evaluation of systematic desensitization and social skills training for socially inadequate psychiatric patients, *Behaviour Research and Therapy*, **14**, 225–238.

Mathews, A. M., Gelder, M. G., and Johnston, D. W. (1981). *Agoraphobia*, Guildford Press, New York.

Mavissakalian, M. (1983). Agoraphobia: the problem of treatment, *Behavior Therapist*, **5**, 173–175.

Mechanic, D. (1976). *The Growth of Bureaucratic Medicine*, Wiley, New York.

Meichenbaum, D. H. (1972). Cognitive modification of test anxious college students, *Journal of Consulting and Clinical Psychology*, **39**, 370–380.

Meichenbaum, D. (1975). Self-instructional methods. In *Helping People Change: A Textbook of Methods* (eds F. H. Kanfer and A. P. Goldstein), pp. 399–422, Pergamon Press, New York.

Meichenbaum, D. (1977). *Cognitive-Behavior Modification: An Integrative Approach*, Plenum Press, New York.

Meichenbaum, D., and Genest, M. (1980). Cognitive behavior modification: an integration of cognitive and behavioral methods. In *Helping People Change: A Textbook of Methods*, 2nd ed (eds, F. Kanfer and A. Goldstein), Pergamon Press, New York.

Meichenbaum, D. H., Gilmore, J. B., and Fedoravicius, A. (1971). Group insight versus group desensitization in treating speech anxiety, *Journal of Consulting and Clinical Psychology*, **36**, 410–421.

Milgram, S. (1965). Some conditions of obedience and disobedience to authority, *Human Relations*, **18**, 57–76.

Milgram, S. (1974). *Obedience to Authority*, Harper and Row, New York.

Modigliani, A. (1966). Embarrassment and social influence. Unpublished doctoral dissertation, University of Michigan, Ann Arbor, Mich.

Modigliani, A. (1968). Embarrassment and embarrassibility, *Sociometry*, **31**, 313–326.

Modigliani, A. (1971). Embarrassment, facework, and eye contact: testing a theory of embarrassment, *Journal of Personality and Social Psychology*, **17**, 15–24.

Modigliani, A., and Blumenfeld, R. (1979). A developmental study of embarrassment and self-presentation. Unpublished research proposal.

Mowrer, O. H. (1950). *Learning Theory and Personality Dynamics*, Arnold Press, New York.

Nadler, A. (1980). 'Good looks do not help': effects of helper's physical attractiveness and expectations for future interaction on help-seeking behavior, *Personality and Social Psychology Bulletin*, **6**, 378–383.

Nadler, A. (1983)., in *New Directions in Helping*, vol. 2: *Help Seeking* (eds B. DePaulo, A. Nadler, and J. D. Fisher), Academic Press, New York.

Nadler, A., and Porat, I. (1978). Names do not help: effects of anonymity and locus of need attribution on help seeking behavior, *Personality and Social Psychology Bulletin*, **4**, 624–626.

Nadler, A., Fisher, J. D., and Streufret, S. (1976). When helping hurts: effects of donor recipient similarity and recipient self-esteem on reactions to aid, *Journal of Personality*, **44**, 392–409.

Nadler, A., Shapira, R., and Ben-Itzhak, S. (1982). Good looks may help: effects of helper's physical attractiveness and sex of helper on males' and females' help-seeking behavior, *Journal of Personality and Social Psychology*, **42**, 90–99.

Newton, A., Kindness, K., and McFadyen, M. (1983). Patients and social skills groups: do they lack social skills? *Behavioural Psychotherapy*, **11**, 116–126.

Nichols, K. A. (1974). Severe social anxiety, *British Journal of Medical Psychology*, **74**, 301–306.

O'Banion, K., and Arkowitz, H. (1977). Social anxiety and selective memory for affective information about the self, *Social Behavior and Personality*, **5**, 321–328.

Orleans, C. T., Shipley, R. H., Williams, C., and Haac, L. A. (1981). Behavioral approaches to smoking cessation. I. A decade of progress 1969–1979, *Journal of Behavior Therapy and Experimental Psychiatry*, **12**, 125–137.

Öst, L-G., Jerremalm, A., and Johansson, J. (1981). Individual response patterns and the effects of different behavioral methods in the treatment of social phobia, *Behavior Research and Therapy*, **19**, 1–16.

Pasquarelli, B., and Bull, N. (1951). Experimental investigation of the body-mind continuum in affective states, *Journal of Nervous and Mental Diseases*, **113**, 512–521.

Paul, G. L. (1968). Two-year follow-up of systematic desensitization in therapy groups, *Journal of Abnormal Psychology*, **73**, 119–130.

Pavio, A., and Lambert, W. E. (1959). Measures and correlates of audience anxiety ('stage fright'), *Journal of Personality*, **27**, 1–17.

Perlman, R. (1975). *Consumers and Social Services*, Wiley, New York.

Phillips, G. M., and Metzger, N. J. (1973). The reticient syndrome: some theoretical considerations about etiology and treatment, *Speech Monographs*, **40**, 220–230.

Piliavin, I. M., Piliavin, J. A., and Rodin, J. (1975). Costs, diffusion, and the stigmatized victim, *Journal of Personality and Social Psychology*, **32**, 429–438.

Pilkonis, P. A. (1977). Shyness, public and private, and its relationship to other measures of social behavior, *Journal of Personality*, **45**, 585–595.

Plutchic, R. (1980). *Emotion: A Psychoevolutionary Synthesis*, Harper and Row, New York.

Plutchic, R. (1984). Emotions: a general psychoevolutionary theory. In *Approaches to Emotion* (eds K. R. Scherer and P. Ekman), pp. 197–219, Lawrence Erlbaum Associates, Hillsdale, Jew Jersey.

Pomazal, R. J., and Clore, G. L. (1973). Helping on the highway: the effects of dependency and sex, *Journal of Applied Social Psychology*, **3**, 150–164.

Rachman, S., and Teasdale, J. D. (1968). Aversion therapy. In *Assessment and Status of the Behavior Therapies and Associated Developments* (ed. K. M. Franks), McGraw-Hill, New York.

Rehm, L. P., and Marston, A. R. (1968). Reduction of social anxiety through modification of self-reinforcement: an instigation therapy technique, *Journal of Consulting and Clinical Psychology*, **32**, 565–574.

Reitz, W. E., and Keil, W. E. (1971). Behavioral treatment of an exhibitionist, *Journal of Behavior Therapy and Experimental Psychiatry*, **2**, 67–69.

Richardson, F. C., and Tasto, D. L. (1976). Development and factor analysis of a social anxiety inventory, *Behavior Therapy*, **7**, 453–462.

Robinson, V. M. (1983). Humor and health. In *Handbook of Humor Research, vol. 2: Applied Studies* (eds, P. E. McGhee and J. H. Goldstein), pp. 109–128, Springer-Verlag, New York.

Ross, A. S., and Braband, J. (1973). Effect of increased responsibility on bystander intervention: II. The cue value of a blind person, *Journal of Personality and Social Psychology*, **25**, 254–258.

Rothbart, M. K. (1976). Incongruity, problem-solving and laughter. In *Humour and Laughter: Theory, Research and Applications* (eds A. J. Chapman and H. C. Foot), pp. 37–54, John Wiley & Sons, London.

Rutledge, L. L., and Hupka, B. B. (1985). The facial feedback hypothesis: methodological concerns and new supporting evidence, *Motivation and Emotion*, **9**, 219–240.

Salter, A. (1952). *Conditioned Reflex Therapy*, Allen and Unwin, London.

Samerotte, G. C., and Harris, M. B. (1976). Some factors influencing helping: the effects of a handicap, responsibility, and requesting help, *Journal of Social Psychology*, **98**, 39–45.

Sarason, I. (1958). The effects of anxiety, reassurance, and meaningfulness of material to be learned in verbal learning, *Journal of Experimental Psychology*, **56**, 472–477.

Sarason, I. G. (1975). Anxiety and self-preoccupation, in *Stress and Anxiety*, vol. 2 (eds I. G. Sarason and C. D. Spielberger), pp. 165–186, Hemisphere Publishing (Wiley), Washington, D. C.

Sarason, I. G. (1978). The test anxiety scale: concept and research. In *Stress and Anxiety*, vol. 5 (eds C. D. Speilberger and I. G. Sarason), pp. 193–215, Halsted-Wiley, New York.

Sarnoff, I., and Zimbardo, P. (1961). Anxiety, fear and social affiliation, *Journal of Abnormal and Social Psychology*, **62**, 356–366.

Sartre, J. P. (1956). *Being and Nothingness*, Philosophical Library, New York.

Sattler, J. (1965). A theoretical development and clinical investigation of embarrassment, *Genetic Psychology Monographs*, **71**, 19–59.

Sattler, J. (1966). Embarrassment and blushing: a theoretical review, *Journal of Social Psychology*, **69**, 117–133.

Saul, L. J. (1966). Embarrassment dreams of nakedness, *International Journal of Psychoanalysis*, **47**, 552–558.

Schachter, S. (1964). The interaction of cognitive and physiological determinants of emotional state. In *Advances in Experimental Social Psychology*, vol. 1 (ed. L. Berkowitz), pp. 49–80, Academic Press, New York.

Schachter, S., and Singer, J. E. (1962). Cognitive, social and physiological determinants of emotional state, *Psychological Review*, **69**, 379–399.

Schaefer, H. H. (1976). Stimulus generalization treatment for exhibitionism. In *Behavioral Counselling: Cases and Techniques*, 2nd edn (eds J. D. Krumboltz and C. E. Thoresen), Holt, Rinehart and Winston, New York.

Scheier, M. F. (1976). Self-awareness, self-consciousness, and angry aggression, *Journal of Personality*, **44**, 627–644.

Scheier, M. F., and Carver, C. S. (1977). Self-focused attention and the experience of emotion: Attention, repulsion, elation and depression, *Journal of Personality and Social Psychology*, **35**, 625–636.

Scheier, M. F., and Carver, C. S. (1982). Cognition, affect and self-regulation. In *Affect and Cognition* (eds M. S. Clark and S. T. Fiske), Erlbaum, Hillsdale, N. J.

Scheier, M. F., Carver, C. S., and Matthews, K. A. (1983). Attentional factors in the perception of bodily states. In *Social Psychophysiology: A Sourcebook* (eds J. T. Cacioppo and R. E. Petty), pp. 510–542, Guildford Press, New York.

212

Scherer, K. R. (1982). Emotion as a process: function, origin and regulation, *Social Science Information*, **21**, 555–570.

Scherer, K. R. (1984). Emotion as a multicomponent process: a model and some cross-cultural data. In *Review of Personality and Social Psychology, vol. 5: Emotions, Relationships and Health* (ed. P. Shaver), pp. 37–63, Sage, Beverley Hills, London, and New Delhi.

Schlenker, B. R. (1980). *Impression Management: The Self Concept, Social Identity, and Interpersonal Relations*, Brooks/Cole, Monterey, California.

Schlenker, B. R. (1982). Translating actions into attitudes: an identity analytic approach to the explanation of social conduct. In *Advances in Experimental Social Psychology*, vol. 15 (ed. L. Berkowitz), pp. 193–247, Academic Press, New York.

Schlenker, B. R. (1983). Identities, identifications, and relationships. In *Communication, Intimacy, and Close Relationships*, (ed. D. J. Derlega), pp. 71–104, Academic Press, New York.

Schlenker, B. R., and Darby, B. W. (1981). The use of apologies in social predicaments, *Social Psychology Quarterly*, **44**, 271–278.

Schlenker, B. R., and Leary, M. R. (1982). Social anxiety and self-presentation: a conceptualization and model, *Psychological Bulletin*, **92**, 641–669.

Schonbach, P. (1980). A category system for account phases, *European Journal of Social Psychology*, **10**, 195–200.

Scott, M. B., and Lyman, S. B. (1968). Accounts, *American Sociological Review*, **33**, 46–62.

Semin, G. R., and Manstead, A. S. R. (1981). The beholder beheld: a study of social emotionality, *European Journal of Social Psychology*, **11**, 253–265.

Semin, G. R., and Manstead, A. S. R. (1982). The social implications of embarrassment displays and restitution behaviour, *European Journal of Social Psychology*, **12**, 367–377.

Semin, G. R., and Manstead, A. S. R. (1983). *The Accountability of Conduct: A Social Psychological Analysis*, Academic Press, London.

Serber, M. (1970). Shame aversion therapy, *Journal of Behavior Therapy and Experimental Psychiatry*, **1**, 213–215.

Shahar, A., and Merbaum, M. (1981). The interaction between subject characteristics and self control procedures in the treatment of interpersonal anxiety, *Cognitive Therapy and Research*, **5**, 221–224.

Shapiro, E. G. (1978). Help seeking: effects of visibility of task performance and help seeking, *Journal of Applied Social Psychology*, **8**, 163–173.

Shapiro, E. G. (1980). Is seeking help from a friend like seeking help from a stranger?, *Social Psychology Quarterly*, **43**, 259–263.

Shapiro, E. G. (1983). Embarrassment and help-seeking. In *New Directions in Helping*, vol. 2: *Help Seeking* (eds B. Depaulo, A. Nadler, and J. D. Fisher), pp. 143–163, Academic Press, New York.

Shapiro, E. G. (1984). Help seeking: why people don't, *Research in the Sociology of Organisations*, **3**, 213–236.

Shaw, P. (1979). A comparison of three behaviour therapies in the treatment of social phobia, *British Journal of Psychiatry*, **134**, 629–623.

Simmons, R., Rosenberg, F., and Rosenberg, M. (1973). Disturbance in the self-image at adolescence, *American Sociological Review*, **38**, 553–568.

Skinner, B. F. (1953). *Science and Human Behavior*, Macmillan, New York.

Smith, R. E., Smythe, L., and Lien, D. (1972). Inhibition of helping behavior by a similar or dissimilar nonreactive fellow bystander, *Journal of Personality and Social Psychology*, **23**, 414–419.

Smith, T. W., Ingram, R. E., and Brehm, S. S. (1983). Social anxiety, anxious self-preoccupation, and recall of self-relevant information, *Journal of Personality and Social Psychology*, **44**, 1276–1283.

Smith, T. W., Snyder, C. R., and Perkins, S. C. (1983). The self-serving function of hypochondriacal complaints: physical symptoms as self-handicapping strategies, *Journal of Personality and Social Psychology*, **44**, 787–797.

Snyder, C. R., and Smith, T. W. (1982). Symptoms as self-handicapping strategies: on the virtues of old wine in a new bottle. In *Integration of Clinical and Social Psychology* (eds G. Weary and H. L. Mirels), pp. 104–127, Oxford University Press, New York.

Snyder, C. R., and Smith, T. W. (1983). On being 'Shy like a fox'; a self-handicapping analysis. In *A Sourcebook on Shyness: Research and Treatment* (eds W. H. Jones, J. M. Cheek, and S. R. Briggs), pp. 161–172, Plenum, New York.

Snyder, C. R., Smith, T. W., Augelli, R. W., and Ingram, R. G. (1985). On the self-serving function of social anxiety: shyness as a self-handicapping strategy, *Journal of Personality and Social Psychology*, **48**, 970–980.

Snyder, M. (1974). Self-monitoring of expressive behavior, *Journal of Personality and Social Psychology*, **30**, 526–537.

Snyder, M. (1979). Self-monitoring processes. In *Advances in Experimental Social Psychology*, vol. 12 (ed. L. Berkowitz), pp. 85–128, Academic Press, New York.

Snyder, M. (1981). Impression management: the self in social interaction. In *Social Psychology in the 80s*, 3rd edn (eds L. S. Wrightsman and K. Deux), pp. 92–123, Brooks/Cole, Monterey, California

Sroufe, R., Chaikan, A., Cook, R., and Freeman, V. (1977). The effects of physical attractiveness on honesty: a social desirability response, *Personality and Social Psychology Bulletin*, **3**, 59–62.

Stokes, S. J., and Bickman, L. (1974). The effects of physical attractiveness and role of the helper on help seeking, *Journal of Applied Social Psychology*, **4**, 286–294.

Stratton, T. T., and Moore, C. L. (1977). Application of the robust factor concept to the fear survey schedule, *Journal of Behavior Therapy and Experimental Psychiatry*, **8**, 229–235.

Strom, J. C., and Buck, R. W. (1979). Staring and participants' sex: physiology and subjective reactions, *Personality and Social Psychology Bulletin*, **5**, 114–117.

Sutton-Simon, K., and Goldfried, M. R. (1979). Faulty thinking patterns in two types of anxiety, *Cognitive Therapy and Research*, **3**, 193–203.

Tedeschi, J. T. (ed.) (1981). *Impression Management Theory and Social Psychological Research*, Academic Press, New York.

Tedeschi, J. T., and Riess, M. (1981a). Identities, the phenomenal self, and laboratory research. In *Impression Management Theory and Social Psychological Research* (ed. J. T. Tedeschi), pp. 3–22, Academic Press, New York.

Tedeschi, J. T., and Riess, M. (1981b). Verbal strategies in impression management. In *Ordinary Explanations of Behaviour* (ed. C. Antaki), pp. 271–326, Academic Press, London.

Tedeschi, J. T., Riordan, C. A., Gaes, G. G., and Kane, T. (1983). Verbal accounts and attributions of social motives, *Journal of Research in Personality*, **17**, 218–225.

Teichman, Y. (1973). Emotional arousal and affiliation, *Journal of Experimental Social Psychology*, **9**, 591–605.

Thompson, T. L. (1982). Gaze towards and avoidance of the handicapped: a field experiment, *Journal of Nonverbal Behavior*, **6**, 188–196.

Thorpe, G. L., Amatu, H. T., Blakey, R. S., and Burns, L. E. (1976). Contributions of overt instructional rehearsal and 'specific insight' to the effectiveness of self-instructional training: a preliminary study, *Behavior Therapy*, **7**, 504–511.

Thyer, B. A., Himle, J., and curtis, G. C. (1985). Blood–injury–illness phobia: A review, *Journal of Clinical Psychology*, **41**, 451–459.

Tice, D. M., Buder, J., and Baumeister, R. F. (1985). Development of self-consciousness: at what age does audience pressure disrupt performance?, *Adolescence*, **78**, 301–305;

Timms, M. W. H. (1980). Treatment of chronic blushing by paradoxical intention, *Behavioral Psychotherapy*, **8**, 59–61.

Tobey, E. L., and Tunnell, G. (1981). Predicting our impression of others: Effects of public self-consciousness and acting: a self monitoring subscale, *Personality and Social Psychology Bulletin*, **7**, 661–669.

Tomkins, S. S. (1962). *Consciousness, Imagery and Affect*, vol. 1, Springer, New York.

Tomkins, S. S. (1982). Affect as amplification: some modifications in theory. In *Emotion: Theory, Research and Experience* (eds R. Plutchik and H. Kellerman), pp. 141–161, Academic Press, New York.

Tomkins, S.S. (1981). The role of facial response in the experience of emotion: a reply to Tourangeau and Ellsworth, *Journal of Personality and Social Psychology*, **40**, 355–367.

Tourangeau, R., and Ellsworth, P. C. (1979). The role of facial response in the experience of emotion, *Journal of Personality and Social Psychology*, **37**, 1519–1531.

Trower, P. (1982). Towards a generative model of social skills: a critique and synthesis. In *Social Skills Training: A Practical Handbook for Assessment and Treatment* (eds J. Curran and P. Monti), pp. 399–427, Guildford Press, New York.

Trower, P., Bryant, B., and Argyle, M. (1978a). *Social Skills and Mental Health*, Methuen, London.

Trower, P., Yardley, K. Bryant, B. M., and Shaw, P. (1978b). The treatment of social failure: a comparison of anxiety-reduction and skills-acquisition procedures on two social problems, *Behavior Modification*, **2**, 41–60.

Turner, R. G. (1978). Self-consciousness and speed of processing self-relevant information, *Personality and Social Psychology Bulletin*, **4**, 456–460.

Twentyman, C. T., and McFall, R. M. (1975). Behavioral training of social skills in shy males, *Journal of Consulting and Clinical Psychology*, **43**, 384–395.

Vallelonga, D. (1976). Straus on shame, *Journal of Phenomenological Psychology*, **7**, 55–69.

Van den Berg, J. H. (1955). *Phenomenological Approach to Psychiatry*, Thomas, Springfield, Illinois.

Ward, C., Beck, A., and Roscoe, E. (1961). Typical dreams, *Archives of General Psychiatry*, **5**, 606–615.

Wardlaw, G. R., and Miller, P. J. (1978). A controlled exposure technique in the elimination of exhibitionism, *Journal of Behavior Therapy and Experimental Psychiatry*, **9**, 27–32.

Watson, D., and Friend, R. (1969). Measurement of social-evaluative anxiety, *Journal of Consulting and Clinical Psychology*, **33**, 448–451.

Watson, J., and Raynor, R. (1920). Conditioned emotional reactions, *Journal of Experimental Psychology*, **3**, 1–22.

Weinberg, M. S. (1968). Embarrassment: its variable and invariable aspects, *Social Forces*, **46**, 382–388.

West, S., and Brown, T. (1975). Physical attractiveness, the severity of the emergency and helping: a field experiment and interpersonal simulation, *Journal of Experimental Social Psychology*, **11**, 531–538.

Wicklund, R. A. (1975). Objective self-awareness. In *Advances in Experimental Social Psychology*, vol. 8 (ed. L. Berkowitz), pp. 233–275, Academic Press, New York.

Williams, K. B., and Williams, K. D. (1983). Social inhibition and asking for help: the effects of number, strength and immediacy of potential help givers, *Journal of Personality and Social Psychology*, **44**, 67–77.

Williamson, J. B. (1974). The stigma of public dependency: a comparison of alternative forms of public aid to the poor, *Social Problems*, **22**, 213–238.

Wolpe, J. (1958). *Psychotherapy by Reciprocal Inhibition*, Stanford University Press, Stanford, California.

Wolpe, J. (1976). *Themes and Variations: A Behavior Therapy Casebook*, Pergamon Press, New York.

Wolpe, J. (1982). *The Practice of Behavior Therapy*, 3rd edn., Pergamon Press, New York.

Zanna, M. P., and Pack, S. J. (1975). On the self-fulfilling nature of apparent sex differences in behavior, *Journal of Experimental Social Psychology*, **11**, 583–591.

Zimbardo, P. G. (1977). *Shyness*, Addison-Wesley, Reading, Massachusetts.

Author index

Ables, B., 111–112
Adams, H. E., 172
Altman, L. L., 7
Amies, P. L., 2
Argyle, M., 2, 42, 45, 47, 48, 75–76, 78–79, 172, 178
Arkin, R. M., 25–26, 124, 125
Arkowitz, H., 116, 158, 161, 164, 168
Arluke, A., 150–151
Armstrong, W. D., 46, 132
Asch, S. E., 43
Ascher, L. M., 182
Asendorpf, J., 4, 82, 93
Aspler, R., 141–142
Austin, J. L., 54, 57
Ausubel, D. P., 13–14

Baldwin, A., 13
Baldwin, A. L., 5
Bandura, A., 160, 161, 178
Barlow, D. H., 172, 174, 176
Baumeister, R. F., 100, 114–115
Beck, A., 8
Bellack, A. S., 172
Bem, D. J., 99
Ben-Itzhak, S., 145–146, 149, 150
Benedek, T., 8
Benson, D. F., 90
Berglas, S., 26
Bergler, E., 8
Berlyne, D., 82, 83
Berscheid, E., 147
Bickman, L., 146
Biedel, D. C., 159–160, 163, 170–171, 173
Biernat, J. J., 102
Biglan, A., 172
Birdwhistell, R. L., 75, 82
Blaney, P. H., 102
Blumenfeld, R., 110, 112, 114
Blumer, D., 90
Borkovec, T. D., 170
Bowen, R., 114

Braband, J., 135, 136
Brehm, S. S., 164–165
Briggs, S. R., 37, 124, 125
Brockner, J., 189–190
Brown, B. R., 31, 136, 148
Brown, T., 139
Bryant, B., 2, 172, 178
Buck, M., 71–72
Buck, R. W., 71–72, 73, 76, 96
Buder, J., 114–115
Bull, N., 94
Bull, R., 140
Buss, A. H., 1, 2, 3, 6, 20, 28, 29, 34, 37, 47, 50–51, 68, 70, 76, 108–109, 112–113, 115–117, 124, 125, 126, 128
Buss, E. H., 108–109
Butler, G., 172, 185, 188
Buytendijk, F., 10

Cacioppo, J. T., 161, 162, 168
Calhoun, K. S., 172
Cannon, W.B., 89
Capon, M., 124
Carlsmith, J. M., 74–75
Cartwright-Smith, J., 96
Carver, C. S., 20, 21, 28, 38, 97, 100–102
Cautela, J. R., 193
Chambless, D. J., 7
Chapman, A. J., 82
Cheek, J. M., 37, 76, 124, 125, 127, 128–129
Cialdini, R. B., 141
Ciminero, A. R., 172
Clark, J. V., 161, 168
Clark, R. D., 136–137
Clore, G. L., 139
Colby, C. Z., 96
Coleman, J. C., 111
Collett, P., 42–43
Cook, M., 75–76, 78–79
Cooper, J., 100
Coser, L. A., 143

216

Crowne, D. P., 35
Curran, J. P., 2, 161–162, 173, 177, 178
Curtis, G. C., 153–154

Daly, S., 158, 159
Dancu, C. V., 159–160
Dann, O. T., 7, 8
Darby, B. L., 141
Darby, B. W., 65–66
Darley, J. M., 43, 133, 135, 136
Darwin, C., 69–70, 73–74, 90, 93, 108
Davis, M. H., 128
De Beauvoir, S., 10
DePaulo, B. M., 143, 148
Devins, G. M., 103
Devinsky, O., 89–90
Dixon, N. F., 85
Donaldson, M., 113, 114
Dow, M. G., 172
Druian, P. R., 148
Duval, S., 20, 28, 100

Edelmann, R. J., 17, 26, 29, 47, 48,
    51–53, 54, 56, 59, 61, 63, 64–65, 66,
    68, 71, 75–76, 79–82, 83, 84, 85–86,
    87, 93, 104, 120, 122–123, 124, 125,
    126, 127, 128, 129–130, 138, 140–141,
    151, 166–170, 189, 190
Edelstein, B. A., 172
Ekehammar, B., 3
Ekman, P., 75, 80, 95, 96–97
Elkind, D., 114, 115
Ellis, A., 163, 184
Ellsworth, P. C., 74–75, 78, 95–96
Emerson, J. P., 85
Emmelkamp, P. M. G., 172, 176–177,
    178, 181, 185, 186, 190
English, F., 5, 12, 117–118
Exline, R. V., 74, 77
Eysenck, H. J., 12, 128, 156
Eysenck, S. B. G., 128

Farrell, A. D., 158
Fedoravicius, A., 177, 184
Feldman, S., 8
Felling, J. P., 3
Fenichel, O., 9
Fenigstein, A., 20, 29, 37, 125, 126, 189
Finch, A. J., 129
Fink, E. L., 83–84, 129
Fischetti, M., 161–162
Fish, B., 78
Fisher, J. D., 143–150
Flavell, J. H., 113

Foa, E. B., 181
Foddy, M., 158, 163
Frankl, V. E., 182
Fremouw, W. J., 185
Freud, S., 7
Friend, R., 26, 36, 128, 158, 161, 162,
    173, 185, 188
Friesen, W. V., 75, 80
Furnham, A., 42, 45, 124

Gabrenya, W. K., 124, 125
Garfinkel, H., 42, 48
Garland, H., 31, 136, 148
Gelder, M. G., 2, 176
Genest, M., 190–191
Gerard, H. B., 20, 21
Gibbs, D. N., 182–183
Gilbert, F. S., 177
Gillan, P., 176
Gilmore, J., B., 177, 184
Ginsburg, G. P., 44–45
Glaser, S. R., 172
Glasgow, R. E., 161
Glass, C. R., 161, 162–163, 168
Glogower, F., 185
Goldberg, D., 177, 179
Goffman, E., 5, 6, 14, 19, 20, 24–25,
    41–42, 54, 55, 104, 132, 139, 198
Goldfried, M. R., 161, 163–164,
    184–185, 186
Goldstein, A. J., 7
Gordon, J. E., 11
Gough, H. J., 129
Graham, J. A., 42, 45
Gray, D., 74, 77
Greenberg, D., 153
Greenberg, M. S., 142–143
Greenley, J. R., 143–144
Greif, E. B., 129
Gross, A. E., 144
Gross, E., 47–48
Gutheil, E., 7, 8

Hafler, D. A., 89–90
Hager, J. C., 95
Halford, K., 158, 163
Hall, R., 177, 179
Hampson, S. E., 48, 75–76, 79–82, 84,
    104
Hardwick, S., 190
Harkins, S., 32, 136
Harper, R. A., 163
Harris, M. B., 139
Hasdorf, A., 141

Hayes, B. J., 184, 185, 190
Heath, M., 78
Heider, F., 13, 51
Heimberg, R. G., 177, 184, 185, 187
Hellpach, W., 13
Herold, E. S., 117
Hersen, M., 172
Himle, J., 153–154
Hitschmann, E., 8
Hodges, W. F., 3
Hogan, R., 129
Hollon, S. D., 172
Horowitz, E., 109–110
Hull, J. G., 100
Hulton, A. J. B., 189–190
Hupka, R. B., 95

Ingram, R. E., 164–165
Iscoe, I., 108–109
Izard, C. E., 90, 95

Jackson, M. J., 32, 136
James, W., 89, 93–94
Jerremalm, A., 103, 173, 180
Johansson, J., 103, 173, 180
Johnson, J. A., 127, 128–129, 130
Johnston, D. W., 176
Jones, E. E., 20, 21, 22, 23–24, 26
Jones, W. H., 37

Kamhi, A. G., 77
Kane, T. R., 85
Kanter, N. J., 184–185, 186
Karabenick, S. A., 78
Karch, F. E., 9
Kazdin, 172
Keil, W. E., 193, 194
Kellet, J. A., 177
Kendall, P. C., 129, 172
Kindness, K., 158–159, 172
Kleck, R. E., 96, 102, 141
Konecni, V. J., 139
Kraut, R. E., 94
Krout, M. H., 75

Lacey, J. I., 72
Laird, J. D., 95–96
Lambert, C., 177
Lambert, W. E., 130
Lang, P. J., 170
Lanzetta, J. T., 96, 102
Latane, B., 32, 43, 133, 134, 135–136,
  144, 145

Leary, M. R., 1–2, 3, 15, 19, 21, 33, 36,
  37, 76–77, 87, 130
Lefcourt, H. M., 85
Lent, R. W., 184
Leventhal, H., 90, 91, 96, 97, 104
Levin, H., 5
Levin, J., 150–151
Levy, A. S., 100
Lieberman, M. A., 143
Lien, D., 135, 136
Lowy, S., 7
Lyman, S. B., 54, 57–58, 60, 65, 66
Lynd, H., 5

McCroskey, J. C., 4, 185
McCusker, G., 120, 122–123, 127, 128,
  129–130, 170
McEwan, K. L., 103
McFadyen, M., 158–159, 172
McFall, R. M., 158
McOsker, T. G., 77
Magnusson, D., 3
Mandler, G., 99, 186
Mandler, J. M., 186
Manstead, A. S. R., 4, 15, 45, 54, 55,
  57, 59, 61, 62–63, 104
Marks, I. B., 2
Marlowe, D., 34
Marshall, W. C., 184, 185, 190
Marston, A. R., 162
Martin, R. A., 85
Martinez-Diaz, J. A., 172
Marzillier, J. S., 177
Mathews, A. M., 176
Matthews, K. A., 100–101, 102
Mavissakalian, M., 7
Mechanic, D., 142, 143–144
Meichenbaum, D., 162, 177, 184,
  190–191
Merbaum, M., 184, 186
Merluzzi, T. V., 161
Metzger, N. J., 4, 26
Meyer, F. W., 139
Milgram, S., 43
Miller, P. J., 193–194
Modigliani, A., 5, 6, 14–15, 43, 47, 50,
  59, 63, 74, 104, 110, 112, 114,
  119–123, 129, 130, 150
Montgomery, L. E., 129
Monti, P. M., 173
Moore, C. L., 3
Mosbach, P. A., 90, 91, 104
Mowrer, O. H., 12, 156
Mullan, J. T., 143

Nadler, A., 143, 144, 145–147, 149, 150
Newton, A., 158–159, 172
Nichols, K. A., 36
Nida, S., 133, 134, 135

O'Banion, K., 133, 134, 135
Ono, H., 141
Orleans, C. T., 193
Ost, L-G., 103, 173, 180, 186
Oster, O., 96–97

Pack, S. J., 147
Park. R. D., 71–72, 76
Pasquarelli, B., 94
Paul, G. L., 177
Pavio, A., 130
Perkins, S. C., 27
Perlman, R., 144
Phillips, G. M., 4, 26
Piliavin, I. M., 140
Piliavin, J. A., 140
Pilkonis, P. A., 34, 37, 76, 128, 130
Pittman, T. S., 20, 22, 23–24
Plutchic, R., 90, 91
Pomozal, R. J., 139
Porat, I., 144–145

Rachman, S., 176, 192
Raynor, R., 12, 156
Rehm, L. P., 162
Reitz, W. E., 193, 194
Richardson, F. C., 3
Riess, M., 21, 22, 54, 55, 56, 57, 58–59, 61, 104
Robinson, V. M., 85
Rodin, J., 135, 136, 140
Roscoe, E., 8
Rosenberg, F., 114
Rosenberg, M., 114
Ross, A. S., 135, 136
Rothbart, M. K., 83
Russell, R. K., 184
Russell, W. D., 37
Rutledge, L. L., 95

Salter, A., 181–182, 183–184
Samerotte, G. C., 139
Sarason, I., 190
Sarnoff, I., 77–78
Sartre, J. P., 10
Sattler, J., 7, 14, 47, 49–50, 53
Saul, L. J., 8
Schachter, S., 89, 98
Schaefer, H. H., 193

Scheier, M. F., 20, 28, 37, 38, 97, 100–102, 126
Scherer, K. R., 90, 91–92, 106
Schlenker, B. R., 1–2, 3, 15, 19, 20–21, 22, 28, 29, 33, 54, 55, 58, 60–61, 64, 65–66, 76, 87, 104
Schonbach, P., 57, 58, 60
Schuette, D., 74, 77
Scott, M. B., 54, 57–58, 60, 64, 66
Semin, G. R., 4, 15, 45, 54, 55, 57, 59, 61, 62–63, 104
Serber, M., 193, 194
Shahar, A., 184, 186
Shapira, R., 145–146, 149, 150
Shapiro, E. G., 133, 134, 143, 144, 148–149
Shaw, P., 2, 177, 179–180
Simmons, R., 114
Singer, J. E., 98
Skinner, B. F., 11
Smith, R. E., 135, 136
Smith, T. W., 27, 164–165
Smither, R., 127, 128–129
Symthe, L., 135, 136
Snyder, C. R., 27
Snyder, M., 38, 39, 124, 125
Sroufe, 139
Stevens, J., 140
Stokes, S. J., 146
Stone, S. P., 47–48
Stratton, T. T., 3
Stavinski, A., 153
Streufret, S., 150
Strom, J. C., 73
Suls, J., 85
Sutton-Simon, K., 161, 163–164

Tasto, D. L., 3
Teasdale, J. D., 192
Tedeschi, J. T., 21, 22, 54, 55, 56, 57, 58–59, 61, 85, 104
Teichman, Y., 77
Thompson, T. L., 139
Thorpe, G. L., 184, 185
Thyer, B. A., 114–115
Tice, D. M., 114–115
Timms, M. W. H., 97, 173, 183
Tobey, E. L., 124
Tomkins, S. S., 90, 95, 97–98, 197
Tourangeau, R., 95–96
Trower, P., 2, 169, 172, 177, 178, 179
Tunnell, G., 124
Turner, R. G., 127

220

Turner, R. M., 182
Turner, S. M., 159–160
Twentyman, C. T., 158

Uviller, E. T., 186

Vallelonga, D., 5, 6
Van den Berg, J. H., 11
Victor, J., 89–90
Vincent, J. E., 141

Walker, B. A., 83–84
Wallander, J. L., 161–162
Walster, E., 147
Ward, C., 8
Wardlaw, G. R., 193–194

Watson, D., 26, 36, 128, 158, 161, 162,
    185, 188
Watson, J., 12, 156
Weinberg, M. S., 43–44
West, S., 139
Wicklund, R. A., 20, 28, 100
Williams, K. B., 145
Williams, K. D., 145
Williamson, J. B., 143
Witcher-Alagna, S., 143
Word, L. E., 136–137
Wolfe, B. E., 174, 176
Wolpe, J., 156, 176, 183, 192

Zamostny, K. P., 184
Zanna, M. P., 147
Zimbardo, P. G., 4, 20, 29, 30, 33, 34,
    76, 77–78, 127, 130, 153, 156

Subject index

accounts, verbal, 17, 54–67
  see also apologies; excuses;
    justifications; remedial tactics
adolescence, 49, 108–110, 117–118
  and blushing, 10–11
  and self-consciousness, 114–116
  and self-presentation, 34
  and role novelty, 34
affiliation, 76–79, 87, 93
age differences, 108–119
  and blushing, 108, 112
  and role-taking, 113–114, 116
  and self-consciousness, 114–116
  and self-presentation, 111–113
  see also adolescence
agoraphobia, 2, 7, 153, 174
ambiguous situations, *see* situations,
    ambiguity of
amusement, facial expression,
    79–80
anxiety management training, 188
apologies, 54–57, 60, 64–66, 151, 168
assumptions, disturbance of, 47–48, 51,
    56, 60
audience anxiety, 1, 3–4, 7, 34, 37, 130,
    153
audience evaluation
  and adolescent egocentrism, 114–115
  and embarrassment, 13–14, 20, 31–32,
    197
  and protective self-presentation, 27,
    30–33
  and public self-attention, 29, 38
  and self-monitoring, 39
  and self-presentation, 25, 111
  and social anxiety, 30, 33
  see also help-giving; help-seeking
aversive conditioning, *see* conditioning,
    aversive

behavioural, approach, 11–13
blood pressure, changes in, 170–171
blushing, 6–11, 18, 68–71, 73, 87, 89–91,

93, 97–101, 103, 106, 108, 112, 119,
153, 155, 170–173, 182–184, 191,
197
  see also temperature, changes in;
    vasodilation, cutaneous body
  motion, 73, 84, 93, 101, 106, 197
  and emotion, 79–80
  see also foot movements gestures;
bystander intervention, *see* help-giving,
    social inhibition of

California Psychological Inventory, 129
cognitive bias, *see* irrational beliefs;
    memory; self-evaluation; self-
    statements
cognitive restructuring, 176–177, 185
cognitive therapy, 184–192
  see also cognitive restructuring;
    Rational–Emotive Therapy; Self-
    Instructional Training
communication apprehension, *see*
    reticence
conditioning
  aversive, 192–194
  classical, 12, 155–157, 160, 176
conformity, 43, 111, 113, 129–130

differences, individual, 119–131,
    150–152
  and protective self-presentation,
    35–39
diffusion of responsibility, 135, 136

embarrassibility, 15, 18, 119–124,
    125–131, 150
  see also Modigliani's Embarrassibility
    Scale
embarrassment
  age differences in, 108–111, 114–116
  and dreams, 7–8
  and non-verbal behaviour, 73–79,
    80–87, 93–98
  and related constructs, 1–7

and self-presentation, 19–27
and social-rules, 41–47
as an emotion, 89–91
categories of, 47–54
contraceptive, 117
empathic/vicarious, 50–51, 60, 122,
  128, 129–130
mature, 114, 119
primary, 93
primitive, 114, 116, 119
recognition of, 17, 79–80
secondary, 93
the physiology of, 68–73
theories of, 7–16
emotions, 104
and cognitive appraisal, 98–101
as a muilticomponent construct, 91–92
expression of, 90
intensity of and self focus, 101–103
Leventhal's perceptual-motor theory
  of, 104–105
theories of, 89–91
see also facial expression, feedback
  from
empathy, 127, 128–130
environmental focus, 100–101
equity theory, 142
erythrophobia, see blushing
excuses, 54, 57–66, 168
exhibitionism, 8–9, 18, 193–194
existential, approach, 10–11
exposure based treatments, 174,
  176–177, 186–188, 190
see also flooding; systematic
  desensitization
extraversion, 125, 127–130
eye contact, 68, 84, 87, 93, 141,
  158–160, 197
see also gaze, aversion of
Eysenck Personality Questionnaire, 128

face, covering of, 6, 14
face-saving strategies, 85, 87
see also accounts, verbal; humour;
  remedial tactics
facework, 59, 61, 63
facial expression, 87, 99
emotion and, 79–80
feedback from, 93–98, 102, 106, 197
Fear of Heights Survey, 164
Fenigstein et al.'s Self-Consciousness
  Scale, 125–126, 192
fidgeting, see gestures
flooding, 176, 178

flushing, see blushing
foot movements, 75
see also body motion; leg movements
frontal lobe disorder, 90

gaze, aversion of, 6, 14, 17, 56, 73–80,
  82, 101, 159
see also eye contact; staring
gestures, 17, 29, 56, 68, 73–76, 79, 87,
  103, 158
see also body motion
grinning, see smiling

heart rate, changes in, 68, 71–73, 76,
  170, 197
help-giving, social inhibition of
and ambiguity, 20, 133, 136–138
and audience effects, 133–136, 151
and disablement, 131, 133, 139–141
and disfigurement, 139–141, 151
and embarrassing situations, 138–139,
  151
and emotional state, 141–142
help-seeking, social inhibition of
and age, 148, 151
and ambiguity, 20, 133
and attractiveness, 146–147, 151
and audience effects, 133, 144–146,
  151
and disablement, 133
and emotion, 150–151
and personality, 150, 151–152
and relationship with helper, 148–149
and self-esteem, 143, 150
Hogan's Empathy Scale, 129–130
Horowitz's Embarrassment
  Questionnaire, 109
humour, 83–84
as a coping response, 85–87
see also face saving; joking; laughter

identity, 17, 19–22, 25, 28, 36–37, 70,
  85, 104, 111, 136, 144, 155
inappropriate, 47–48, 51, 59
impression management, see self-
  presentation
individual differences, see differences,
  individual
interaction anxiety, see shyness
internal dialogue, see self-statements
interpersonal, approach, 13–16
intimacy, level of, 76, 82, 84
introversion, 127–128, 150
irrational beliefs, 161, 163–164, 185–186

Irrational Beliefs Test, 164, 173, 186–187

joking, 85, 168
justifications, 54, 57, 60–66, 168

laughter, and expressed embarrassment, 6, 17, 56, 68, 73, 76, 80–84
    and incongruity, 83
    as a coping response, 84–87, 168
    as ridicule, 12, 116–117
    see also humour; joking; smiling
Leary's Interaction Anxiousness Scale, 36
leg movements, 80
    see also foot movements
Literature Empathy Test, 129

Marlowe–Crowne Social Desirability Scale, 35–36
memory, selectivity of, 161, 164–166
meshing, failure of, see assumptions, disturbance of
Minnesota Multiphasic Personality Inventory, 129
modesty, 116–117
Modigliani's Embarrassibility Questionnaire, 50, 120–124, 128–130, 166, 192
muscles, tension of, 68, 71, 76, 98

neuroticism, 127–129, 150
novel situations, see situations, novelty of

obsessive–compulsive disorders, 174
other-directedness, 125, 150
overpraise, 50–51, 59

paradoxical intention, 176, 182–184, 188
personality, 119–131, 197
    and help-seeking, 134
poise, loss of, 47–48, 50–53, 59–60
privacy, invasion of, 49–51, 60
psychoanalytic, approach, 7–10
public speaking anxiety, see audience anxiety

Rational–Emotive Therapy, 176, 184–186
rational restructuring, see cognitive restructuring
reciprocal inhibition, 182
relationships, interpersonal, 115–116

see also social anxiety, heterosexual
relaxation, 176–177, 179–180, 185, 188, 190
remedial tactics, 22, 59, 61
    see also face-saving strategies
reticence, 4, 26, 34, 37, 153
    see also shyness
ridicule, 12, 116–117, 153–154, 156
role-taking ability, 113–116
rules, social, 15–18, 39, 41–44, 88, 192, 196
    acquisition of, 117–118
    transgression of, 44–46, 53–54, 66, 132

scopophilia, 8–10
self, phenomenal, see identity
self-attention, 15, 20, 27–29, 37, 97, 101, 106, 154, 160
    public, 17, 29, 54, 77, 106
    reduction of, 189–192
self-awareness, 28, 37
    private, 28
    public, 29, 114
self-concept, 21, 92, 143
self-control, 116–117
self-control desensitization, see systematic desensitization
self-consciousness, 13, 26–29, 36–38, 100, 113–119, 125, 197
    private, 37, 102, 125–126
    public, 37–38, 114, 125–127, 150, 163, 165
self-esteem, 6, 15, 22, 130, 150, 189–190
    individual, 14, 130
    public, 14, 130
self-evaluation, 161–164, 166
self-focus, 100–101, 104, 106, 189
    and emotional intensity, 101–103
    see also self-attention
self-image, 5, 14
    public, 15, 18, 131
Self-Instructional Training, 184–186, 190
self-monitoring, 38–39, 100, 113, 124–125, 172
self-perception, 83, 99, 161
self-presentation, 3–6, 14–20, 47, 50, 83–84, 87–88, 111–119, 121, 124–125, 144–151, 160, 163, 165, 168–169, 171–172, 192, 198
    and self-awareness, 28–30
    styles of, 23–27, 132
    acquisitive, 29

exemplification, 24–25
ingratiation, 23–25, 34
intimidation, 23–24, 34
protective, 25–28, 30–39, 54, 131,
    136, 154, 170, 196
self-handicapping, 25–27, 31, 33,
    196
self-promotion, 23–24, 34
supplication, 24–25
self-statements, 161–164, 190–191
self-touching, see gesturing
sensitivity, 129–130
sexual deviance see exhibitionism
sexuality, 117
shame, 1, 3–6, 11–13, 73–75, 77–78, 92,
    98, 118, 193–194
shyness, 1, 3–4, 7, 13, 27, 29, 34, 37, 98,
    125–126, 129, 153–154, 196
    see also reticence
situations, novelty and ambiguity of, 133
    and audience anxiety, 34
    and embarrassment, 17, 33–35, 132
    and protective self-presentation, 27,
        33–35
    and public self-consciousness, 29, 38
    and self-monitoring, 39
    and self-presentation, 17, 33–34
    and shyness, 34
    and social anxiety, 34
    see also help-giving; help-seeking
Situations Questionnaire, 162, 164
skills deficit, see social skills, deficit of
skin conductance, 71–73
    see also temperature, changes in
smiling and expressed embarrassment,
    6, 17, 68, 73, 76, 80–84, 86–87, 196
    and coping, 82, 85
    and social skills, 158–159
    see also laughter
Snyder's Self Monitoring Scale, 38–39,
    124–125, 128, 150, 192
social anxiety, 12–13, 15, 19, 26–27, 30
    34, 36–37, 76–78, 87, 103, 125–128,
    130, 150, 166–170, 196
    as fear of embarrassment, 2, 153–154
    heterosexual, 3, 116–117, 154
    subtypes of, 1–7, 153
    theoretical explanations, of, 155–166
    treatment of, 174–181, 184–192

Social Behaviour Role Playing Test, 158
social desirability, 34–35
social impact theory, 135–136, 145–146
social influence theory, 135
Social Interaction Self-Statement Test,
    162–163, 173
social norms, see social rules
social phobia, see social anxiety
Social Situations Questionnaire, 172
social skills, 12, 161–162, 169
    deficit of, 157–160
    failure of, see poise, loss of
    training, 174, 178–181, 186–187,
        189
socialization, 116–117
speech, disturbance of, 17, 68, 73,
    75–77, 79, 84, 87, 93, 101, 196
speech anxiety, 4, 27, 177, 190
stage fright, see audience anxiety
stammering, see speech, disturbance of
staring, 56, 84, 151
    see also gaze
stimulus evaluation checks, 91–93, 106
symptomatic erythema, see blushing
systematic desentization, 174, 176–177,
    180–181, 185–186

temperature, changes in, 68
    blood, 70–71
    skin, 71, 73, 97–98, 102, 197
    see also blushing; vasodilation,
        cutaneous
test anxiety, 27, 130, 190
trembling, see body movement

vasodilation, cutaneous, 70
    see also blushing; temperature,
        changes in
verbal accounting strategies, see
    accounts, verbal
vocal cues, 158–159
    see also speech disturbances

Watson and Friend's Fear of Negative
    Evaluation Scale, 36, 161, 188
Watson and Friend's Social Avoidance
    and Distress Scale, 36, 158,
    161–166, 173, 187–188, 192